Nose

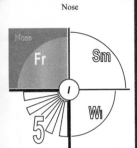

M000306083

| Cereal : C |
| Dulcet : D |
| Floral : Fl |
| Fruity : Fr |
| Grassy : G |
| Marine : Ma |

Aromas

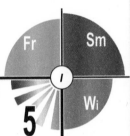

| Mi : Mineral |
| O : Oily |
| Sm : Smoky |
| Su : Sulphurous |
| Wi : Winey |
| Wo : Woody |

Notation Scale

1 Acceptable	2 Noticeable	3 Good	4 Very good	5 Remarkable	6 Excellent	7 Magnificent	8 Exceptional	9 Ultimate
75-79	80-82	83-84	85-86	87-88	89-90	91-92	93-95	96-100

Rating equivalent/100

11	12	13	14	15	16	17	18	19-20

Rating equivalent/20

Notation: Nose-Palate-Finish

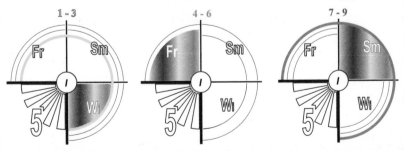

1 - 3   4 - 6   7 - 9

R

Pine Resin
Rancio
Cedar
New wood
Pepper
Ginger
Cinnamon
Clove
Cigar box
Coconut
Walnut
Hazelnut
Liquorice
Chocolate
Coffee
Roasted almond
Bourbon vanilla
Mocha
Crème brûlée
Meringue
Resedà
Fruit brandy
Cognac
Calvados
Rhubarb wine
Walnut wine
Peach wine
Blackcurrant wine
Vins doux naturels
Port
Marsala
Madeira
Sherry vinegar
Oloroso
Pedro Ximénez
Fino
Sauternes
Pinot Noir
Chardonnay
Cabernet Sauvignon
Plastic
Rubber
Used matches
Barbecued meat
Meat pie
Iberico ham
Broth
Worcestershire sauce
Black olive
Onion
Cabbage
Soot
Burnt leaves
Ash
Embers
Smoky sauna
Kippery
Lapsang suchang
Wood smoke
Incense
Peat oil
Tar
Peat smoke
Creosote
TCP antiseptic
Bandage
Camphor
Arnica
Leather upholstery
Musk
Russian leather
Boiled pork
Old Parmesan
Comté
Danish pastry
Shortbread
Butter
Yogurt
Eggnog
Coconut milk
Double (heavy) cream
Olive oil
Flaxseed oil
Lemon essential oil
Condiment
Copper
Bronze
Metallic rails
Cast iron
Ink
Silex
Flint
Striking strip
Hot sand
Graphite
Wet rock
Pebble
Slate
Chalk
Shell
Chablis
Limestone
Anchovy
Salty liquorice

F

I

G

N

Wood
Spicy
Nutty
Roasted
Vanilla

Woody: Wo

Fruit Wine
Spirit
Fortified
Sherried
Wine

Winey: Wi

Rubbery
Meaty
Vegetable

Sulphurous: Su

Burnt
Smokehouse
Peaty
Medicinal

Smoky: Sm

Leathery
Cheesy
Buttery
Milky
Plant Oil

Oily: O

Pot Still
Metallic
Silex
Beach
Calcareous

Mineral: Mi

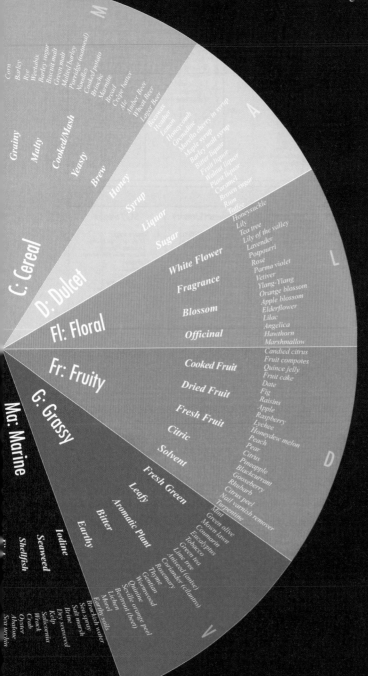

Ma: Marine

IO / Iodine	SW/ Seaweed	SF / Shellfish	FI / Fishy
1. Borage flower 2. Brackish water 3. Brine 4. Salt marsh 5. Sea spray	1. Dry seaweed 2. Kelp 3. Nori 4. Salicornia 5. Samphire 6. Wakame 7. Wrack	1. Abalone 2. Clam 3. Crab 4. Dried shellfish 5. Lobster 6. Oyster 7. Scallop 8. Sea urchin	1. Anchovy 2. Pickled herring 3. Salty liquorice

Mi: Mineral

CA / Calcaerous	BE / Beach	SI / Silex	MT / Metallic	PS / Pot Still
1. Cement 2. Chablis 3. Chalk 4. Egg shell 5. Lime 6. Limestone 7. Plaster 8. Shell	1. Clay 2. Fresh laundry 3. Hot sand 4. Lava stone 5. Pebble 6. Rope 7. Sail locker 8. Sandy beach 9. Salt 10. Silica 11. Slate 12. Wet rock 13. Wet sand	1. Flint 2. Graphite 3. Striking strip 4. Silex	1. Aluminium 2. Cast iron 3. Electric cable 4. Garlic metallic 5. Iron 6. Ink 7. Lead 8. Magnesium 9. Metallic rails 10. Musty metallic 11. Rust 12. Steel 13. Zinc	1. Bronze 2. Copper

O: Oily

PL Plant Oil	MI Milky	BT Buttery	CH Cheesy	LU Leathery
1. Almond oil 2. Candlewax 3. Corn oil 4. Eucalyptus oil 5. Flaxseed 6. Hemp oil 7. Lemon essential oil 8. Walnut oil 9. Olive oil 10. Pumpkin seed oil 11. Sesame oil 12. Shea butter 13. Sunflower oil	1. Coconut milk 2. Crème fraîche 3. Curdled milk 4. Double (heavy) cream 5. Eggnog 6. Floral cream 7. Milk jam 8. Panna cotta 9. Sour cream 10. Yogurt	1. Butter 2. Salted butter 3. Butter cookie 4. Danish pastry 5. Shortbread	1. Butyric 2. Boiled pork 3. Comté 4. Gym shoes 5. Old Parmesan	1. Ambergris 2. Chamois leather 3. Cowhide 4. Gamey 5. Labdanum 6. Lanolin 7. Leather 8. Leather upholstery 9. Mousey 10. Musk 11. Russian leather 12. Suede

Sm: Smoky

ME Medicinal	PE Peaty	SM Smokehouse	BU Burnt

1. Arnica
2. Bandage
3. Camphor
4. Carbolic acid
5. Hospital
6. TCP antiseptic
	1. Creosote
	2. Diesel oil
	3. Farmyard
	   Chicken coop
	   Farm yard
	   Horse stable
	   Manure
	4. Kerosene
	5. Peat moss
	6. Peat oil
	7. Peat smoke
	8. Peated malt
	9. Petrol (gas)
	10. Tar
	11. Tar rope
	12. Tobacco pipe juice
		1. Incense
		2. Kippery
		   Haddock
		   Smoked eel
		   Smoked herring
		   Smoked mackerel
		   Smoked oysters
		   Smoked salmon
		   Smoked shellfish
		   Smoked sturgeon
		3. Lapsang suchang
		4. Burning pine needle
		5. Smoky mezcal
		6. Smoky sauna
		7. Vine shoot smoke
		8. Wood smoke
		   Beech smoke
		   Birch bark smoke
		   Fir smoke
		   Hickory smoke
		   Liquid smoke
		   Maple smoke
		   Oak smoke
			1. Ash
			2. Beach fire
			3. Bonfires
			4. Burnt grass
			5. Burnt leaves
			6. Burnt rubber
			7. Burnt stick
			8. Burnt toast
			9. Burnt wood
			10. Coal
			11. Charcoal
			12. Embers
			13. Pencil-lead
			14. Rimed
			15. Soot

Wi: Winey

WI Wine	SH Sherried	FO Fortified	FW Fruit Wine	SP Spirit

1. Barbarossa
2. Barbera
3. Cabernet Franc
4. Cabernet
    Sauvignon
5. Carignan
6. Champagne
7. Chardonnay
8. Chasselas
9. Chenin
10. Dregs
11. Gamay
12. Gewurztraminer
13. Grenache
14. Malbec
15. Merlot
16. Mourvèdre
17. Nebbiolo
18. Old wine
19. Pinot Gris
20. Pinot Noir
21. Primitivo
22. Riesling
23. Sangiovese
24. Sauternes
25. Sauvignon
26. Savagnin
27. Sémillon
28. Sylvaner
29. Syrah
30. Tannat
31. Tempranillo
32. Trebbiano
33. Viognier
34. Zinfandel
	1. Amontillado
	    Dry Amontillado
	    Medium
	    VORS
	2. Fino
	3. Manzanilla
	    Manzanilla
	    Amontillada
	    Manzanilla Fina
	    Manzanilla Olorosa
	    Manzanilla Pasada
	4. Moscatel
	5. Pale cream sherry
	6. Palo Cortado
	    VORS
	7. Pedro Ximénez
	    Brown sherry
	    Cream sherry
	    VORS
	8. Oloroso
	    Oloroso seco
	    Amoroso
	    Oloroso
	    VORS
	9. Sherry vinegar
	10. Yellow wine (Jura)
		1. Artichoke wine
		    (Cynar)
		2. Madeira
		    Malvasia
		    Bual
		    Verdelho
		    Sercial
		3. Malaga
		4. Marsala
		    Marsala Alla
		    Mandorla
		    Marsala All'uovo
		    Marsala Oro
		    Marsala Solera
		5. Port
		    White
		    Old white
		    Rosé
		    Ruby
		    Tawny
		    Colheita
		    Vintage
		6. Vermouth
		    Extra dry
		    Dry
		    Rosso
		    Punt E Mes
		7. Vins doux
		    naturels
		    Banyuls
		    Cap Corse
		    Frontignan
		    Maury
		    Muscat
		    Rivesaltes
		8. Liqueur (Liquor)
		    wine
		    Floc de Gascogne
		    Macvin
		    Pineau des
		    Charentes
		    Ratafia
			1. Blackcurrant wine
			2. Cherry wine
			3. Fig wine
			4. Mulberry wine
			5. Peach wine
			6. Raspberry wine
			7. Rhubarb wine
			8. Seville orange
			    wine
			9. Strawberry wine
			10. Umeshu
			11. Walnut wine
				1. Armagnac
				2. Bourbon
				3. Calvados
				4. Cognac
				5. Fruit brandy
				6. Marc / Grappa
				7. Tequila

Wo: Woody

VA Vanilla	RO Roasted	NU Nutty	SP Spicy	WO Wood

1. Creamy
    Crème brûlée
    Crème anglaise
    Liquorice cream
    Pastry cream
2. Pastry
    Meringue
    Lemon meringue
    Mango meringue
3. Vanilla
    Bourbon vanilla
    Reseda
    Tahitian vanilla
    Vanilla cream
	1. Chocolate
	    Bitter chocolate
	    Cocoa
	    Dark chocolate
	    Fudge
	    Gianduja
	    Ganache
	    Milk chocolate
	2. Coffee
	    Coffee ground
	    Chicory root
	    Espresso
	    Mochaccino
	    Mocha
	    Ristretto
	    Ricoré
	    Robusta coffee
	3. Liquorice
	    Zan
	4. Roasted nut
	    Roasted almond
	    Roasted cocoa bean
	    Roasted hazelnut
	    Roasted sesame
		1. Coconut
		2. Kernel
		3. Macaroon
		4. Marron glacé
		5. Marzipan
		6. Peanut
		7. Nuts
		    Brazil nut
		    Cashew
		    Hazelnut
		    Fresh walnut
		    Macadamia nut
		    Pecan nut
		    Pine nut
		    Pistachio
		    Sweet almond
		    Sweet chesnut
		    Walnut
		8. Praline
			1. Chilli
			    Cayenne pepper
			    Espelette chilli
			    pepper
			2. Cigar box
			3. Cinnamon
			4. Clove
			5. Pepper
			    Black pepper
			    Cubeb
			    Grains of Selim
			    Green pepper
			    Long pepper
			    Sichuan pepper
			    Voatsiperifery
			    White pepper
			6. Satay
			7. Spices
			    Allspice
			    Cardamom
			    Gingerbread
			    Green curry
			    Mace
			    Nutmeg
			    Paprika
			    Saffron
			    Turmeric
			8. Spicy root
			    Galangal
			    Ginger
			    Horseradish
				1. Amber
				2. Balsamic vinegar
				3. Cade oil
				4. Conifer
				    Cedar
				    Cypress
				    Fir
				    Pine
				    Spruce
				    Thuja
				5. Libraries
				6. New wood
				    Cardboard
				    Cork
				    Green wood
				    Plywood
				7. Oak
				    French oak
				    Japanese oak
				    Spanish oak
				    White oak
				8. Balsam of Peru
				9. Rooibos tea
				10. Resinous
				    Armenian paper
				    Benzoin
				    Encaustic
				    Frankincense
				    Incense
				    Mastic
				    Myrrh
				    Pine Resin
				    Propolis
				11. Root beer
				12. Rancio
				13. Old wood
				    Agarwood
				    Mahogany
				    Old hull
				    Panelling
				    Rosewood
				    Sandalwood
				    Sailing deck
				    Wintergreen

Su: Sulphurous

VE Vegetable	MY Meaty	RU Rubbery

1. Sour
    Garlic
    Onion
    Shallot
2. Cabbage
3. Kitchen garden
    Artichoke
    Black olive
    Brussels sprout
    Carrot
    Leek
    Parsnip
    Radish
    Turnip
4. Worcestershire
    sauce
	1. Barbecued meat
	    Bacon
	2. Broth
	    Beef broth
	    Chicken broth
	3. Gravy
	4. Ham
	    Cooked ham
	    Iberico ham
	5. Meat pie
		1. Plastic
		    Heated plastic
		    Oilskin
		    Vinyl
		2. Rubber
		3. Used matches

ICONIC
WHISKY

TASTING NOTES & FLAVOUR CHARTS FOR
1,000 OF THE WORLD'S BEST WHISKIES

Quarto is the authority on a wide range of topics.

Quarto educates, entertains and enriches the lives of
our readers – enthusiasts and lovers of hands-on living.

www.QuartoKnows.com

Special thanks
to Davin de Kergommeaux
and to Richard Liogier,
without whom this book would not exist.

First published in the UK, USA and Australia in 2016 by
Jacqui Small LLP
74–77 White Lion Street
London N1 9PF

Title of the original edition: ICONIC WHISKY, single malts and more
Copyright © 2015 Editions de la Martinière – EDLM, Paris

Translated from French by Anne McDowall

ISBN: 978 1 910254 63 9
A catalogue record for this book is available from the British Library.

2018 2017 2016
10 9 8 7 6 5 4 3 2 1

Printed in France

ICONIC WHISKY

CYRILLE MALD &
ALEXANDRE VINGTIER

jacqui
small

CONTENTS

III. Exploring the different aspects of whisky 348

APPENDICES 389

INTRODUCTION

'Truth is far superior to any story.'
Antonin Artaud

Today more than ever, whisky has reached a record peak in the history of spirits. Whisky has forged the destiny of men and women, their joys and their friendships. Some have fashioned their pleasures from it, others their palates. Others have built remarkable empires in incredible circumstances. This, indeed, is what lies at the heart of the expertise of tasters who have an intimate knowledge of whisky: an understanding of this exceptional diversity.

Whisky tasting began to become fashionable in the 1960s. Since that time scientific research has continued to reveal the infinite richness and complexity of this beverage. The presence of hundreds of flavour compounds had already been proven and experts were becoming increasingly interested in their formation and in the mechanisms, practices and ingredients that lead to precisely this diversity.

This book brings a new perspective to the exploration of the world of whisky by placing aromas at its heart, and not least by introducing a new flavour wheel, which aims to make these scientific findings easy to understand. This has enabled us to offer a graphic rendering of the dominant aromas of each of the 1,000 selected whiskies to make them more accessible and to help you understand their nuances, providing guidelines, as it were, that aim to develop, as far as possible, a common language. In addition, in order to help you compare, differentiate or match them, we have created a label that assembles the aromatic families that dominate the nose, palate and finish of each whisky.

This educational approach is also a feature of the other sections of this book, of those concerning the history and manufacture of whisky, of course, but also of the introduction to tasting techniques and pairing whisky with food. There is also an introduction to travel, to the heart of whisky lands, to discover the skills and *terroirs* that have created it, via those who make it. This book is a chance for us to pass on our knowledge of the keys and codes of this prolific and passionate world.

Mald-Vingtier

PREFACE

Many books have been written about whisky. But aside from two or three old seminal works and a few technical volumes, most have settled for regurgitating the history of whisky and distilleries, relating anecdotes that are already well known, and reeling off tasting notes that are often perplexing.

Ultimately, the literary landscape of whisky – and I am including here the myriad of specialist and amateur websites – has been divided between numerous books for beginners and a few very daunting semi-professional works. There remained, then, a large gap to fill and Cyrille and Alexandre have proven to be up to the challenge, offering a new approach to whisky – serious without being off-putting and entertaining without being trivial – in a way that is methodical, knowledgeable and eloquent.

Thanks to them, whisky literature has at last reached the heights of that of wine! Thank you, Cyrille and Alexandre!

Serge Valentin

PART I

WHISKY:
from making it to tasting it

DEFINING WHISKY

Whisky is a high-alcohol content spirit that was first made in the British Isles many centuries ago. It is made solely from grain and yeast, i.e. from ale, and aged in barrels. Whisky is not made from fruit like fruit-, wine- or cider-based spirits such as brandies (Cognac, Armagnac, Calvados), from sugar-cane juice, molasses or syrups like rum, or even from honey. Its characteristic taste is derived from its raw ingredients and from wood and it should not be sweetened. Among the vast family of grain-based spirits, this minimalist definition enables us to distinguish, on the one hand, true whiskies from artificial ones – those artificial, neutral-alcohol-based ersatz whiskies whose organoleptic characteristics come from additives rather than from their raw materials – and, on the other hand, whisky from so-called neutral spirits with little flavour such as vodka, distilled at more than 95% ABV. The use of yeast, its high alcohol content and barrel ageing distinguishes it, too, from traditional Asian spirits such as the Chinese *baijiu* (the top category of spirits worldwide in terms of volume), Korean *soju* and Japanese *shochu* as well as from Western grain-based eaux-de-vie. The absence of flavouring to modify its aromas prevents confusion with gin, Jenever, akvavit and beer-based distilled spirits, to which juniper berries, dill seed, caraway or hops are added. So much for what whisky is not.

If we want to present it in a more positive way, whisky is generally defined in traditional whisky-producing countries as a spirit:
– made from one or more types of grain
– wholly or partially malted
– fermented mainly by the action of yeast
– then distilled to less than 94.8% (or 95% in America and Japan) alcohol by volume (ABV) so as to retain the characteristics of its raw ingredients
– aged for several years in wooden casks of less than 700 litres (185 gallons)
– and finally bottled at at least 40% ABV in order to preserve the organoleptic qualities in the bottle.

ALL GRAINS

Moreover, any type of grain can be used: not only barley, wheat, rye and corn but also oats, spelt and more recently triticale (an artificial cross between wheat and rye) and even millet, sorghum or rice. The Distillerie des Menhirs in Brittany even offers a buckwheat-based whisky while the Corsair distillery in Tennessee produces a whiskey made from quinoa; yet buckwheat and quinoa are pseudograins, that is they are not true grasses yet their seeds are nevertheless recognized as grains in the commercial sense. However, the Catskill Distilling Co. in New York State also makes a spirit from buckwheat using the same techniques as whisky but does not use this label, considering that only grains can be used as the basis for true whisky. Scottish regulations expressly prohibit the use of pseudograins in the manufacture of Scotch Whisky.

SACCHARIFICATION AND MALT

The issue of the definition of grains is central insofar as whisky must retain the characteristics of its raw ingredients during its manufacturing process. Indeed, to this end, the saccharification phase is very often regulated. As grains have complex carbohydrates, the use of malted grains, and in particular barley, is vital in order for its enzymes, such as diastase, to simplify sugars without consuming them or turning them into alcohol. In Scotland, only this enzymatic system endogenous to malt is allowed while in other countries, it can be supplemented (or replaced) by other natural enzymes.

FERMENTATION, YEAST AND...

The EU and Japan require that fermentation should occur only under the action of yeast. In the United States, the use of recycled yeast, via the sour-mash method – in other words by reusing the 'starter' – enables the accumulation of lactic acid bacteria, which also ferments the sugars in the grain. Generally, the deliberate addition of other types of bacteria or fungi that compete with the yeast is prohibited, although wild yeast, some bacterial flora and fungi naturally present in the atmosphere will influence the character of a whisky. (Indeed, these factors, along with the quality of the water used during mashing and fermentation, the climate during the ageing process and even the quality of the peat will to a large extent define the uniqueness or *terroir* of a whisky.) The water quality may be controlled, in particular its pH. Most often, the use of defoamers during fermentation and distillation is permitted in order to prevent overflows in the tanks and stills.

GREAT FREEDOM IN DISTILLATION

Distillation techniques and equipment may be imposed for certain categories of whisky, but, in general, great freedom exists in this area: both very traditional and very modern stills are used throughout the world as long as the ABV does not exceed 40% and the distillate is not adulterated by excessive modification, above 94.8% ABV in Europe or 95% in America or Japan. The number of distillations is only very rarely specified: simple, double, triple or even more if necessary. Usually, rich whiskies such as malt and bourbon are distilled between 55 and 80% ABV and lighter or grain whiskies from 80–94% ABV.

AGEING IN (OAK) CASKS

The ageing of whisky is a characteristic that is both identified by the regulations in effect and expected by consumers. It is generally carried out in oak casks of tens or hundreds of litres (gallons), the maximum capacity often being limited to 700 litres (185 gallons), except in the case of named exemptions and local exceptions. Some US designations demand the use of new casks, which moreover must be charred, or of old ones, and require that the whiskey be diluted to 62.5% ABV before being casked. Nevertheless, oak is not always mandatory; some regulations require only that the ageing be carried out in wood casks: chestnut, false acacia or ash are permitted, although their use remains marginal. Used casks may have contained other spirits, wines, beers or ciders, and will notably transfer their colours, aromas and sometimes their sugars to the whisky. The cask can thus impart other characteristics to the whisky in addition to those of the grain used to make it and the wood used in the cask construction. The minimal ageing period is established at three years in Europe and Canada and two years for American straight whiskies and Australian whiskies, but elsewhere a single day can suffice for simple qualities.

MARKETING CONDITIONS

With the exception of Japan and Australia, where, for their domestic markets, whisky can be bottled at a lower ABV, whisky is bottled at a minimum of 40% ABV (or even 43% in some countries) although there are some rare exemptions for very old Scottish single malts such as Littlemill and Macallan. It can also be bottled at cask strength (or barrel proof), that is to say at the alcoholic strength recorded in the cask, without dilution, and thus can easily exceed 60% ABV. The use of caramel (from burnt sugar) is also permitted as a colorant, generally to give the whisky the colour when bottled that it had in the cask prior to dilution. Any sweetening or addition of sugar is prohibited.

DEFINITIONS IN THE TRADITIONAL COUNTRIES

Whisky-producing countries have implemented definitions, which vary in their precision, to describe the whiskies produced locally and protect the mention of their origin on the labels. Moreover, the main economic free-trade zones and other important domestic markets have established whisky definitions in their laws.

Scotland

Scotch whisky is undeniably the highest and most demanding whisky production standard as well as the model for many producers worldwide. Above and beyond the characteristics already mentioned, note that fermentation and distillation must take place at the distillery and that, during ageing, only casks that have been emptied of all liquid are permitted. Also, consequently, the use of oak shavings, sugar, caramel, boise (an infusion of shavings in distilled water permitted in Cognac) and *paxaretta* (a very sweet condensed Spanish wine used in Scotland until the 1980s to treat the casks) are prohibited. Moreover, any innovation in the ageing cellars must be previously authorized by Her Majesty's Customs and Excise. Finally, it is prohibited to produce whisky in Scotland that does not adhere to the regulations of Scotch Whisky. All whisky must belong to one of five defined categories.

Single Malt Scotch Whisky must be made in a single distillery exclusively from malted barley and must be distilled in pot stills. If several Single Malts are blended, whatever the proportions (one drop of a single malt in the cask of another single malt is enough), the whisky then becomes a **Blended Malt Scotch Whisky**. These were also known in the past as Vatted Malts. The reference Pure Malt is now banned since it could designate either a Single Malt or a Blended Malt. Single Malt Scotch Whisky must be bottled in Scotland.

Single Grain Scotch Whisky is made in a single distillery from malted barley and possibly another grain and is generally distilled in a column still. Even if 100% malted barley wort is distilled in a column still, or a wort of several grains is distilled in a pot still, the description Single Grain Scotch Whisky still applies. The blending of several Single Grain Scotch Whiskies gives a **Blended Grain Scotch Whisky**. In Scotland, mainly wheat has been used since the 1980s, only the North British distillery continuing the traditional use of high levels of corn – creating a lighter whisky, which can be a much appreciated quality in a blend as it allows the malt to express itself more fully. It is sometimes said that the higher the proportion of malted barley, the higher the quality of a Grain Whisky will be.

Finally, and this is by far the most important category in terms of volume, **Blended Scotch Whisky** is the result of blending one or more Single Malts with one or more Single Grains.

If the whisky is entirely produced in one of the protected areas or regions, the name can be placed in front of these classifications: **Campbeltown, Islay, Highland, Speyside** or **Lowland**.

Ireland

Irish Whiskey (Ireland and the US both use whiskey rather than whisky), also called *Uisce Beatha Eireannach* in Irish, is a Protected Geographical Indication of Ireland following the regulations common to Scotch whisky with regards its manufacture. Although Ireland is often associated with triple distillation, double distillation is also still used and authorized. There are four types of Irish Whiskey:

– **Malt Irish Whiskey**, made from 100% malted barley and distilled in pot stills

– **Grain Irish Whiskey**, made from a maximum of 30% malted barley and other unmalted grains, most commonly corn, wheat or barley, and distilled in a column still

– **Pot Still Irish Whiskey**, made from a mash containing at least 30% malted barley and 30% unmalted barley (generally in proportions from 50:50 to 40:60) supplemented with usually about 5% of other unmalted grains – rye or oats – and distilled (two or three times) exclusively in a large pot still

– **Blended Irish Whiskey**, made by blending two or three of the whiskey types mentioned above. Thus Irish Blended Whiskey is not necessarily, as in Scotland, a blend of grain and malt whiskies but might also be a blend of Malt and Pot Still Whiskeys, for example.

Note that with Irish Malt Whiskey, it is quite permissible to use peat in drying the malt. It is therefore possible, technically speaking, to produce the same types of whisky as in Scotland.

Finally, and this is a drink consumed worldwide, **Irish Cream** is a cream liqueur made with at least 1% Irish Whiskey; the remainder of the alcohol may come from other agricultural sources.

United States

The outstanding feature of American whiskies is that they are made from a blend of grains, distilled at less than 80% ABV then, with some exceptions, aged in new charred casks. These definitions are not necessarily based on a type or number of distillations as with Scottish or Irish whiskies. The main distinction between the different types produced lies in the predominance of a particular type of grain in the mash. The words Whisky and Whiskey are used interchangeably on the labels.

Bourbon Whiskey must be made with at least 51% corn, **Rye Whiskey** is based on 51% rye, **Wheat Whiskey** is based on 51% wheat, **Malt Whiskey** is based on 51% malted barley (barley is not specified but is implied) and **Rye Malt Whiskey** is based on 51% malted rye. There are also unregulated designations such as Spelt, Oat, Millet and Triticale Whiskey.

With the exception of malted barley or rye whiskies, which can be made from a single type of grain, American whiskies contain another malted grain, usually malted barley, plus one or two other grains. This choice in the proportions of grains used is called the Mash Bill, like the ingredients in a recipe. Thus, for example, we find Four Grain Bourbon Whiskies, made with a majority of corn supplemented with malted barley, rye and wheat. As a general rule, a high proportion of corn is used to make classic bourbon, along with rye and a little malted barley, but the presence of rye can be accentuated or the rye can be replaced with wheat so that these cereals have a significant influence (for example 30–40%); such whiskies are then known as High Rye Bourbon or Ryed Bourbon or Wheated Bourbon, for example. The Buffalo Trace distillery in Kentucky has even experimented with oats and rice instead of rye and barley. A distillery in Brooklyn recently launched a range called Widow Jane that emphasizes different varieties of corn, the grain that is central to American whiskey.

Tennessee Whiskey follows the same rules as Bourbon Whiskey but, in accordance with the law of May, 13 2013, must be distilled in the state of Tennessee and filtered through a layer of maple charcoal chips before being casked. This process is known as the Lincoln County Process, from the name of the county where the original Jack Daniel's distillery was located.

Finally, **Corn Whiskey** is also made from corn but with a minimum proportion of 80% and also differs from Bourbon Whiskey in its optional ageing, which is carried out in uncharred new casks or in casks that have already been used. This is the only American whiskey for which no ageing or casking is required. That said, a short casking period, of no minimum duration, is sufficient for all other types of American whiskey: whereas in Europe and Canada, three years ageing are required before the spirit is allowed to be called whisky, a single day suffices in the United States!

What about a whisky made from a mash in which no single grain prevails? Producers often use the simple label American Whiskey, and as such whiskies are often made from four different cereals in more or less equal proportions, they sometimes state Four Grain on the label.

All these types of whiskey must be casked at a maximum 62.5% ABV, even though by evaporating water at a faster rate than the alcohol during ageing in a very dry cellar, the final ABV before bottling can rise to around 70%. If a whiskey is produced following the rules previously mentioned but aged in old casks or with a level of alcohol higher than 62.5% ABV, it carries the wording 'whiskey distilled from xxx mash', for example, Whiskey Distilled from Bourbon Mash.

The word **Straight** describes, in the United States, a whiskey that has been aged for at least two years (four years if the age is not specified) and, if it is the result of a blend of different whiskies, these must come from a single state (for example, Kentucky Straight Bourbon Whiskey).

There are also other categories that have less to do with quality and more with economics and that are normally aimed at the domestic market. For example, if a whisky is distilled at between 80 and 95% ABV, it will carry the label **Light Whiskey**. Such whiskies are very often made from 99% corn and 1% malted barley. This is the American equivalent of Scottish grain whiskies.

The label **Blended Whiskey** denotes a blend of at least 20% Straight Whiskey, in other words a mature whiskey with rich aromas, with another type of whiskey, younger and lighter, or even with neutral alcohol (distilled at at least 95% ABV and sometimes lightly aged). If the whiskey is supplemented with one of the superior categories (Bourbon, Rye, Wheat, Corn, Malt or Rye Malt), this category must represent at least 51% of the blend. For example, a Blended Bourbon Whiskey must contain at least 51% of Straight Bourbon Whiskey, supplemented, where required, with other types of whiskey or even with neutral alcohol.

Finally, the label **Spirit Whiskey** denotes a blend of neutral alcohol with at least 5% of Whiskey and a maximum of 20% of Straight Whiskey. If the whiskey has been flavoured, it can display the label **Flavored Whiskey** provided it has not been sweetened, that it has been bottled at at least 30% ABV and that its flavours are natural. There are also liqueurs made from 51% Bourbon or Rye Whiskey, which are called Bourbon or Rye Liqueurs/Cordials and, along the lines of flavoured rums, whiskey-based drinks such as Rock and Rye and Rock and Bourbon. It is also possible to produce a spirit called **Imitation Whiskey**, which is obtained by artificially flavouring a neutral alcohol.

Canada

Canadian Whisky or **Canadian Rye Whisky** is a style of whisky that is generally, and erroneously, confused with American Rye Whiskey: there are several types of whisky produced in Canada, made from malt, wheat and, of course, rye, as well as blends of different whiskies. The regulations surrounding production methods in Canada are substantially similar to those relating to American, Scottish and Irish whiskies, the law requiring that whisky be aged for three years in casks, as in Europe. The addition of flavouring substances is allowed but the whisky must retain the flavour characteristics of a Canadian whisky.

Originally made from wheat, gradually replaced by corn, Canadian whisky is renowned for its spiciness derived from the use of rye and new and old casks. Rye cultivated on these northern lands is considered to be more flavoursome and spicy than that of its American counterpart, and the producers therefore do not necessarily use 51% of rye to make **Canadian Rye Whisky**. Finally, in order to retain as much of the characteristics of the different grains as possible, they may be fermented and distilled separately before being blended at the liquid phase.

Canadian **Malt Whisky** follows the minimal requirements of Scottish Malt Whisky except that the limited addition of flavouring is not excluded.

DEFINITIONS IN THE REST OF THE WORLD

The fourth largest producer of whisky in the world in terms of volume, **Japan** has developed minimal definitions for several categories, which are based on Scotch Whisky not only for historical reasons but also because the major Japanese groups have distilleries in Scotland. Thus we find references to **Single Malt**, **Single Grain** (mainly corn) and **Blended Whisky** as well as the label **Pure Malt**, which denotes a whisky made from 100% malted barley.

India is the world's largest whisky market with around 1.5 billion litres (0.4 billion gallons) consumed every year (in terms of alcoholic drinks, only beer exceeds whisky in volume, and only by 40%), so much so that eight out of ten of the biggest (by volume) whisky brands are Indian (only the Scottish brands Johnnie Walker and Ballantine's make it into the top ten, at third and tenth place, respectively)! The Indian taste for whisky, which was imported in the 19th century, is highly developed and the domestic market accounts for the major part of its production, but Indian whisky is not necessarily made from grains. Most often, neutral alcohol made from molasses (the viscous by-product of sugarcane production), as well as whisky essences, are used – for economic reasons and the availability of raw ingredients – both for entry-level whiskies and to give the whiskies a very light, even neutral, flavour. Nevertheless, more and more producers are developing whiskies made from 100% grains, not only malted barley but also corn, rice, sorghum and millet. Thus to create premium blends, several tens of millions of litres of Scotch Whisky are imported each year. (The situation is virtually identical in **Thailand**, but on a smaller scale.) Remarkably, India now has several malt distilleries that use pot stills: Amrut in Bangalore and Paul John and McDowell's, both in Goa, all produce single malts that have won numerous awards for the quality of their products.

Australia formulated a definition of its whiskies, namely the **Australian Standard Malt Whisky** and the **Australian Blended Whisky** in 1901, but this definition that was revoked in 2006 and replaced by the label **Australian Whisky**, guaranteeing the exclusive use of grains, a minimum ageing of two years and that its flavour, aroma and other characteristics are those of a whisky (which presupposes a Scotch Whisky).

South Africa recognizes several types of whisky: **Whisky**, **Malt Whisky** and **Blended Whisky** and refers expressly to its domestic product in its laws. Its definition of whisky is in accordance with European standards; nevertheless the category Blended Whisky is a blend containing at least 25% Malt Whisky, whereas no such minimum requirement exists elsewhere. In particular, it imposes a minimum ABV of 43%.

The **EU** and **Switzerland** have based their regulations on the definition given above, defending of the historical identity of whisky but nevertheless with far fewer constraints than Scotch Whisky. Remarkably, beyond the traditional Geographical Indications of Scotch Whisky and Irish Whiskey, three other production areas are defined and protected, namely in Spain, **Whisky Español** (Spanish whisky), where a malt and grain distillery run along Scottish lines has existed since 1958, the Destilerías y Crianza del Whisky (DYC), and in France, where **Whisky de Bretagne** and **Whisky d'Alsace** were defined in late 2014. One of the features of these two French PGIs is the exclusion of the use of genetically modified grains and the imposition of a content of volatile substances exceeding 150 grams per hectolitre (5 ounces per gallon) of pure alcohol (HLPA). **Whisky d'Alsace** is a malt whisky exclusively distilled in pot stills with a maximum capacity of 2,500 litres (660 gallons) and with an ABV of between 60 and 80% when leaving the still. Finally, it must be bottled at between 40 and 65%. **Whisky de Bretagne** must be produced in Brittany or certain communes in the Loire-Atlantique department and be made from barley, wheat, triticale, rye, spelt, corn, oats and/or buckwheat (a pseudograin is thus lawful here). Fermentation should last from between 35 hours and 12 days, which is extremely long compared to the maximum five days observed in Scotland, the stills' boilers should have a maximum volume of 6,000 litres (1,585 gallons) and the column stills a maximum production level of 20,000 litres (5,283 gallons) per 24 hours. Alscace and Brittany have thus opted for production using small pot stills. **Whisky Español** adopted a very comprehensive legislation in 1973 that imposes, notably, a minimum of three years ageing in oak casks of a maximum volume of 650 litres (172 gallons). Tannins must have been previously eliminated from the casks with white wine or spirits, whose residual flavours and aromas do not harm the whisky. Whisky Español is above all a blend of at least 25% malt whisky, **Whisky Malta**, distilled to between 60 and 80% ABV, and grain whisky, **Destillado de Cereales**, produced at between 80 and 96% ABV, and must be bottled at between 40 and 58% ABV. The law also limits the proportions of acetic acid, ethyl acetate, aldehyde, furfural, higher alcohol and methanol as well as solids (3 per 1,000 by weight). Treatment with active carbon is authorized. Finally, the label **Whisky elaborado en España** (whisky made in Spain) denotes a blended whisky for which up to 75% of the malt whisky used can be imported.

Brazil, one of the principal export markets for traditional whiskies and itself a whisky producer, defines three domestic categories that must have an ABV of between 38 and 54%: malt whisky aged for at least two years in casks of a maximum of 700 litres (185 gallons) known as **Whisky Puro Malte** or **Uísque Malte Puro**, whose volatile congeners must exceed 350 grams/HLPA (12 ounces/HLPA); grain whisky aged for at least two years, or **Uísque de Cereais**, whose volatile congeners must exceed 100 grams/HLPA (3½ ounces/HLPA); Blended Whisky or **Uísque Cortado**, a blend of at least 30% malt whisky with an alcohol of agricultural origin (grain or otherwise) that must be modified at more than 95% ABV and/or aged, whose volatile congeners must exceed 100 grams/HLPA (3½ ounces HPA). Finally, **Raw Grain Whisky** must be aged for at least two years in casks and bottled at between 54 and 95% ABV.

HISTORICAL EVENTS

1. Uisge Beatha

432	Saint Patrick returns to Ireland to evangelize the people of Ireland, and, according to legend, carries out the first distillation here.
1130	At the Schola Medica Salernitana (Italy), Magister Salernus writes the *Mappae Clavicula* (a work annotated and completed by Adelard de Bath). It provides the first known description of the distillation of alcohol. Two medical treaties also mention this same discovery: *Practica Chirurgiae* (The Practice of Surgery) by Rogerius and the *Compendium Magistri Salerni*. The use of distilled spirits is therapeutic and is lent support by the observation that alcohol enables the preservation of herbs and plants and prevents the decomposition of flesh.
1200-1300	The technique of condensation has been sufficiently mastered to enable distillation to be developed for taste purposes. Methods for producing distilled spirits spread throughout wine-producing countries: Italy, France and Spain.
1245-1311	Arnaud de Villeneuve, a doctor and alchemist influenced by the Schola Medica Salernitana, perfects distillation methods at Montpellier. He establishes the retention of aromatic and flavouring ingredients from herbs that are macerated in the distilled spirits to obtain aromatic spirits, and popularizes their use in medicine.
1276	With the support of King Henry II of England, De Courcy, with 22 Norman knights and 300 soldiers, invades Ireland in 1177. In 1276, Sir Robert Savage, the eldest son of William Savage, a powerful baron who controls the region of Bushmills, allegedly gives his troops *Uisge Beatha* (distilled spirits) to drink to give them courage before they go into battle against the Irish.
1360	The *Red Book of Ossory*, a Celtic manuscript by Richard Ledred, Bishop of Ossory, describes the recipe

for making *Uisge Beatha*. It provides the first conclusive evidence of distillation in Ireland, which is probably confined at this time to the distillation of wine in the monasteries.

1405   According to the *Annals of Clonmacnoise*, the chieftain Richard MacRaghnaill died from the consequences of an excess of *Uisge Beatha*.

1488   King James IV of Scotland acquires large quantities of whisky to conduct his experiments.

1494   An accounting note from the treasury of Brother John Cor of the Lindores Abbey (Fife) relating to the acquisition of eight bolls of malted barley for the production of *Uisge Beatha* provides the first conclusive evidence of distillation in Scotland.

1505   The Guild of Barber Surgeons of Edinburgh obtains the right to make and sell distilled spirits.

1609   Under James VI of Scotland, the Statutes of Iona, which prohibit strong drink, nevertheless make provision for the inhabitants of the Hebridean islands to distill their own grain and drink their own local produce.

2. Expansion

1617   Walter Raleigh, on his way to Guyana, is offered a cask of 32 gallons of barley spirit, distilled in Cork, by Richard Boyle, Earl of Cork.

1620   At Burkeley Hundred, which he founds in Virginia, James Thorpe distills a spirit made from corn for the first time.

1644   The Scottish Parliament establishes the first system of taxation on malted barley, which is improved in 1661.

1713   The Malt Tax that is part of the rationalization of the tax on spirits following the integration of the Scottish Parliament into the English one (the Acts of Union of 1707), is not applied in Scotland until ten years later, after the riots provoked by the Acts have been crushed. In the Highlands, contraband whisky – made by local, small-scale producers – is rife. It is also of better quality than that produced in the Lowlands, where it is more difficult to evade the tax authorities and where commercial distilleries therefore use other cereals to circumvent the tax.

		Distilleries (foundation)
1742-1746	In Scotland, nearly 100 people are arrested for crimes of illegal distillation.	
1755	Captain Edward Burt of the General George Wade's army is responsible for the first written evidence of the word *usky*, in a letter dated 1736. *Uisge Beatha* has become *Uisce*, then *Usky* and finally *Whisky*. This word enters Johnson's dictionary in 1755.	1779 Bowmore 1780 Jameson
1782	The Highlands are devastated by famine. Fleeing poverty, many Scots and Irish leave for America, where they settle as farmers.	
1783	The first distillery is founded in the United States by Evan Williams at Louisville (now Kentucky). Almost simultaneously, Marker's Mark and Jim Beam are also founded (1785).	
1784	Established to encourage legal distillation in the Highlands, the Wash Tax enables distillers here to benefit from a more favourable tax regime than that imposed in the Lowlands.	
1785	Creation of Bourbon County in honour of the French royal family who supported the United States during the War of Independence. Originally part of Virginia, it is now in the state of Kentucky. Jacob Spears names his distilled spirit Bourbon Whiskey to indicate that it is a whisky made from corn and not rye like those produced in northeastern states such as Pennsylvania.	1785 Marker's Mark Jim Beam 1786 Strathisla 1789 Elijah Craig 1790 Balblair
1791-1794	The Whiskey Rebellion is waged in the United States in opposition to the introduction of the tax on whisky	1794 Oban

production (the Whiskey Excise Act of 1791). This tax is later abolished by Thomas Jefferson.

1797 Glen Garioch

1798 Glenkinchie

1808 Abolition of slavery in the United States and of the triangular trade that enabled the development of the rum trade. Americans turn their back on rum, and whiskey becomes the national drink.

1810 Isle of Jura

1815 Ardbeg Laphroaig

1823 The Excise Tax Act lays the foundations of modern taxation by marginalizing clandestine distillation. In 1824, 337 distilleries obtain licences in Scotland. The quantities produced increase and the quality of whisky – like rail and maritime transportation routes – improves.

1816 Lagavulin

1819 Clynelish

1824 The Port Ellen distillery trials the Spirit Safe, which is then adopted by all other distilleries.

1824 Cardhu Glenlivet Macallan

1825 The Lincoln County Process filtration system is developed by Alfred Eaton, who founds the Tennessee Whiskey brand.

John Walker sells whisky from his shop in Kilmarnock.

1826 Aberlour Old Pulteney

1826 Robert Stein, of the Kilbagie distillery, patents the Patent Still, the first method of continuous distillation.

1828 Springbank

1831 Talisker

1827 George Ballantine sells whisky from his shop in Edinburgh.

1833 Glengoyne

1830 Aeneas Coffey patents the Coffey Still, a column still that outperforms the Patent Still.

1836 Glenfarclas

1837 Edradour Glenkinchie

1839 Dalmore

1840 Glen Grant

1843	James Chivas becomes purveyor to Queen Victoria and begins storing casks in the cellar of his shop in Aberdeen.	1843 Glenmorangie 1846 Caol Ila
1847	John Dewar bottles his first whisky.	
1853	The first law authorizing the blending of casks of whiskies from the same distillery but of different ages.	
1860	The Spirit Act is the first law authorizing the blending of casks of malt whisky with grain whisky in order to make whisky more accessible and to standardize production.	
1864	The *phylloxera* epidemic that is raging on the European continent leads the British to turn away from wine, Cognac and sherry in favour of blended whisky and single malt Scotch.	1866 Jack Daniel's 1870 Cragganmore
1877	The Distillers Company Ltd is founded by six Lowland grain distilleries in order to gain an influence at a time of rapid change in the whisky industry. In 1919, John Haig joins the Distillers Company, as do Dewar, Buchanan and Johnnie Walker in 1925 and, in 1927, White Horse.	1878 Glenrothes 1881 Bruichladdich Bunnahabhain 1887 Glenfiddich 1892 Balvenie 1897 Dalwhinnie Tomatin 1898 Knockando
1915	The first law compelling distillers to age whisky for at least two years in cask.	
1919-1933	Prohibition in the United States (Volstead Act).	
1920	Masataka Taketsuru returns to Japan having studied whisky production for two years in Scotland. He works with Shinjiro Torii, who founds Suntory.	

1923

The first whisky distillery in Japan, Yamazaki, is founded by Torii and managed by Taketsuru. It begins production in 1924. In 1929, the first Japanese whisky is released: Suntory Shirofuda, a peaty whisky that does not find a market in Japan.

1923
Yamazaki

1934

Masataka Taketsuru founds his own company, which becomes Nikka in 1952. He creates the first distillery on the island of Hokkaido: Yoichi.

1934
Yoichi

1949
Tullibardine

1995
Isle of Arran

2006
Kilchoman

2007
Chichibu

2009
Abhainn Dearg

2010
Roseisle

2013
Wolfburn

THE COMPONENTS OF THE TERROIR

O ver and above its technical and technological aspects, whisky production is based on natural ingredients that give it, in part, its taste characteristics: grain, water, yeast and sometimes peat. These are the elements that contribute to the definition of the *terroir* of a whisky.

GRAIN

Whisky can be made from all types of grain: principally barley, wheat, rye and corn, but also oats, spelt, triticale, millet, sorghum and rice. Some regulations even allow whisky making from pseudograins such as buckwheat or quinoa. The four main grains used by whisky producers are wheat, barley, rye and corn. Malted barley is the only or main grain used by malt and Irish single pot distillers, while grains such as wheat and corn are used by grain distilleries. In North America, malted rye may be used for rye whiskey (Rye Malt Whiskey), but most mash recipes (known as mash bills) for Bourbon or other American whiskies use malted barley to ensure the conversion of starch into sugars.

Malted barley is used to make single malts with complex aromas. Barley (*Hordeum*) is a grain with a bearded ear and is the earliest known grain to have been cultivated. There are two main types of barley: spring two-row barley, which has more fermentable sugars and is thus better adapted for making whisky, and winter barley, which has six rows. Barley is the grain in which activation (and activity) of enzymes is easiest. It is this activation that will transform the starch into fermentable sugars and in particular into maltose, which itself will be consumed by the yeast during the fermentation stage, to be converted into alcohol. Like Macallan, which cultivates over 120 hectares (297 acres) of a barley variety called Golden Promise, Kilchoman, which has its own barley fields on Islay and Bruichladdich, which notably uses barley from parcels of land on eight farms located in different regions of Scotland that between them produce 100 tonnes (110 tons) of the barley variety Concerto, many distilleries attach importance to the *terroir* and use barley produced by specifically localized parcels of land. Indeed, the different nature of the soils in different cultivation areas (whether the region is coastal and affected by the sea or, conversely, inland; the exposure of the fields; the acidity level, the pH, of the soil; the amount of rainfall; the altitude; etc.) will give the same barley variety different aromas. The Scotch whisky industry alone currently depends on 800,000 tonnes (881,849 tons) of malted barley per year. And consumption is expected to grow by 20% over the next five years. Demand is such that in 2015, a third of the total barley production in the

UK is destined for malting, brewing and distilling. In addition, for nearly a century, most distilleries have also used barley imported from all over the world to make their whisky. Today, France and Germany are the main barley producing and exporting countries.

In the same way that there are many grape varieties used in making wine, there are also different varieties of barley, which impart their different aromatic profiles to whisky. The selection, testing and development processes for a new barley variety are long (15 years on average) and costly. A range of considerations are taken into account in the selection of different barley varieties:

– the yield per hectare of the barley variety (for example, the variety Archer yielded 3 tonnes per hectare/1.4 tons per acre as opposed to the 8 tonnes per hectare/3.23 acres per acre of the most recent barley varieties)
– the alcohol yield per tonne of barley harvested (LPA/T)
– its resistance to illness, parasites and climate
– the aromatic profiles developed
– a high starch content and high germination capacity that make it possible to achieve higher levels of alcohol
– a high malt carbohydrate content (the higher this is, the lower the proportion of protein and fat)
– a low level of nitrogen. The concentration of nitrogen should fall within the percentage range from 1.4% (for the Concerto and Minstrel varieties) to 1.65%.

Varietal diversity in the main barley strains used by the whisky industry since its origins

Barley variety	Period of use	Yield
Odyssey	2012–*currently in use*	435–460 LPA/T
Concerto	2008–*currently in use*	430 –460 LPA/T
NFC Tipple	2006–*currently in use*	420–435 LPA/T
Decanter	1998–*currently in use*	420–435 LPA/T
Chalice (organic)	1997–*currently in use*	400–405 LPA/T
Optic	1994–*currently in use*	400–410 LPA/T
Prisma	1994–*currently in use*	410–420 LPA/T
Chariot	1992/2000	410–440 LPA/T
Pipkin	1991–*still in use*	405–410 LPA/T
Puffin	1987–*still in use*	405–410 LPA/T
Camargue	1985–90	405–410 LPA/T
Triumph	1980–5	395–405 LPA/T
Golden Promise	1968–80–*in use again*	385–395 LPA/T

Barley variety	Period of use	Yield
Marris Otter	1965–85–*in use again*	350–370 LPA/T
Zephyr	1950–68	370–380 LPA/T
Proctor (Plumage-Archer x Kenia)	1950–65	370–380 LPA/T
Pioneer (Kenia x Australian Tshermarks)	1950–65	370–380 LPA/T
Plumage-Archer	Interwar years to 1950	360–370 LPA/T
Spratt-Archer	Interwar years to 1950	360–370 LPA/T
Archer	1906	– – –
Spratt	1905	– – –
Goldthorpe	1880–1935	– – –
Annat	1830 to early 20th century	– – –
Chevalier	1819 to early 20th century	– – –
Bere	Original–1926, *in use again since 1985*	

Other grains and their choice depending on country All types of grains can be used to make grain whiskies. In Scotland, wheat replaced corn in the production of grain whiskies in the early 1980s. Conversely, in the United States, mash bills for Bourbon generally use 70–80% corn with varying proportions of rye, malted barley and wheat depending on whether the whiskey is a Traditional Bourbon (Jim Beam, Elijah Craig, Heaven Hill, etc.), High Rye (Bulleit, Four Roses, etc.) or a Wheated Bourbon (Van Winkle, Maker's Mark). Obviously, the latter grains are found in the different types of American whiskies at at least 51% (Straight Rye Whiskey, Straight Wheat Whiskey, etc.) The use of corn gives a milder aromatic profile, while rye tends to have a more spicy taste and dry finish and wheat brings out a lighter palette of flavours. Experiments aim to integrate the two worlds. Such is the case with Miya-gikyo in Japan and Loch Lomond in Scotland, two of a handful of distilleries that produce single malt and grain whiskies at the same production site and are thus able to combine the two to make what can be called a single blended whisky. Here we are at the limits of the exercise.

WATER

It is commonly held that brewing beer requires 10 litres (2.6 gallons) of water for every litre (0.26 gallon) of ale produced whereas it takes 100 litres (26 gallons) of water to produce a litre (0.26 gallon) of whisky. The ready supply and quality of water are essential for whisky production. Indeed, it is the exploitation of a spring, stream, river or loch – and the assurance of owning the rights to do so – that is the primary factor that dictates the location of a distillery. Much more than simply an ingredient, water is a necessity at all stages. It is important, too, that it is of high quality, as pure as possible (rendered such by osmosis or mechanical or natural filtration in the case of springs without input) and available all year round. Availability is a key factor and the water cycle during the summer can impose a 'silent season' during which the distillery is obliged to cease its production of whisky. It is during this season that major control and maintenance operations are carried out, along with any necessary repairs. In fact, the flow and temperature of the water have an effect, in particular, on the cooling capacity of the condensers and hence on the rate of distillation. The pace of life in distilleries therefore varies between winter and summer.

Although its influence is relatively slight, the mineralization of the water will have some effect on the aromatic profile of a whisky. Indeed, water will take on particular qualities according to its mineral content (calcium, magnesium, zinc, iron), which themselves result from the geological formations that the water has flowed through (sedimentary or volcanic layers, limestone ridge or alkaline peat). It is this mineralization that will define the total hardness of the water and thus its influence on the aromatic profile of the whisky. From the soft water of Yamazaki, Hakushu and the granitic areas of Speyside, and the affect of quartzite at Cardhu, red sandstone at Inchgower and Midleton, basalt rock at Talisker, basalt and clay at Bushmills, peat at Yoichi and limestone at Jack Daniel's, to the very hard water used by Glenmorangie, which is loaded with mineral salts from the limestone and sandstone layers it has crossed, there is a whole range of mineralization to be discovered.

This influence can become apparent at different times due to the fact that water is used at each stage of the production process:
– during germination to reactivate dormant barley by immersing it into successively heated water baths to reproduce the natural development and activate diastase enzymes that will make the grain germinate. At this stage, soaking the barley in peaty water is likely to impart smoky notes to the malt
– during the mashing in the mash tuns, the ground malt (grist) is mixed with hot water to obtain a paste (mash) to extract the soluble compounds and convert the starch into fermentable sugars. Water that is rich in calcium enables the diastase enzymes to play their catalytic role in the mashing process, which will promote the action of the yeast during the following fermentation stage
– for indirectly heating the steam stills
– to cool the condensers during the distillation process and re-liquefy the evaporated alcohol
– during the blending process to lower the alcohol content of the whisky when it is being casked (around 63%) and potentially reducing it before bottling.

YEAST

Yeast is an essential element in the aromatic profile of a whisky and the future of innovation in terms of aromas. Indeed, if we accept, to simplify things, that the aromatic profile of a whisky is 60% as a result of its ageing and 40% from its ingredients and the production methods used by the distillery, at least half of this 40% results from the type of yeast used. This gives us a clearer understanding of the possibilities presented by the action of yeast during fermentation when the sugars are converted to alcohol and carbon dioxide.

Yeasts are living micro-organisms (unicellular fungi of the Ascomycetes family). There are two types of yeast: (i) natural yeasts: lambics, resulting from spontaneous fermentation, very aromatic but sensitive to climate changes as well as to the microbial environment, and (ii) cultured yeasts: strains selected based on their increased tolerance to ethanol, their ability to ferment more complex sugar molecules and on the correct formation of aromatic congeners (metabolites). The varieties of yeast chosen and the proportions used at each fermentation are specific to each distillery and they will determine the alcohol content and the aromatic profile. Moreover, as fermentation can take place in either open or closed, wooden or steel tanks, the choices made at this stage will also have an effect on the aromatic palette: open tanks allow indigenous yeasts present in the air to enter the tank, while wooden tanks enable bacteria and natural yeasts to grow from one tankful to another.

The yeast used by the distilleries (*Saccharomyces cerevisiae*) is baker's yeast. This yeast is also used by ale breweries (while lager brewers use another type of yeast, *Saccharomyces pastorianus*). The yeast is in liquid form but can also be compressed or in powder form to facilitate transportation. The most commonly used distiller's yeasts are *S. cerevisiae* strain M, which has been modified several times, strain MX, which allows faster fermentation, and the Pinnacle from Maury, which creates even faster fermentation times while retaining the particular character of the fermentation aromas. Brewer's yeast is used in a complementary way to distiller's yeast. It allows the fermentation congeners, the chemical compounds produced during fermentation, to be accentuated. These include fusel alcohol, fatty acids and their esters, aldehydes and ketones as well as sulphur compounds. These congeners vary depending on the varieties of yeast used and more than 90 fermentation esters have been distinguished, which impart the characteristic fruity or floral aromas. The formation of these aromatic compounds is affected by the fermentation temperatures; the higher these are, the fewer esters are produced.

Fermentation congeners
Esters
Ethyl acetate
Apple, pear, white fruits, varnish, solvent
Isoamyl acetate
Banana, pineapple, strawberry, liquorice allsorts
2-phenylethanol
Rose, geranium, hyacinth, lily, honey, neroli, Parma violet
3-mercaptohexanol acetate
Boxwood, tropical fruits
Aldehydes
Malt, cinnamon, almond, salted caramel, porridge (oatmeal), bread
Damascenone
Prune, rose, apple, jasmine, lavender
Guaiacols
Clove, smoke, boise, pine, bacon

The lees can be partially retained in the brew: a draw at the end of the fermentation eliminates the largest and retains the fine lees (dead yeast, bacteria and foculated and precipitated organic compounds). The constituent components of the lees will hydrolyze into much smaller and more soluble elements. Once distilled, they will impart qualities to the aromatic profile of the whisky by increasing the fatty acids and their esters, which will give it body and refine its liveliness and aromas – in particular fruit and rancio ones.

Future strains of yeast will be selected in accordance with their ability not only to improve the aromatic profiles of whiskies but also to reduce their fermentation times and to meet the requirements of high-density worts.

PEAT

Peat is a fossil matter formed by accumulation in an environment that is saturated in water and low in oxygen (anaerobic) of:
– plant debris such as sphagnum moss (bryophytes), algae and aquatic plants (helophytes), woody plants, heather, etc., and of
– dead micro-organic matter (microfauna and arthropods, bacteria and fungi).

Because it grows at a rate of only about 1mm ($\frac{1}{32}$in) per year, a peat bog can take a period of between 1,000 and 5,000 years to form.

Scottish peat bogs contain greater quantities of sphagnum moss and heather than of any other plant species. The surface layer is thin and the deeper the underlying layer, the more phenolic aromatic compounds it contains.

The peat used during the kilning phase comes from alkaline peat bogs. It is mainly composed of (i) brown peat (from the fibrous layer lying directly below the surface layer of the peat bog), (ii) a small fraction of black peat (from the deeper and more fertile layer, rich in mineral particles), sometimes supplemented with (iii) peat caff (macerated peat debris), which is a smoke accelerator.

In order that the malt absorbs fully the aromatic compounds released by the burning of the peat, this is done at the beginning of the kilning phase, when the moisture content of the malt exceeds 25%. The generation of smoke (peat reek) depends on the composition of the bricks used and their moisture content: the more humid the peat, the more smoke and less heat it will generate (and vice versa). The extraction of the aromas of smoke and lignin derivatives (wood compound) is all the more important in that peat burns at a relatively low temperature and without flames. The smoke that is generated increases the number of aromatic compounds (phenols), the concentration levels of which are measured in ppm (phenol parts per million).

Concentration in ppm of malt				
0 ppm	2–3 ppm	8–15 ppm	20–50 ppm	50+ ppm
Unpeated	Slightly peaty	Moderately peaty	Very peaty	Powerfully peaty

The phenolic concentration of the whisky is ultimately about half that of the malt that was used to make it. This concentration will, however, depend on the distillation method used. Assuming an equal phenolic concentration level in the wort, the longer the middle cut, the peatier the whisky will be. It will also depend on (i) the length of time the whisky is aged (the longer the duration, the greater the loss of phenols) and (ii) the casks used for this ageing and on whether or not they have previously been used to age peaty whisky. From a practical standpoint, a whisky that has suffered substantial oxidation (i.e. because the bottle was opened several months earlier) will also lose phenolic concentration.

Peat has its own characteristics depending on the components that have formed it (fern, moss, pinewood, algae, etc.) So, it will impart particular aromas to the whisky depending on its place of origin. Peat from Islay is richer in phenols, guaiacols (an organic compound that is found in wood creosote) and in vanilla compounds than mainland peat due to a greater amount of sphagnum.

Other smoking processes are also possible, such as those practised notably in Sweden, for example, where the Mackmyra distillery, in its Svensk Rök whisky, adds juniper branches to the Karinmossen peat during the kilning phase in order to impart a specific juniper aroma to the malt. In the future, the variation in types of smoking will have a natural tendency to increase, as is currently seen in the United States, where using hickory wood in smoking, with gastronomic accents, is making an appearance.

THE PROCESSES OF WHISKY MAKING

MALTING: GERMINATION

Malting is the first stage in the transformation of the grain into alcohol. Its objective is the conversion and simplification of the starch in the barley (or rye or wheat for some whiskies) into sugar. The enzymes are activated to germinate the grain and split the cell walls. They will transform the starch into fermentable sugars and especially into maltose. It is this malt sugar that will later be consumed by the yeast, during the fermentation stage, to be converted into alcohol. Since the 1970s, most malt production is undertaken outside the distilleries themselves by mechanized malt houses, which have developed industrial processes. Only a few distilleries, such as Balvenie, BenRiach, Bowmore, Chichibu (in progress), Highland Park, Kilchoman, Laphroaig and Springbank, carry out the malting of some of the barley that they use themselves. This is more common in the United States, where artisanal distilleries such as Copper Fox, Coppersea, Corsair, Hillrock, Leopold Bros, Maine Craft, Orange County and Rogue Spirits, have their own malting floors.

Reception

1 **Barley silo** • The barley is stored in the silo after delivery.

2 **Screener-Grader** • The barley is cleaned to remove any impurities (plant debris, straw and stones).

Germination

3 **Steeping tanks** • Dormant barley is reactivated with water and oxygen. The process consists in reproducing, by artificial means, the natural development of the barley by immersing it in successively hotter baths in order to activate the diastase enzymes (amylases) that will germinate the grain.

4 **Malting floors** • The barley is spread out to extract the moisture from the germs. The barley is turned regularly to aerate it and maintain it at a stable temperature. This process encourages the green shoots that will split the cell walls and simplify the starch. The process is usually automated in saladin boxes or rotating drums called malting drums, which also prevent the roots of the germs from becoming matted. Germination must be interrupted before the shoot consumes the fermentable sugars. The green malt obtained therefore needs to be dried.

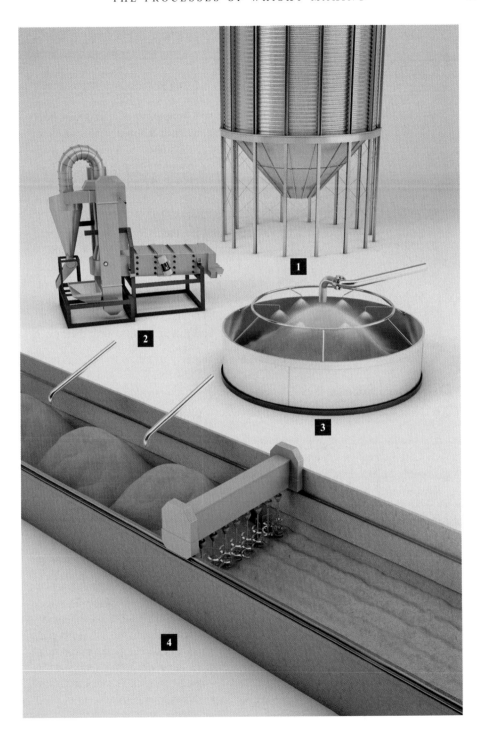

MALTING: KILNING

Kilning / Drying

5 **Kiln** • The green malt is dried in buildings with pagoda-like roofs (to provide adequate ventilation) by aerating it with hot air to reduce its moisture content from 45 to 4%. The heat is supplied by the kiln's fireplace. The heat

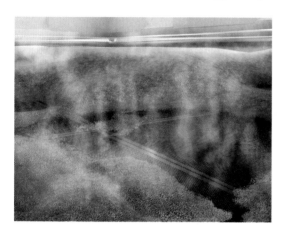

passes up the chimney flue and through the grating of the drying room where the green malt is spread out. The temperature of the ventilated air is increased towards the end of the drying phase to reveal the malt's aromas. By varying the malting process and the malt roasting levels, it is possible to obtain different colourings and flavours, for example caramel malt, chocolate malt, etc.

Smoking with peat/charcoal: the principle of drying is the same but is done by smoking peat or charcoal, which imparts its smoky aromas to the whisky. The smoke that is generated increases the number of aromatic compounds (phenols), the concentration levels of which are measured in ppm (phenol parts per million).

Deculming / Destoning

6 **Deculmer-Destoner** • The malt is cleaned by passing it through a rotating drum that removes any remaining traces of root (rootlets, culms) and stones before it is put into sacks.

FERMENTATION

Milling

7 **Grist / Malt mill** • The weighing of the malt and the extraction of the starch: the malt is ground into 'grist'.

Grist hopper • The ground malt (grist) is stored in the grist hopper.

Mashing

8 **Mash tun** • The ground malt (grist) is mixed with hot water then stirred with the blades of the mash tun to extract the soluble elements of the malt. The speed of rotation of the blades will determine whether the resulting wort is clear or cloudy (with bits of grain in suspension). The solid residue or draff is then collected and used in the production of farm feed.

9 **Underback** • Control of the grist in the mash tun and straining of the wort, which is retrieved by gravity. Two draws are made per operation.

10 **Wort cooler (Heat exchanger)** • The wort is cooled from 63–20°C (145–68°F).

Fermentation

11 **Washback** • The sweet wort is mixed with yeast, which transforms the sugar into alcohol and carbon dioxide. Mechanical blades stir the wort constantly in order to prevent a critical rise in temperature, which would kill the yeast. This fermentation also creates aromatic congeners: thus the first fruity notes are developed (for example pineapple, apple, peach and raspberry), as well as floral ones (including jasmine, lavender or ylang-ylang) and other aromas such as butter, pine, glue, parsnip and cinnamon.

12 **Wash charger** • Reception of the fermented wort, the wash, which has an ABV of 6–8°. Preheating of the wash.

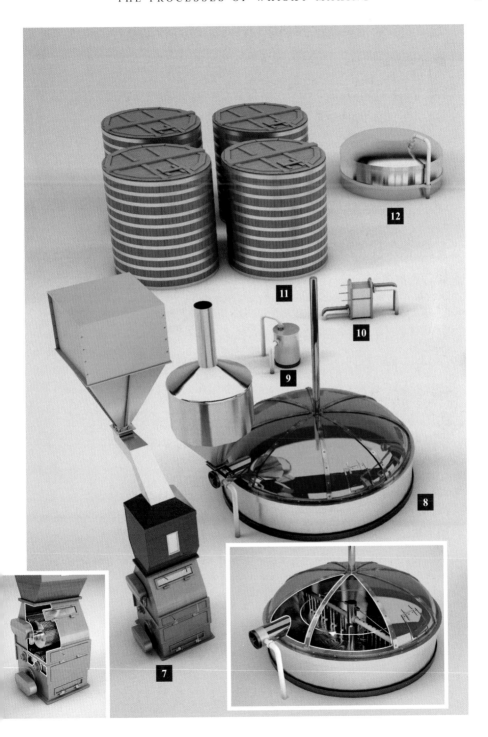

POT STILL: FRACTIONAL DISTILLATION

The stills room is the heart of a single malt distillery. The use of copper for making stills is due to this metal's many properties: it is malleable and excellent as a heat conductor, as a catalyst and at purifying alcohol by eliminating undesirable sulphurated substances.

The indirect heating of the stills by steam has become widespread as it facilitates even heat distribution. But the traditional method of direct heating, either with a naked gas flame (as at Glenfarclas and Glann Ar Mor distilleries) or with coal (still used at Yoichi distillery) is considered by some to give more character to the whisky.

First distillation

13 **Wash still** • The fermented wort is distilled to concentrate the alcohol it contains. Alcohol separates from water because of its lower boiling point (78°C/172°F) and its vapours rise into the 'swan neck' then pass into the 'lyne arm'. The charge level, size and shape of the still, the neck height and the gradient of the lyne arms affect the amount of reflux and therefore the discrimination between light and heavy compounds.

14 **Condenser (Worm tub)** • Condensation of the alcoholic vapours by cooling from 90 to 20°C (194 to 68°F).

15 **Wash safe (Intermediate spirit safe)** • Collection of 'low wines', containing 20–25% ABV.

16 **Low wine receiver** • Storage of the low wine before distillation.

Second distillation

17 **Spirit still** • Distillation of the low wines, to which may be added the 'foreshots' and 'feints' of a previous second distillation.

18 **Condenser (Worm tub)** • Condensation of the alcoholic vapours by cooling.

19 **Spirit safe** • Collection of the distillation ('new make spirit') after condensation of the vapours. The degree of alcohol is checked and the distiller ('stillman') directs the heads and feints into a different vat from the 'heart'. How these cuts are determined affects the whisky's aromatic profile. The heart is usually collected at 73–61% ABV, but for peated malts ABV may drop below 60%.

20 **Spirit receiver** • Storage of the spirit before casking

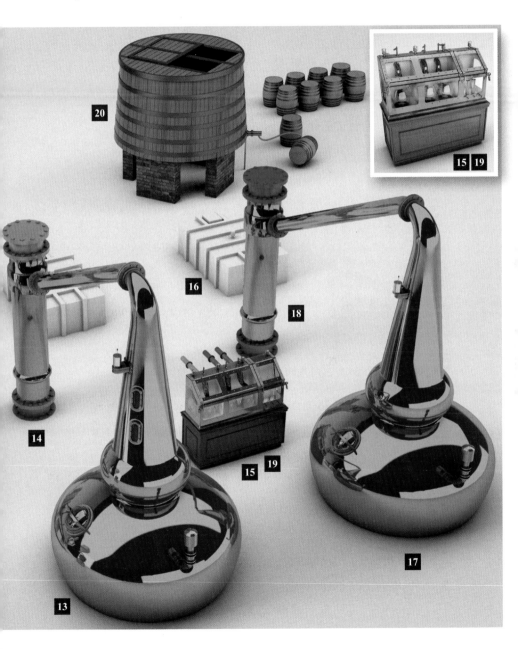

COFFEY STILL: CONTINUOUS DISTILLATION

Column Stills were invented towards the end of the 18th century and became widespread during the 19th century. They enable the very rapid and efficient production of a high-purity distillate in a single operation and are now used for the bulk of whisky production worldwide. The Coffey Still, which was invented around 1830, is probably the most commonly used model in the industry. In continuous distillation, the columns are continuously fed with fermented wort (wash) to be concentrated and separated. Continuous multistage distillation is used, in particular, for making grain whiskies and for many American whiskies.

Continuous distillation

21 **Analyzer** • Tiering of the column by plates over which the wash flows (the lower plates are supplied by overflow). Valves in these plates allow steam injected at the base of the analyzer to rise. The steam and the wort come into contact at the perforations of the plates. The vapour takes on al-

cohol on contact with the wort then, when it reaches the top of the first column, is directed towards the 'rectifier'. It discharges some of its water, which is driven by gravity to the base of the column.

22 **Rectifier** • Injection of the water vapour/alcohol mixture from the bottom of the rectifier. Condensation of alcohol vapours occurs on the copper plates layered in the column. The more volatile alcohols, or 'foreshots' are collected

at the top of the column. Further down flows the distillate with a maximum ABV of 94%, sometimes considerably less. The feints are collected right at the bottom and are then fed back into the top of the analyzer. The heavy 'fusel oils' may also be collected from the lower part of the rectifier. These are then redistilled by bringing them to the boil separately and are then re-injected into the analyzer. The wash, meanwhile, is injected at the top of the rectifier in a through tube and rises in temperature, to higher than 90°C (194°F), at the same time as serving as a coolant for the alcohol vapours in the worm tub before being directed towards the analyzer.

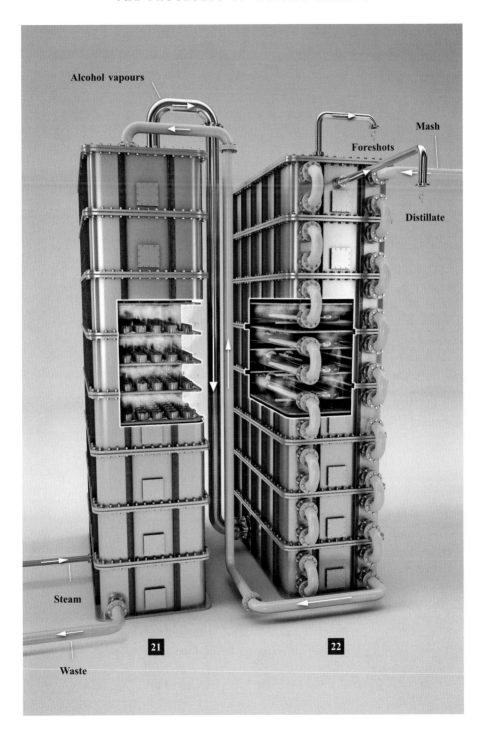

Alcohol vapours

Mash

Foreshots

Distillate

Steam

Waste

21

22

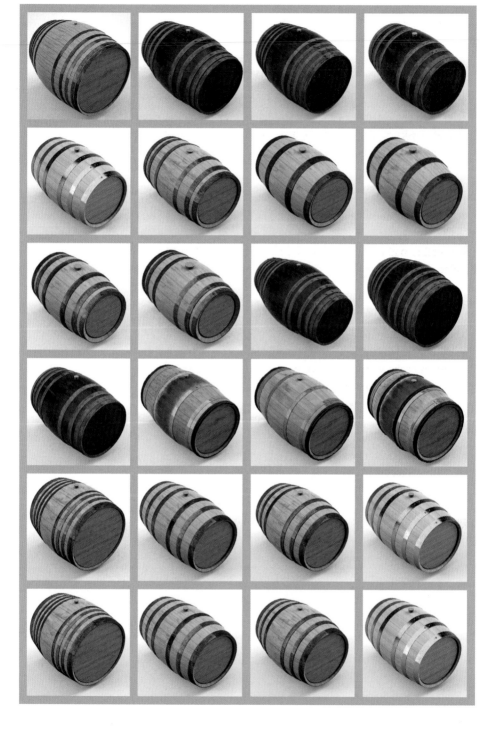

CASKS

TRADITIONAL BRITISH CASKS

U ntil the beginning of the 20th century, producers used a variety of sizes of casks for transporting and ageing whisky. It was logical to use for whisky casks of sizes that were already in use for beers, ales and ciders, along with those used for the wines and spirits that had been imported from all over Europe since the Middle Ages.

In fact, since the Magna Carta in 1225, the English Parliament had been trying to regulate the trade of goods such as wine and beer by imposing standard measures and from 1380 all containers had to be measured. From 1454 to 1825, the ale or beer gallon had a volume of 4.621 litres (1.221 gallons). In 1826, this measure was replaced by the Imperial (UK) gallon, equivalent to 160 fluid ounces, 4.54609 litres or 10 Imperial pounds. This system was definitively replaced by the metric system (litres) in 1985.

In order to understand these volumes and sizes, we need to take into account the historical context of the use of these traditional casks. In fact, the advantages of ageing in casks were not developed until later: the cask was first simply a container in which to store and transport goods and became a measure that could be divided up to resell (or transport on horseback or carry on the back) its contents in equal parts, often split into two or three. It is believed that ageing whisky was developed by merchants and noblemen, who were able to buy the whisky in large quantities and store it for several months or years, which led, as we know, to its rise in popularity in the 19th century.

Thus the system of traditional British casks could be seen as the model of a pyramidal system, of which the 'tun' or the 'butt' were the standard measures and the other casks their divisors.

Tun

216 or 210 Imperial (UK) gallons / 259 or 252 US gallons / Volume ~ 982 or 955 litres

Originally, the tun, a type of cask that had been used at least since the 15th century (the term itself has been in use for over a thousand years in England), contained about 252 wine gallons, a measure corresponding to 3.791 litres. If we break down this number mathematically, we find that $252 = 2 \times 2 \times 3 \times 3 \times 7$ and thus has as divisors 2, 3, 4, 6, 7, 8, 9, 12, etc.

It is believed that the Tun could also contain 256 gallons, since $256 = 2^8$. Converted into 210 Imperial (UK) gallons, this number is itself divisible by 2, 3, 5, 6, 7, 10, etc. since $210 = 2 \times 3 \times 5 \times 7$. The volume of 216 Imperial (UK) gallons (259 US gallons) is itself equal to the volume of two butts of whisky.

	Tun	Butt / Pipe	Puncheon	Hogshead	Barrel	Quarter	Kilderkin	Rundlet	Octave	Anker	Firkin	Bloodtub	Pin	Steckan
Divisor	1	2	3	4	6	8	12	14	16	20	24	28	48	52
Imp. (UK) gallons	216	108	72	54	36	28	18	15	13½	10	9	7½	4½	4¼
Litres	982	491	327	245	164	127	82	68	61	45	41	34	20	19

Butt / Pipe

½ Tun / 108 Imperial (UK) gallons / 130 US gallons / Volume ~ 491 litres

The butt is both a standard measure for liquids and a large cask used for transporting wine or water on board ship. While the English Wine Butt contains 105 Imperial (UK) gallons (477 litres/126 US gallons), the Whisky Butt is slightly bigger, at almost 500 litres/130 US gallons), like the *bota de exportación* of Jerez (sherry). It is hardly surprising that the volume of this *bota* should be the same as that of the butt since Great Britain was the major export market of the wines of Jerez (sherry), which were bottled in the British ports.

British Puncheon

⅓ Tun / 72 Imperial (UK) gallons / 86 US gallons / Volume ~ 327 litres

The British puncheon is a measure and a type of cask used since the 15th century in England, for wine then beer. Whisky appropriated the size and adapted it, to 112 or 120 Imperial (UK) gallons (509–546 litres/135–144 US gallons) in the 19th century. Today, the Japanese use Puncheons of 480 litres (106 US gallons).

Hogshead

½ Butt / 54 Imperial (UK) gallons / 65 US gallons / Volume ~ 245 litres

Sometimes pronounced 'hox-head', this English measure also used for wine and ale dates back to at least the 15th century. It was natural for this measure to be adopted by whisky producers. Five American Standard Barrels of 200 litres (53 US gallons) enabled the manufacture of four Bourbon Hogsheads, probably the most commonly used type of cask in Scotland.

British (Ale) Barrel or (Wine) Tierce

⅓ Butt / 36 Imperial (UK) gallons / 43 US gallons / Volume ~ 164 litres

The barrel of ale is a measure that has been used since the 15th century and has experienced a few variations over the centuries. Now obsolete for whisky, it has been replaced by the Bourbon Barrel, which holds about 180 litres (48 US gallons), and the American Standard Barrel, which holds 200 litres (53 US gallons).

Quarter

¼ Butt / 28 Imperial (UK) gallons / 34 US gallons / Volume ~ 127 litres

This quarter of a butt is practical for transportation on horse-back but also for ageing. It was used for sherry and port wines but also for brandy (at sizes of 126, 132 and 136 litres/33, 35 and 36 US gallons respectively). The term is still employed and generally denotes casks of 110–130 litres (30–34 US gallons), although some use it to mean a quarter of an American Barrel, in other words 50 litres/13 US gallons (cf. Octave).

Kilderkin

⅙ Butt or ½ Barrel / 18 Imperial (UK) gallons / 22 US gallons / Volume ~ 82 litres

Borrowed from the Middle Dutch *kindekijn*, of *kinde* 'quintal', this size of cask has been used since the 16th century at least in the UK, and still exists in Scotland.

Rundlet

½ Butt / 15 Imperial (UK) gallons / 18 US gallons / Volume ~ 68 litres

A deformation of the word *rondelet* (French for rotund), the rundlet has been used since the 15th century. It was originally a wine cask, but the word was also used to refer to all sorts of small casks used for wine, vinegar and distilled spirits. Its volume can vary from 3–20 gallons.

Octave

⅛ Butt / 13 ½ Imperial (UK) gallons / 16 US gallons / Volume ~ 61 litres

Common in the early 20th century, an octave then corresponded to an eighth of a butt of whisky or sherry. Nowadays, the word is used to refer to casks of about 50 litres (13 US gallons).

Anker / Anchor

¹⁄₁₀ Butt / 10 Imperial (UK) gallons / 12 US gallons / Volume ~ 45 litres

An anchor of spirits, an old measure used by maritime powers of the North and Baltic Seas, was used to denote a size of cask (that used to hold about 32 litres/7 US gallons of ale or 38 litres/8 US gallons of wine) that was sometimes carried by smugglers on their backs. There also existed Half-Anker and Quarter-Anker casks, of 5 and 2½ Imperial (UK) gallons respectively (about 23 and 11 litres/6 and 3 US gallons).

Firkin

¹⁄₁₂ Butt or ¼ Barrel / 9 Imperial (UK) gallons / 11 US gallons / Volume ~ 41 litres

A deformation of the Middle Dutch word *vierdekijn* meaning 'quart', this type of cask was originally used to transport and store beer, eels, herrings, soap and even butter and was still in use in Scotland in the early 20th century. Nowadays it is very rare.

Bloodtub

¼₄ Butt or ½ Rundlet / 7 ½ Imperial (UK) gallons / 9 US gallons / Volume ~ 34 litres

Oval in shape and proportionally longer to facilitate transport on horseback or mule, these casks are still sometimes used, although today the word Bloodtub is more often used to refer to kegs of 40 or 50 litres (10½ or 13 US gallons) in Scotland or 20 litres (5 US gallons) in Australia.

Pin

¼₄ Butt or ½ Firkin / 4 ½ Imperial (UK) gallons / 5.3 US gallons / Volume ~ 20 litres

In the 19th century, these kegs of beer, ale, porter or whisky enabled the division of a Firkin into two Pins. They can still be found today in the United States, along with many other small formats referred to simply as small barrels.

Steckan or Steekan

¼₅ Butt or ½ Anker / 4 ¼ Imperial (UK) gallons / 5 US gallons / Volume ~ 19 litres

A transportation cask, formerly used by smugglers (tubmen), who unloaded their goods on their backs. These casks were usually flattened and elliptical in shape for easy transportation, and carried in pairs, linked together by ropes: one on the back, the other on the chest. This was for a long time a standard measure for Dutch merchants.

SPANISH SHERRY CASKS

The British have been crazy about the wines from Xérès, sherry (*jerez* in Spanish) – dry fortified and naturally sweet wines from Andalusia at the southern tip of Spain – for centuries. Until the early 1970s, most wines were shipped in casks to Great Britain where the wine was then bottled. But from the 1960s onwards, wineries started to equip themselves with bottling plants. Scottish whisky producers were then no longer able to simply reuse the casks that had been used to transport these wines but had to buy them directly from the Andalusian bodegas. They then developed their own standard, 480–500-litre (127–132-gallon) casks or 'sherry butts' destined for export based on the model of the old transportation casks. In fact, the standard cask size for maturing their wines is 600 litres (159 gallons) for their *bota gorda*, which enables them to mature 500 litres (132 gallons) of wine and leave sufficient space for ageing under a layer of yeast ('*sous-voile*') or exposed to oxygen (oxidative ageing).

Moreover, while the bodegas almost exclusively use American oak casks, whisky producers have traditionally preferred English oak. Although whisky producers sometimes buy bodega barrels, they mostly follow a practice known as seasoning: they commission Spanish coopers to make casks to their specifications that the bodegas fill with fermented grape wort then with young wines for two or three years, which will absorb the tanines and other undesirable aromas of the new cask, while the staves absorb several litres (gallons) of this wine. Sometimes the bodega may be asked to fill the casks with aged sherry again. Since the 1990s, it has become increasingly common to see American oak sherry casks.

The type of sherry particularly favoured by whisky producers worldwide is oloroso, due to its dried-fruit aromas and amber to mahogany colour, but all types of sherry are now used. We present them here with definitions supplied by their appellations of origin and invite you to taste them so that you understand the advantages of this type of ageing and the impact it can have on whiskies.

Sherry hogshead   **Puncheon**   **Sherry butt**

Fino

Dry wine with a bright colour, from straw yellow to pale gold

Resulting from the complete fermentation of Palomino grape musts, the basic wine obtained is fortified to 15% ABV in order to encourage the development of a layer of flor yeast. The natural protection of the yeast will prevent oxidation of the wine during the ageing process and will impart very special organoleptic characteristics. This organic ageing lasts for at least three years and takes place in American oak casks.

Aromas: Yeast, breadcrumb, sea spray, herb/rosemary, almond, green apple.

Manzanilla

Dry, very pale wine, bright straw yellow in colour

Manzanilla follows the same process as Fino but must be aged only in the bodegas of Sanlucar de Barrameda. The unique microclimate of this town, which is situated at the mouth of the Guadalquivir, encourages the development of a layer of *flor* with unique characteristics.

Aromas: Chamomile, green apple, almond, bread, salt, chalk, green olive, lemon peel, sea spray.

Amontillado
Dry wine, topaz to amber in colour

Resulting from the complete fermentation of Palomino musts, Amontillado is a wine that is produced from the fusion of two types of ageing, organic and oxidative. This unique ageing process begins, as with Finos and Manzanillas, with an intial phase beneath a layer of *flor*, then, after a certain period of time, the *flor* is killed off by fortification, prompting a second, oxidative phase of ageing.

Aromas: Solvent, hazelnut, aromatic herbs, dried fruit, tobacco, bread crust, yeast, almond.

Palo cortado
Dry wine, chestnut to mahogany in colour

Like Amontillado, Palo Cortado is the result of dual ageing process, organic then oxidative, but the latter phase occurs spontaneously rather than as a result of fortification. It is only later that it is fortified to a minimum of 17% ABV.

Aromas: Walnut, Seville orange, rancid butter, tobacco, leather, coffee, dark chocolate.

Oloroso
Dry wine, amber to mahogany in colour

Resulting from the complete fermentation of Palomino musts, Oloroso is fortified to at least 17% ABV then aged with continuous exposure to the slow action of oxygen.

Aromas: Walnut, roasted almond, balsamic vinegar, vegetable, tobacco, fine wood, leather, truffle, raisins, date, fig, chocolate.

Cream sherry
A smooth, sweet wine, chestnut to dark mahogany in colour

Cream sherry is a liqueur wine made from blending sherry that has undergone an oxidative ageing process with a significant amount of *vin doux naturel* or rectified concentrated must. The ageing process is thus entirely oxidative and the result of the blending must have sugar content of at least 115 grams per litre (4 ounces per quart).

Aromas: Walnut, roasted almond, caramel, balsamic vinegar, tobacco, leather, raisins.

Pedro Ximénez (PX)
Ebony-coloured *vin doux naturel*

Pedro Ximénez is made from grapes of the same name that have been left to dry on the vine. Pressing produces a must that is characterized by a high concentration of sugar and dark colour, which is subjected to partial fermentation that may be stopped with the addition of wine alcohol. Its ageing is always oxidative.

Aromas: Raisin, fig, date, molasses/treacle, honey, plum, caramel, liquorice, blackcurrant.

Moscatel
***Vin doux naturel*, chestnust to dark mahogany in colour**

Moscatel is obtained from the grape of the same name (Muscat) and follows the same production process as Pedro Ximénez.

PORTUGUESE CASKS

The British are great fans of the Portuguese fortified wines port and Madeira. So it is hardly surprising that the casks used for these wines are also used for ageing whisky.

Port casks

There are four main types of port, the most well known being the red port wines: ruby and tawny. Ruby port seeks to retain the fruitiness of the wine and is sometimes matured in casks but mainly aged in bottles, particularly in the case of Late Bottled Vintage (LBV) and Vintage ports. Tawny port is aged from between two and 40 years in casks and so takes on oxidative, boise and dried fruit aromas. The two other types of port, which are rarer, are white and rosé.

Aromas: Mulberry, blackcurrant, raspberry, cherry, prune, cocoa, walnut, spices, tobacco, leather, wax.

Maderia casks

The casks of the fortified wines of Madeira have come back into fashion thanks to their inimitable character. The four main grape varieties used – from the driest to the sweetest – are Sercial, Verdelho, Bual or Boal and Malvasia or Malmsey. The first of these, the driest, yields wines that resemble sherry with almond notes, the second is more mineral/smoky, the third has dried-fruit notes while the last has marked pastry aromas.

Aromas: Honey, greengage, dried fruits, caramel, molasses / treacle, coffee, orange peel, mango, nectarine.

FRENCH CASKS

Bordeaux, Burgundy, Cognac – France is full of AOC (denomination of origin) wines and spirits that need no introduction. The British have been partial to these wines for centuries and indeed have contributed to their historic fame. Scottish whisky-makers have thus made the most of French, handmade and toasted, casks for more than 100 years and over the last decade or so have even emphasized the origin of these casks. Today, the quality and particularities of French cooperage and its French Oak Casks are increasingly sought after by whisky producers throughout the world.

Cognac

British merchants have greatly contributed to the high esteem in which the distilled-wine spirit of this region is held. World-renowned cooperages have been created around the vineyards and distilleries, using mainly oak from Limousin and the Forest of Tronçais, and the casks, which have a volume of 280, 350 or 400 litres (74, 94 or 106 gallons), are given a light, medium or heavy 'toast' but without being charred as they are the United States.

Aromas: Vanilla, toast, chocolate, incense, leather, rancio, cedar, cigar box, cinnamon, nutmeg.

Bordeaux or Claret

Red wines from the Bordeaux region are made mainly from Merlot, Cabernet Sauvignon and Cabernet Franc and are aged from between six and 18 months in 225-litre (59-gallon) Bordeaux barrels that are used for several vintages. After the casks have been cleaned of their tartaric deposits by a cooper, distilleries can purchase barrels that have been used by the region's greatest châteaux.

Aromas: Redcurrant, strawberry, raspberry, cherry, mulberry, blackcurrant, parma violet, liquorice, coffee, undergrowth.

Sauternes

A sweet white wine of the Bordeaux region made from Sémillon supplemented with Sauvignon Blanc and Muscadelle grapes, Sauternes is often aged in barrels for several months. It is very advantageous to whisky producers to buy casks from these prestigious châteaux: the appellation includes 16 crus, including the only Premier Cru Supérieur in Bordeaux, Yquem, which sends some of its barrels to Scotland every year.

Aromas: Dried apricot, citrus, white peach, candied fruit, pâte de fruits, acacia flower, honey, wax, pineapple, white pepper.

Burgundy

A grape variety with compact bunches of small, purplish black grapes that is synonymous with the red wines of Burgundy, Pinot Noir has made this region famous by revealing the character of its many climates. The wines are aged for between eight months and two years in 228-litre (60-gallon) Burgundy barrels.

Aromas: Blackcurrant, cherry, grape, prune, orange peel, pepper, thyme, moss, truffle, leather, amber.

AMERICAN CASKS

N ew American casks that are charred to varying degrees are mandatory for most American whiskies whereas second-hand American casks, bought from bourbon producers in Kentucky or whiskey producers in Tennessee, which are usually known as Bourbon Barrels and have a volume of nearly 200 litres (53 gallons), are often used in Canada, Ireland, Scotland and Japan. However, after many trials in the late 20th century, these countries are increasingly looking to use new American casks that have been toasted rather than charred and are known as Virgin Oak Casks. Their volume can range from 200–600 litres (53–159 gallons).

Bourbon Barrel or American Standard Barrel

The casks used by the American whisky industry and reused by other whisky and spirit producers around the world are (almost) all charred. These will display different qualities depending on how their staves were dried (hot air or outside), the degree of charring carried out and whether or not this was preceded by toasting.

Aromas: Vanilla, caramel, banana, coconut, cinnamon, nutmeg, smoke.

Virgin Oak Cask

In Scotland as in Japan, producers have become interested over the last several decades in toasted rather than charred American oak casks. These casks had already become known in the wine world for their aromatic qualities and today, many producers offer whiskies that have been either entirely aged or finished in this type of cask.

Aromas: Vanilla, coconut, banana, ginger, honey, chocolate.

JAPANESE CASKS

Too he Japanese whisky industry developed during the 20th century, using mainly American or Spanish casks, but today many distilleries have their own cooperages.

Mizunara Cask

Around the time of the Second World War, because of the lack of supply, trials were carried out using Japanese oak, *Quercus mongolicus*. At first glance, results were inconclusive, but the whisky was left to age for more than 20 years and it was then that the aromatic potential of this type of oak came to light.

Aromas: Persimmon, sandalwood, aoud, incense, cinnamon, coconut.

CASK REGENERATION

As casks are reused several times, with successive fillings of varying durations (first fill, second fill, third fill, plain), there comes a moment when the aromas (and colours) they impart become weak, virtually non-existent (thus there are 30-year-old whiskies that are almost transparent). Because casks can be costly, and are sometimes in short supply, Scottish coopers have developed ways of regenerating the staves.

In the case of old Bourbon Barrels, they begin by scrubbing the insides to remove the charred layer in order to then reheat them to give them a new layer. These casks are known as recharred casks.

THE FUNDAMENTALS
OF WHISKY TASTING

Although tasting stimulates all the senses, it is not only about sensory pleasure. Whisky tasting is an invitation to move from the sensory sphere to that of analysis, which will help you identify the aromas of a whisky and understand it better. The only real difficulty with this process is that that a whisky is more than the sum of the various components that we perceive. Firstly, because tasting is not confined to the characteristics of the whisky itself but also encompasses the unique perceptions that individual tasters will have depending on their culture, experience and expectations. Secondly, because appreciation of a whisky's characteristics is influenced, too, by external factors, such as the surroundings, as well as the 'aura' that it emits and how each taster perceives it. In any event, tasting a whisky is primarily an experience in which the senses are awakened: the following guidelines will enable you to not only precisely identify aromas but also draw maximum pleasure from them.

TASTING GLASSES

A lot of wine glasses have a tulip shape (to concentrate the aromas) that makes them perfectly suitable for whisky tasting. Conversely, tumblers – wide glasses with no stem that are often considered as the typical whisky glass – are actually inappropriate. A tumbler will reflect only the most ethereal and aggressive notes. Its image as a whisky glass spread with its use in American bars when it was convenient to use to mix blended whisky with ice and soda (club soda) by covering it with the cup of the shaker, which fit to its shape.

For tasting, you need a stemmed glass in order to (i) avoid heating the contents of the glass with your hand and (ii) distance the whisky from any disturbing odours from the skin. The thinness of the lip of the glass (the contour of the opening and the top part of the glass on which you rest your lips) and the absence of a small bulge around the rim of the glass are a sign of quality. Furthermore, the bowl of the glass should not be too deep so that even the heaviest of the volatile compounds can rise to the top of the glass.

Using different types of glasses creates different types of oxidation depending on the surface contact of the whisky with the air. In fact, the wider the shoulder of the glass, the more surface contact the whisky has with the air and the faster the oxygenation. The concentration of aromas and the rate at which volatile particles are diffused will vary depending on the shape of the glass and on how fine it is. However, in order to compare two different whiskies objectively, you should use identical glasses.

ADDING WATER

Adding water needs to be done in stages: (i) after having smelled and tasted, at least once, the pure whisky; (ii) a drop at a time in order to reveal the desired aromas, without diluting the whisky too much. You can do this using either (i) a pipette (or possibly a straw) or, at a pinch, (ii) the cap of the bottle of mineral water you are using.

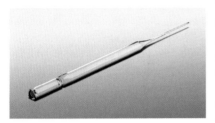

The water you add should be slightly cool or of moderate temperature so as not to disrupt the whisky too much. The aim is to be able to open up the whisky rather than to dilute it or, worse, break its palate, structure or texture.

Only very soft, still water should be added to whisky. Once the water has been added, a transformation will take place on the nose but also on the palate because it will cause a recombination of the fatty substances and aromas. Adding water does not necessarily make the whisky better or worse, but it does reveal or mask certain aromas. In any event, it will reduce the alcohol content of a whisky and will also open it up if it appears closed: water always releases aromas.

APPEARANCE

Whisky should be served at room temperature, between 18° and 22°C (64° and 72°F). Tasting favours quality over quantity and a few centilitres (ounces) of whisky (2 to 4 centilitres/¾ to 1½ ounces maximum) is enough. Tilt the glass sideways and rotate it to make a complete circle. This way you ensure that the whisky is well distributed over the whole inner surface of the bowl. This has the effect of increasing the oxidation surface, obtaining dry residues and bringing out the aromas present at the bottom of the glass. In organoleptic analysis, direct and retronasal olfaction define the aroma, gustation the taste/savour, and flavour the sum of sensations perceived during nosing and tasting, that is to say retro-olfactive, gustative and trigeminal sensations. But having served the whisky in a transparent glass, your first sense to be stimulated will be that of sight, which will enable you to determine:

– **The colour** and thus possibly the type of cask used for ageing the whisky, or even its age, provided, of course, that no colouring agent (caramel E 150) has been used.

Whisky that has not been artificially coloured ('non coloured') is preferable as the legal practice of adding caramel can have a negative impact on its aromatic profile;

– **The clarity** and thus the use (or not) of chill-filtration. In fact, if it has not been chill-filtered, a whisky of less than 46% ABV will tend to become cloudy below a certain temperature, or when you add water to it. This opacity has no bearing on the quality of the whisky. It is not a defect but rather is due to the fact that certain compounds are soluble only above 46% ABV. On the other hand, chill-filtration has an effect on the aromatic profile of whisky, causing it to lose fatty acids, proteins and esters and thus to be deprived of richness and complexity. This practice can reduce the quality of an exceptional whisky just as it can clean a whisky with less balance or even slight defects;

– **The viscosity** of the whisky. Observing the legs (or tears) of a whisky, and the slowness with which they fall, enables you to assess its alcohol content. In fact, these legs are the result of the difference in surface tension between the alcohol and the water contained in the whisky (the Marangoni effect). As the surface tension is lower in alcohol than in water, the higher the alcohol content of the whisky, the more legs there will be and the slower they will form and fall. In the same way, the more fatty acids the whisky contains, the thicker these legs will be. In addition, the longer the whisky was aged in cask, the more they will tend to separate and space out.

Once you have observed the whisky, stand the glass upright again and wait for a few minutes to allow the aromas to become concentrated.

THE NOSE

Olfactory sensations are the result of a structured combination of volatile compounds whose mixture of nuances give the tasted whisky its complexity. Unlike sight, which is a physical sense, smell is a chemical sense. The human olfactory system is capable of analyzing more than a thousand billion different volatile stimuli. These olfactory sensations arise from the combination of 'characteristic' aroma compounds when they alone pick up the olfactory note (for example vanillin for vanilla), or 'merging' ones when a set of volatile compounds contributes to the complete note. These compounds are able to pass into the respiratory tract via the orthonasal pathway (olfaction) or via the retronasal pathway (retro-olfaction).

The nostrils themselves are only the beginning of inhalation. They lead to the upper part of the nasal cavity: the olfactory epithelium. The olfactory molecules are picked up by epithelial mucus (adsorption), which fixes them, by concentrating them, as soon

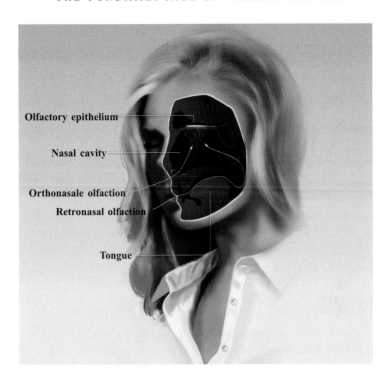

Olfactory epithelium

Nasal cavity

Orthonasale olfaction

Retronasal olfaction

Tongue

as they come into contact. The sensory cells are extended by fibres that continue into the olfactory bulb, which itself is connected to the olfactory regions of the brain.

Perceived aromas result from the production and ageing processes of the whisky: **primary aromas** (varietal and malting) from the type of barley and its malting, such as grain and malt aromas; **secondary aromas** (from fermentation and distillation), such as yeasty, metallic and milky aromas; and finally **tertiary aromas** (from ageing), linked to the redox phenomena to which whisky is subjected during its ageing, as well as the extraction aromas linked to the type of container in which it was aged. These could be vanilla, spicy, winey or woody aromas. The smoky aroma is unusual in that it can be primary (when it comes from the kilning of the barley) and/or tertiary (when it is the result of cask ageing, particularly if these casks were previously used to age peated whiskies or have been heavily toasted). These, then, are the compounds that should be identified.

Where the tasting takes place is also important: the same person will perceive different aromas in the same whisky depending on whether they taste it at the seaside or in a city bar. To limit such influences, it is important, in any event, to avoid non-ventilated rooms. Sometimes it suffices simply to take the time to taste the whisky outside in the open air to better assess the aromatic compounds.

First stage

Hold the glass upright directly above your nose to allow the aromas time to rise. This enables you to experience the first aromas while allowing your nose time to adjust to the level of alcohol. It is important not to ventilate the whisky (by swirling the glass as you would do for wine) if you want the aromas to remain concentrated. The higher the alcohol level, the more important it is to respect this adaptation phase to prevent your nose 'burning'. It is at this stage that the lighter volatile compounds can be detected.

Second stage

While taking care not to spill the contents, turn the glass on its side so that it is perpendicular to your face. Now move the glass upwards in a straight line to assess the different aroma strata. In fact, the aromas from heavier volatile compounds (earthy, smoky, woody, etc. aromas) will remain concentrated at the bottom of the glass. Then, gradually moving up towards the rim, you will notice that the more volatile the particles, the higher they are in the glass: first the spicy, malty and winey aromas, then, higher up, the lighter (and thus more volatile) fruity and floral aromas.

Floral
Fruity
Winey
Malty
Spicy
Woody
Smoky
Earthy

Third stage

Hold the glass perfectly horizontal: your nose should be directly above the top of the glass, a centimetre (½in) from the rim. The circulation of air in the glass will dispel the aromas and the lighter elements will follow the inner surface of the bowl to be deposited at the top of the outer edge of the glass. This technique isolates the very light and volatile elements, such as acidulous and floral aromas, which are barely perceptible when mixed with more powerful aromas.

Fourth stage

Vary the rate of your inhalation throughout the tasting. By doing so, you will vary the detection of molecules (depending on their ability to bind to the olfactory mucus). The molecules that have difficulty in binding to the olfactory mucus (low-sorption odorants) will be difficult to detect when the flow of air is rapid and more easily distinguished when inhalation is slower. Conversely, molecules that bind easily (high-sorption odorants) will be easily detected if the flow is rapid but less perceptible when it is slow, because they saturate the first part of the epithelial zone before they have had time to stimulate the whole of the olfactory surface.

Fifth stage

Sniff using one nostril then the other. Nostrils operate in turn and, generally speaking, while one nostril is responsible for 80% of an inhalation, the other is obstructed by the swelling of the inner nasal concha. This alternation in capacity occurs in regular cycles of two to three hours. The two nostrils thus inhale at different rates and one or other of them will therefore have a higher propensity to convey aromatic molecules depending on the ability of the latter to bind to the olfactory epithelium. Each respiratory canal thus provides a significantly different olfactory perception.

Sixth stage

Determine the aromatic families experienced by referring to the Aroma Wheel. In fact, the way in which we perceive the same aromatic compound may differ, but the element itself will remain unchanged. In the Aroma Wheel, chemical compounds have been grouped into the same family when similarities in their structure reflect aromatic similarities. This method has the advantage of presenting tasters of all levels with a common grammar regarding the characteristics that emerge from the whiskies they are tasting. The Aroma Wheel also enables novice tasters to train their palates by inviting them to learn to taste by processes of deduction – in other words by what a whisky is not in terms of its aromatic profile – as well as by comparison.

THE PALATE

While aromas and flavours possess no nutritional value, the opposite is also true: the nutritional components of drinks contribute neither their aromas nor their flavours. What gives whisky its flavours are the sapid molecules of which it is composed. Gustative perception thus results from the identification of chemical substances in the form of solutions (flavour) via the stimulation of chemo-receptors located on the tongue. Their combination is the origin of gustative effects that will be attributed to the whisky. Each type of taste receptor can be stimulated by a wide range of chemical substances but is particularly sensitive to a certain category: sweet, salty, sour, bitter and savoury (umami, glutamate), astringent, spicy, fatty, mineral (calcium) and metallic.

Seventh stage

It is important to drink some very soft, neutral water at room temperature before beginning tasting (as well as throughout the process) to prevent variations in temperature and acidity affecting the palate. In this regard, it should be noted that the olfactory perception of a drink is inevitably a personal thing as the pH and release of the volatile compounds on the palate of each taster will vary. Before tasting a whisky, you should also avoid consuming any food or drink with strong tastes that would be likely to alter it (for example coffee, liquorice, mint, etc.)

Eighth stage

In order to determine all the gustative compounds, you should taste only a tiny sip of a few millilitres (ounces) at a time. The absorption of tiny sips also has the advantage of accustoming the palate to the strength of the alcohol. The whisky should be 'masticated' for at least 30 seconds to stimulate the salivary glands. In fact, gustation is linked to the stimulation of sensory receptors on the tongue that function only with a liquid medium. During mastication, the aromatic or sapid molecules will be released into the oral cavity and will accentuate the taste of the whisky. The sapid molecules dissolved in saliva will reach the microvilli of each taste cell to bind to their receptors. It is also important to place the whisky at the front, centre and back of the tongue in order to try different positions and optimize the variety of aromatic effects.

THE FINISH

The finish corresponds to the stimulation of the sensory receptors by the aromatic molecules that are released from the mouth to the back of the throat, reaching the olfactory mucosa. Retro-olfaction thus accentuates the taste of the whisky.

Ninth stage

In order to optimize this retro-olfaction process, exhale deeply via the nose as soon as you have swallowed the sip of whisky.

Tasting also involves knowing how to classify the aromatic effects so as not to create confusion. In fact, due to retronasal olfaction, an aromatic effect will persist. Taking another sip will create an aromatic effect that can combine with the previous one if there is perfect harmony, but can also, conversely, be superimposed on it. The persistence of an aromatic effect on the palate will, in itself, modify subsequent olfaction. This is why the aromatic effects of a whisky reveal different notes at different stages of tasting.

THE EMPTY GLASS: THE 'BASE' NOTES

The empty glass contains the dry extract of the whisky, in other words all the substances that do not volatilize. It constitutes a concentrate of the structure around which the aromatic profile of the whisky has developed. A brown deposit corresponding to woody elements may appear at the bottom of the glass. Sometimes the sides of the glass may also have an opaque resinous coating after oxidation.

Tenth stage

It is therefore important, once you have finished tasting a whisky, to hermetically cover the glass in order to concentrate the aromas of the non-volatile residues it contains. The aromas of the dry extract, which will emerge for several minutes, or even several hours, after tasting, constitute the 'base' notes of a whisky. The richer and more woody the aromatic profile of a whisky, the more expressive the aromas it will leave in the empty glass will be.

Pronunciation table

The table below presents the most common pronunciation of Gaelic names of the different distilleries, giving their phonetic transcription in English. The difficulties of Gaelic pronunciation lie, notably, in the fact that spellings are not necessarily phonetic and that the same letter can be pronounced in different ways depending on where it falls within the word and on the letters that surround it. To pronounce the words perfectly, it is worth remembering that in most cases in Gaelic, the accent is placed on the first syllable.

'Och / ach' endings sound as an aspirated 'k', similar to the German 'ach' – these are written here with 'ck' endings.

† Currently not in production.

CAMPBELTOWN
cam-bell-town

Glengyle/Kilkerran
glen-guy/l kill-ker-ran

Glen Scotia
glen sko-sha

Springbank/Hazelburn/Longrow
spring-bank/hazel-burn/long-row

HIGHLAND
hi-lund

Aberfeldy
abur-fell-day

Abhainn Dhearg
a-veen jer-uck

Ardmore
ard-mor

Arran
ar-ran

Balblair
bal-blair

Banff†
banf

Ben Nevis
ben nev-viss

Ben Wyvis†
ben weev-iss

Blair Athol
blair ath-ull

Brora†
bro-ra

Clynelish
kline-leash

Dalmore
dal-mor

Dalwhinnie
dal-whinnay

Deanston	Harris
deen-stun	*ha-riss*
Edradour	Highland Park
ed-radower	*hi-lund park*
Fettercairn	Isle of Jura
fett-ur-care-n	*isle of joo-rah*
Glen Albyn†	Loch Ewe
glen al-bin	*loh yew*
Glencadam	Loch Lomond
glen-cad-am	*loh low-mund*
Glendronach	Lochside†
glen-dro-nack	*loh-side*
Glen Esk†/Hillside	Macduff/Glen Deveron
glen esck/hill side	*mack-duff/glen day-vron*
Glen Garioch	Millburn†
glen gee-reeh	*mill-bur-n*
Glenglassaugh	North Port/Brechin†
glen-glass-ock	*north port/bree-ckin*
Glengoyne	Oban
glen-goyn	*o-bun*
Glenlochy†	Old Pulteney
glen-lock-ee	*old pult-nay*
Glen Mhor†	Royal Brackla
glen moar or glen voar	*royal brack-la*
Glenmorangie	Royal Lochnagar
glen-morrun-jay	*royal loh-na-gar*
Glen Ord	Scapa
glen ord	*ska-pa*
Glenturret	Strathearn
glen-turr-et	*strath-earn*
Glenugie†	Talisker
glen-oo-gee	*tal-iss-kur*
Glenury Royal†	Teaninich
glen-oo-ree royal	*tee-ann-in-ih*

Tobermory/Ledaig
tow-bur-moray/lay-chuck, led-chig

Tomatin
to-ma-tin

Tullibardine
tully-bard-in

Wolfburn
wolf-burn

ISLAY
eye-lah

Ardbeg
ard-beg

Bowmore
bow-mor

Bruichladdich
broo-ick-laddie

Bunnahabhain
bunna-ha-ven

Caol Ila
kool-eye-la or kool ee-la

Kilchoman
kil-ho-man

Lagavulin
laga-voolin

Laphroaig
la-froyg

Malt Mill†
malt mill

Port Ellen†
port el-len

LOWLAND
low-land

Ailsa Bay
ale-sa bay

Annandale
ann-an-dail

Auchentoshan
ock-en-tosh-un

Bladnoch
blad-noh

Daftmill
daf-mill

Eden
ee-den

Glen Flager†/Killyloch
glen fla-gur/kill-ay-loh

Glenkinchie
glen-kinch-ee

Inverleven†
in-ver-le-ven

Kinclaith†
keen-klyte

Kingsbarn
kings-barn

Ladyburn†
lady-burn

Littlemill†/Dunglass
little-mill/dun-glass

Lomond†
low-mund

Rosebank†
row-z-bank

Saint Magdalene†/Linlithgow
saint mag-da-len/lin-lith-go

Strathmore†
strath-mor

SPEYSIDE
spay-side

Aberlour
ah-burl-ow-er

Allt-a-bhainne
alt-a-vain or olt-a-vain

AnCnoc (Knockdhu)
a-nock (nock-doo)

Auchroisk
aw-thrusk

Aultmore
olt-mor

Ballindalloch
balin-dah-loh

Balmenach
bal-may-nah

Balvenie
bal-venny or bal-vee-nee

BenRiach
ben-ree-ack

Benrinnes
ben-rin-ess

Benromach
ben-ro-mack

Braeval-Braes of Glenlivet
bray-val-brayz of glen-liv-it

Caperdonich†
kapper-doe-nick

Cardhu
kar-doo

Coleburn†
coal-bur-n

Convalmore†
kon-val-mower

Cragganmore
crag-an-mower

Craigellachie
craig-ell-ack-ee

Dailuaine
dall-yoo-an

Dallas Dhu†
dallas doo

Dalmunach
dal-moo-nack

Dufftown
duff-town

Glenallachie
glen-alla-ckee

Glenburgie
glen-bur-gee

Glendullan
glen-dull-an

Glen Elgin
glen elg-in

Glenfarclas
glen-fark-lass

Glenfiddich
glen-fidd-ick

Glen Grant
glen grant

Glen Keith
glen key-th

Glenlivet *glen-liv-it*	Mannochmore *man-nack-mor*
Glenlossie *glen-loss-ay*	Miltonduff *mill-ton-duff*
Glen Moray *glen mor-ay*	Mortlach *mort-lack*
Glenrothes *glen-roth-iss*	Pittyvaich† *pit-ee-vay-ick*
Glen Spey *glen spay*	Roseisle *rose-isle*
Glentauchers *glen-tock-ers*	Speyburn *spay-bur-n*
Imperial† *im-pee-rial*	Speyside *spay-side*
Inchgower *inch-gower*	Strathisla *strath-eye-la*
Kininvie *kin-in-vee*	Strathmill *strath-mill*
Knockando *knock-an-doo*	Tamdhu *tam-doo*
Linkwood *link-wood*	Tamnavulin *tam-na-voo-lin*
Longmorn *long-morn*	Tomintoul *tom-in-towel*
Macallan *mack-al-lan*	Tormore *tor-mor*

PART II

TASTING
GUIDE

Highland distilleries

━━━━━━ Boundary of the Highlands

Malt distilleries

Dalmore	Operational distillery
Torabhaig	Proposed distillery
Millburn	Closed distillery

Grain distilleries

| Invergordon | Operational distillery |
| Lochside | Closed distillery |

Abhainn Dearg □

Lewis

Isle of Harris □

Loch Ewe □

Skye

□ Talisker

Isle of Barra □

Torabhaig □

Ben Nevis □
Ben Nevis Grain □

Ardnamurchan

Tobermory □ □   Glenlochy □
Drimnin

Mull

□
Oban

A t l a n t i c

O c e a n

Jura

*Loch
Lomond* D

Jura
□

Islay

Portavadie □

Isle of Arran

□   Loch Lomond
Lomond Grain

Glengo

K i n t y r e

Isle of Arran

North Channel   *Campbeltown*

**NORTHERN
IRELAND**

Speyside distilleries

Boundary of Speyside

Malt distilleries

Glenfiddich Operational distillery

Dallas Dhu Closed distillery

S   C   O   T

Spey

Balmena

Braeval

Tomintoul

Tamnavulin

Glenlivet

Ballindalloch

Torn

Livet

Avon

Spey C

Allt-a'Bhainne

Glenfarclas

Tam

Benrinnes

Imperial

Pittyvaich

Dailuaine

Spey

Dufftown

Glenallachie

Dalmunach

Mortlach

Dufftown

Aberlour

Glendullan

Glenrothes

Macallan

Glenfiddich

Fiddich

Glen G

Balvenie

Craigellachie

Spe

Convalmore

Glen Spey

Rothes

Kininvie

Caperdoni

Strathmill

Glentauchers

Auchroisk

Keith

Strathisla

River Isla

Glen Keith

Aultmore

Spey

Inchgower

Islay distilleries

Malt distilleries

Kilchoman	Operational distillery
Gartbreck	Proposed distillery
Malt Mill	Closed distillery

Firth of Lorn

Colonsay Island

Sound of Islay

Caol Ila

Bunnahabhain ⎯⎯⎯ ☐

Port Askaig

Loch Finlaggan

Loch Gruinart

I

S

l

Bowmore

☐ **Bowmore**

Loch Gorm

Bruichladdich
☐

Loch Indaal

☐

Kilchoman
☐

Gartbreck

Machir Bay

Port Charlotte

Atlantic Ocean

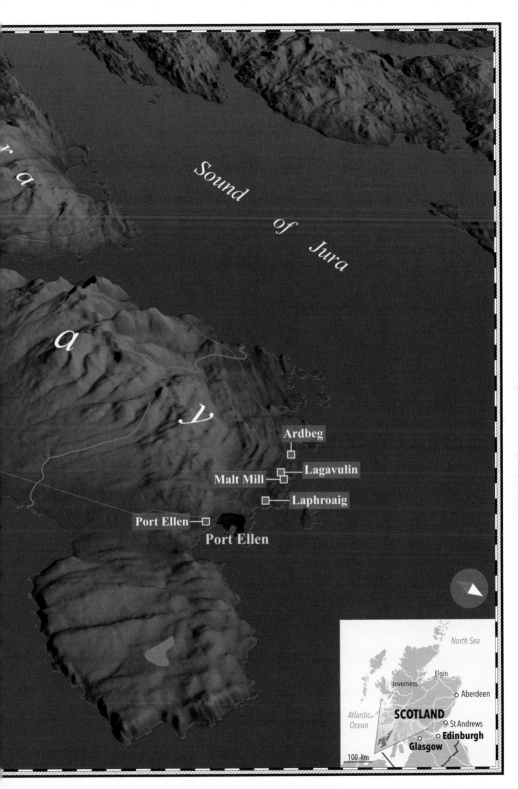

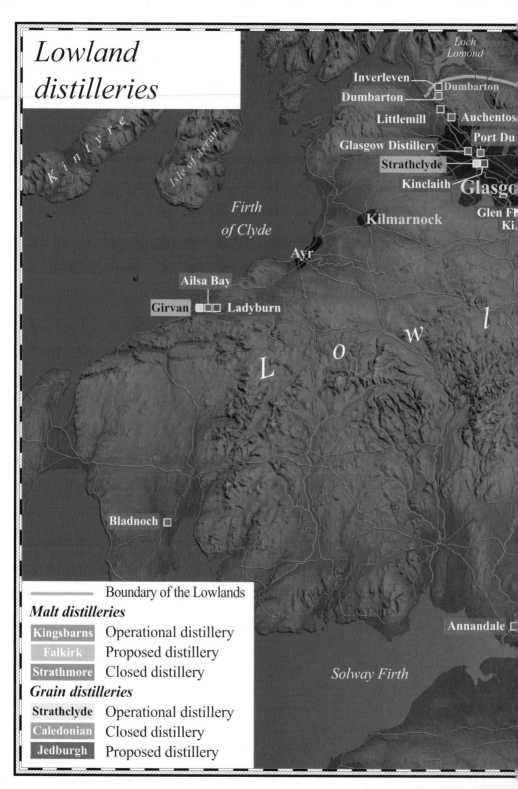

Lowland distilleries

Loch Lomond

Inverleven — Dumbarton

Dumbarton

Littlemill — Auchentos

Port Du

Glasgow Distillery

Strathclyde

Kinclaith — Glasgo

Glen Fl
Ki.

Kilmarnock

Firth of Clyde

Ayr

Ailsa Bay

Girvan — Ladyburn

K i n t y r e

Isle of Arran

L o w l

Bladnoch

Annandale

Solway Firth

Boundary of the Lowlands

Malt distilleries

Kingsbarns	Operational distillery
Falkirk	Proposed distillery
Strathmore	Closed distillery

Grain distilleries

Strathclyde	Operational distillery
Caledonian	Closed distillery
Jedburgh	Proposed distillery

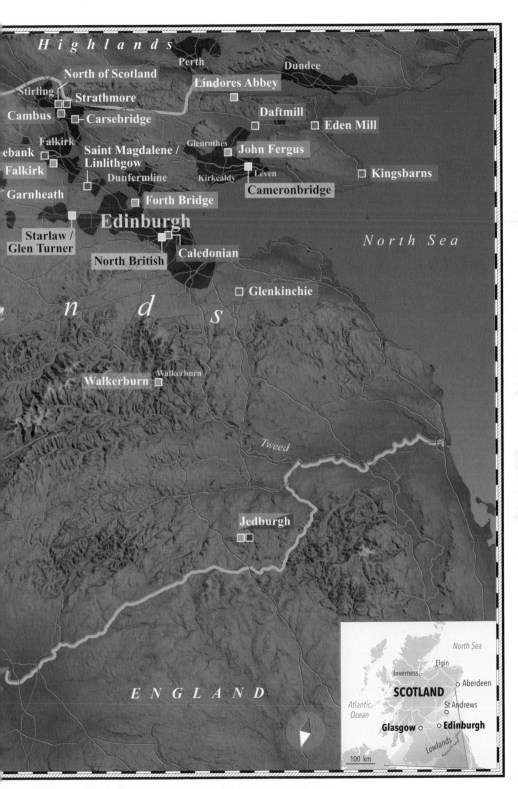

Campbeltown distilleries

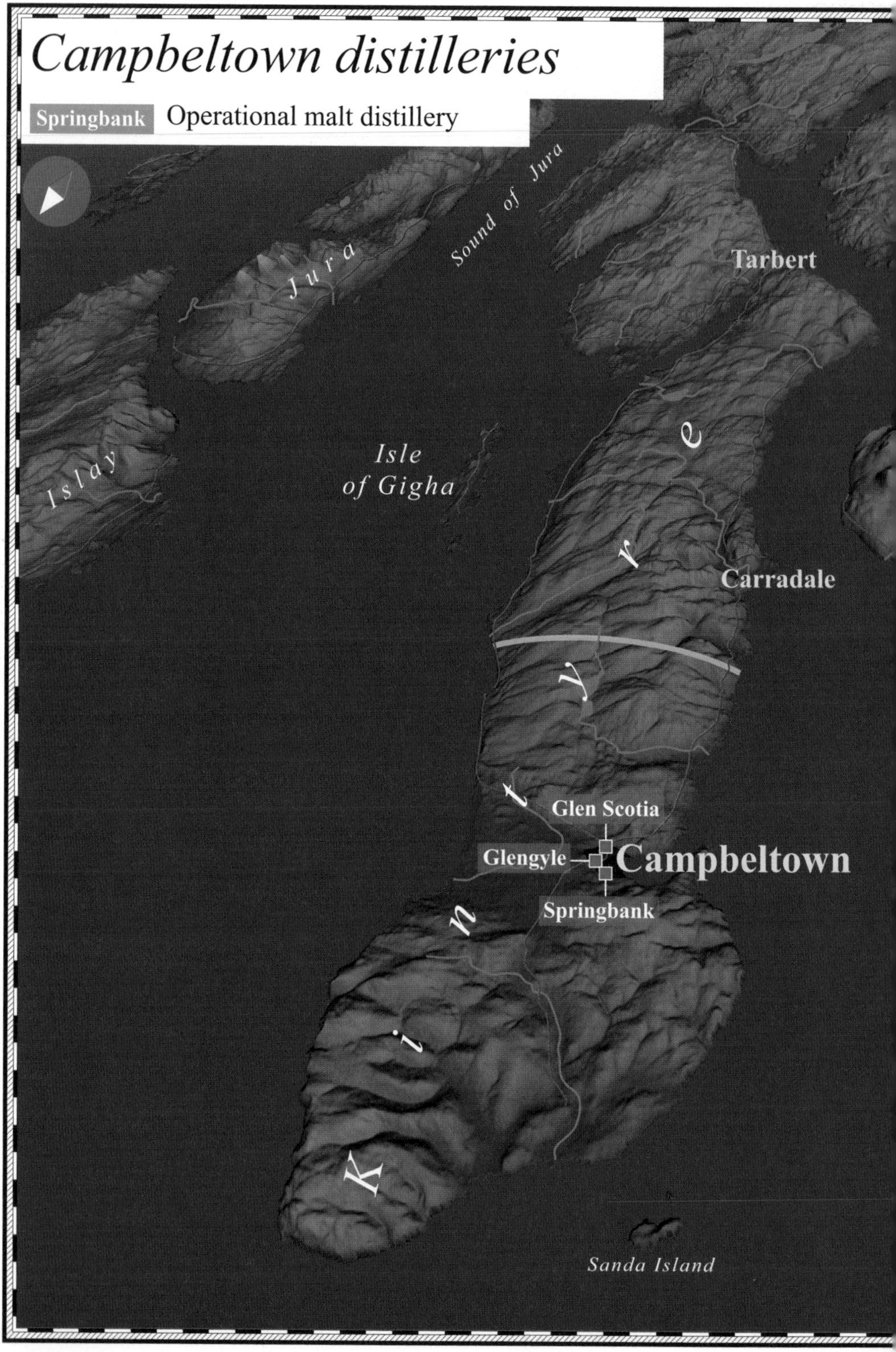

Springbank Operational malt distillery

Jura

Sound of Jura

Tarbert

Islay

Isle of Gigha

Carradale

Glen Scotia

Glengyle — Campbeltown

Springbank

Sanda Island

CONTENTS

Scotland

Aberfeldy
Distillery

Founded in 1896 by John and Tommy Dewar, rebuilt in 1972.
Part of its production is used in the Dewar's blend.

Great vintages: 1975, 1991
4 Stills: 2 wash, 2 spirit – 3.5 million LPA

Aberfeldy, Perthshire PH15 2EB
Central Highland
+44 (0) 1887 822 010
www.dewarswow.com
Owner: John Dewar & Sons Ltd (Bacardi)

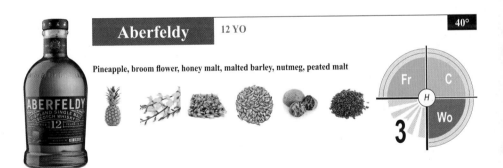

Aberfeldy   12 YO   40°

Pineapple, broom flower, honey malt, malted barley, nutmeg, peated malt

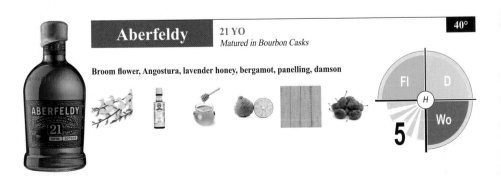

Aberfeldy   21 YO
Matured in Bourbon Casks   40°

Broom flower, Angostura, lavender honey, bergamot, panelling, damson

Ardmore
Distillery

**Founded in 1898 by Adam Teacher.
Part of its production is used in the Teacher's blend.**

Great vintages: 1976, 1992
8 Stills: 4 wash, 4 spirit – 5.5 million LPA

Kennethmont, Huntly, Aberdeenshire AB54 4NH
Eastern Highlands
+44 (0) 1464 831 213
www.ardmorewhisky.com
Owner: Beam Suntory Inc.

Ardmore	Traditional Cask	46° UN
	Quarter Cask Peated	

Crème caramel, pear, peated malt, vanilla cream, burnt grass, mirabelle

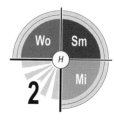

Wo | Sm
H
Sm
4

Ardmore	Teacher's Single Malt	40°
	Quarter Cask	

Mochaccino, mulberry, peated malt, vanilla cream, ink, linseed oil

Wo | Sm
H
Mi
2

Arran
Distillery

Founded in 1993 by Harold Curie.

Great vintages: 1996, 1998
2 Stills: 1 wash, 1 spirit – 0.75 million LPA

Lochranza, Isle of Arran KA27 8HJ
Islands Highland
+44 (0) 1770 830 264
www.arranwhisky.com
Owner: Isle of Arran Distillers Ltd

Arran	10 YO	46° UN

Malted milk, green banana, pear, mirabelle, pomelo, kiwi

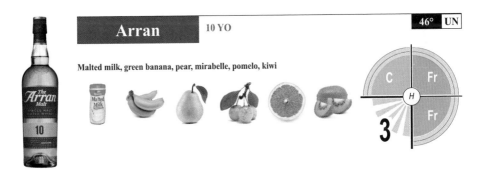

3

Arran	12 YO CS	53.9° UN CS

Pineapple, lychee honey, citrus peel, dark chocolate, ginger, elderberry

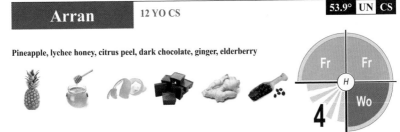

4

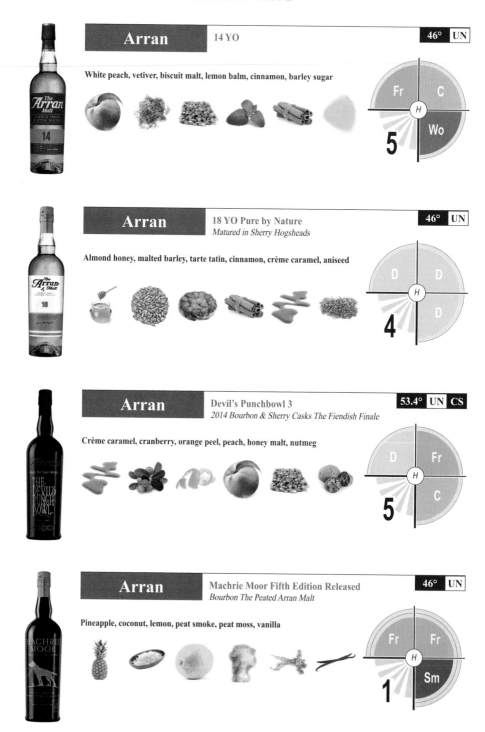

Arran 14 YO 46° UN

White peach, vetiver, biscuit malt, lemon balm, cinnamon, barley sugar

Fr | C
H
Wo
5

Arran 18 YO Pure by Nature 46° UN
Matured in Sherry Hogsheads

Almond honey, malted barley, tarte tatin, cinnamon, crème caramel, aniseed

D | D
H
D
4

Arran Devil's Punchbowl 3 53.4° UN CS
2014 Bourbon & Sherry Casks The Fiendish Finale

Crème caramel, cranberry, orange peel, peach, honey malt, nutmeg

D | Fr
H
C
5

Arran Machrie Moor Fifth Edition Released 46° UN
Bourbon The Peated Arran Malt

Pineapple, coconut, lemon, peat smoke, peat moss, vanilla

Fr | Fr
H
Sm
1

Balblair
Distillery

Founded in 1790 by James McKeddy,
closed from 1911 to 1949, operational since.

Great vintages: 1965, 1966, 1974, 1975
2 Stills: 1 wash, 1 spirit – 1.8 million LPA

Edderton, Tain, Ross-shire IV19 1LB
Northern Highlands
+44 (0) 1862 821 273
www.balblair.com
Owner: Inver House Distillers Ltd (Thai Beverages Plc)

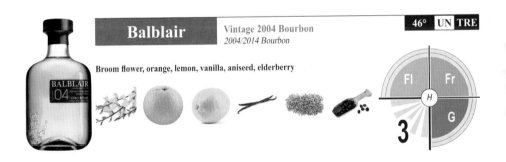

Balblair — Vintage 2004 Bourbon / *2004/2014 Bourbon* — 46° UN TRE

Broom flower, orange, lemon, vanilla, aniseed, elderberry

Balblair — Vintage 2004 Sherry / *2004/2014 Sherry* — 46° UN TRE

Raisin, Seville orange, green apple, suede, cinnamon, dark chocolate

Balblair

Vintage 2003
2003/2013 Bourbon Cask

46° UN

Kiwi, borage honey, caramel malt, orange, coriander, ginger

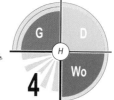

2

Balblair

Vintage 1999
1999/2014 Ex-Bourbon + Ex-Sherry Casks

46° UN TRE

Fern, green apple, spruce honey, marzipan, crème pâtissière, white pepper

4

Balblair

Vintage 1990
1990/2013 2nd Release Spanish Sherry

46° UN

Raspberry, raisin, galangal, milk chocolate, oloroso, berries honey

4

Balblair

Vintage 1983
1983/2013 Bourbon Oak

46° UN

Scented verbena, mango, guava, honeysuckle, honeycomb, galangal

7

Ben Nevis
Distillery

Founded in 1825 by John MacDonald (Long John).
Closed from 1978 to 1984 and from 1986 to 1990, operational since.

Great vintages: 1966, 1967
4 Stills: 2 wash, 2 spirit – 1.8 million LPA

Lochy Bridge, Fort William PH33 6TJ
Western Highlands
+44 (0) 1397 702 476
www.bennevisdistillery.com
Owner: Ben Nevis Ltd (Nikka – Asahi Breweries Ltd)

Ben Nevis 10 YO — 46° UN

Malted barley, plum, Seville orange, clove, mirin, borage flower

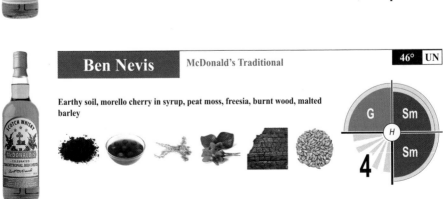

Ben Nevis McDonald's Traditional — 46° UN

Earthy soil, morello cherry in syrup, peat moss, freesia, burnt wood, malted barley

Brora†
Distillery

Founded in 1819 (as Clynelish) by the Marquess of Stafford Duke of Sutherland.
Closed since 1983.

Great vintages: 1972, 1973, 1978
2 Stills: 1 wash, 1 spirit

Clynelish Road, Brora, Sutherland KW9 6LR
Northern Highlands
www.malts.com
Owner: Diageo Plc

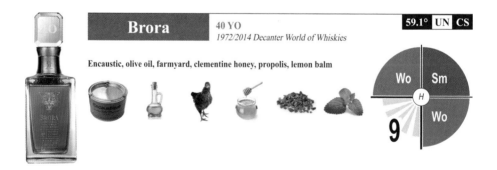

Brora 40 YO **59.1° UN CS**
1972/2014 Decanter World of Whiskies

Encaustic, olive oil, farmyard, clementine honey, propolis, lemon balm

Wo | Sm
H
9 Wo

Brora 12th Release 35 YO **49.9° UN CS**
2013 Edition

Propolis, strawberry tree honey, smoked eel, lemon balm, beach fire, allspice

Wo | Ma
H
9 Sm

Clynelish
Distillery

Old distillery founded in 1819, new distillery founded in 1967.

Great vintages: 1970–1973, 1982, 1996
6 Stills: 3 wash, 3 spirit – 4.8 million LPA

Clynelish Road, Brora, Sutherland KW9 6LR
Northern Highlands
+44 (0) 1408 623 003
www.malts.com
Owner: Diageo Plc

Clynelish	14 YO	46° UN

Candlewax, borage flower, sea spray, peated malt, sandy beach, malted barley

Clynelish	Distiller's Edition *1997/2012 Oloroso Sherry Wood*	46° UN

Amber rum, Angostura, quince, cherry, sea spray, walnut

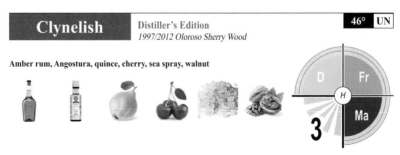

Dalmore
Distillery

Founded in 1839 by Alexander Matheson.

Great vintages: 1928, 1974, 1981
8 Stills: 4 wash, 4 spirit – 3.7 million LPA

Alness, Ross-shire IV17 0UT
Northern Highlands
+44 (0) 1349 882 362
www.thedalmore.com
Owner: Whyte & Mackay Ltd (Emperador Inc.)

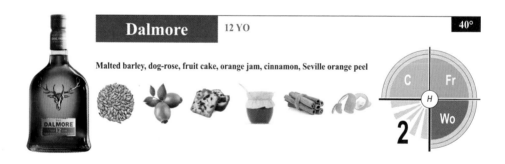

Dalmore 12 YO 40°

Malted barley, dog-rose, fruit cake, orange jam, cinnamon, Seville orange peel

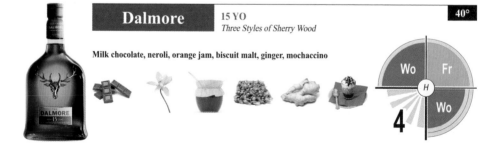

Dalmore 15 YO 40°
Three Styles of Sherry Wood

Milk chocolate, neroli, orange jam, biscuit malt, ginger, mochaccino

Dalmore — King Alexander III

40°

Chocolate malt, kumquat, orange jam, roasted barley, biscuit malt, wormwood

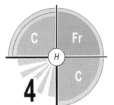

4

Dalmore — Cigar Malt Reserve
Limited Edition

44°

Ganache, mirabelle, gingerbread, orange peel, dark chocolate, bergamot

3

Dalmore — 18 YO
Matusalem Sherry Butt

43°

Rancio, fig, orange jam, preserved lemon, cocoa, almond honey

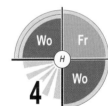

4

Dalmore — 25 YO
Tawny Port Finish Sherry Butt

42°

Candied citrus, honeysuckle, orange jam, blackcurrant, reseda, Grand Marnier®

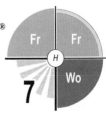

7

Dalwhinnie
Distillery

Founded in 1897 by John Grant, George Sellar and Alexander Mackenzie as Strathspey.
Part of its production is used in the Buchanan's and Black & White blends.

Great vintages: 1966, 1973
2 Stills: 1 wash, 1 spirit – 2.2 million LPA

Dalwhinnie, Inverness-shire PH19 1AB
Central Highlands
+44 (0) 1540 672 219
www.malts.com
Owner: Diageo Plc

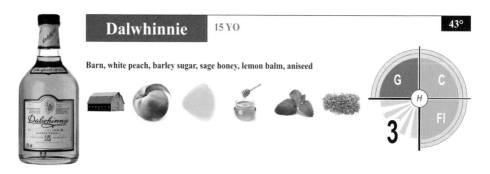

Dalwhinnie 15 YO   43°

Barn, white peach, barley sugar, sage honey, lemon balm, aniseed

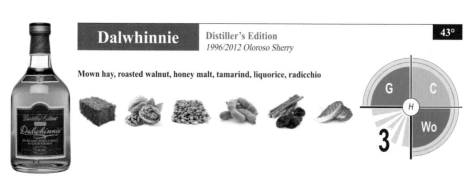

Dalwhinnie Distiller's Edition
1996/2012 Oloroso Sherry   43°

Mown hay, roasted walnut, honey malt, tamarind, liquorice, radicchio

Deanston
Distillery

**Founded in 1965 by James Finlay Co. and Brodie Hepburn Ltd.
Part of its production is used in the Scottish Leader blend.**

Great vintage: 1977
4 Stills: 2 wash, 2 spirit – 3 million LPA

Deanston, Perthshire, FK16 6AG
Central Highlands
+44 (0) 1786 843 010
www.deanstonmalt.com
Owner: Burn Stewart Distillers Ltd (Distell Group Ltd)

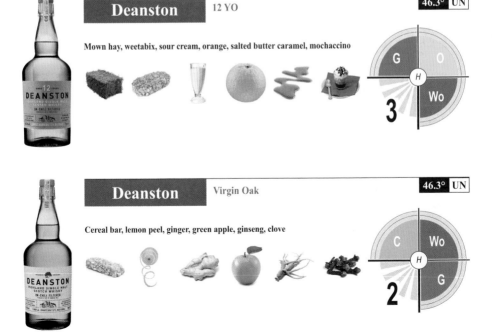

Deanston — 12 YO — 46.3° UN

Mown hay, weetabix, sour cream, orange, salted butter caramel, mochaccino

G | O | H | Wo
3

Deanston — Virgin Oak — 46.3° UN

Cereal bar, lemon peel, ginger, green apple, ginseng, clove

C | Wo | H | G
2

Edradour
Distillery

Founded in 1825 as Glenforres.

Great vintages: 1973, 1983, 1985
2 Stills: 1 wash, 1 spirit – 0.130 million LPA

Pitlochry, Perthshire PH16 5JP
Central Highlands
+44 (0) 1796 472 095
www.edradour.com
Owner: Signatory Vintage Scotch Whisky Co. Ltd

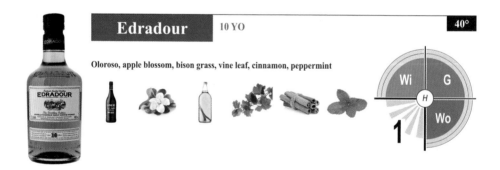

Edradour 10 YO   40°

Oloroso, apple blossom, bison grass, vine leaf, cinnamon, peppermint

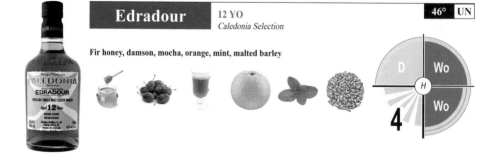

Edradour 12 YO
Caledonia Selection   46° UN

Fir honey, damson, mocha, orange, mint, malted barley

Edradour

2003 Chardonnay
2003/2013 9 YO Chardonnay Matured

 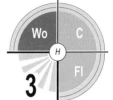

46° UN

Oak, walnut honey, malted barley, white peach, jasmine, nutmeg

Wo | C
H
Fl

3

Edradour

2001 CS
2001/2014 13 YO Port Wood Finish

 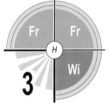

56.3° UN CS

Tayberry, leather, raspberry, chocolate, mulberry wine, cinnamon

Fr | Fr
H
Wi

3

Edradour

1993 Sauternes
1993/2013 19 YO Hogshead Sauternes Cask

 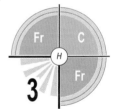

53.2° UN CS

Damson jam, walnut honey, green malt, leather, candied citrus, lily

Fr | C
H
Fr

3

Edradour

Ballechin 10 YO
2014 The Discovery Series

46° UN

Peat smoke, lime, tar, lanolin, peat moss, peppermint

Sm | Sm
H
Sm

3

Fettercairn
Distillery

Founded in 1824 by Sir Alexander Ramsay.

Great vintages: 1967, 1975, 1980
4 Stills: 2 wash, 2 spirit – 2.3 million LPA

Fettercairn, Laurencekirk, Kincardineshire AB30 1YB
Eastern Highlands
+44 (0) 1561 340 205
www.fettercairndistillery.co.uk
Owner: Whyte & Mackay Ltd (Emperador Inc.)

Fettercairn Fasque 42°

Molasses / treacle, mochaccino, candied citrus, cinnamon, roasted cocoa bean,
guarana

1

Fettercairn Fior
Sherry Cask 42°

Pebble, mochaccino, roasted cocoa bean, walnut wine, guarana, dead leaf

2

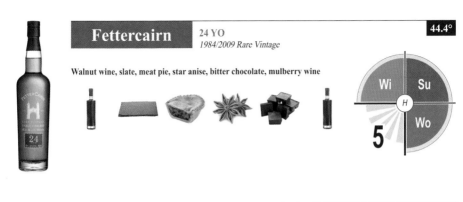

Fettercairn 24 YO
1984/2009 Rare Vintage
44.4°

Walnut wine, slate, meat pie, star anise, bitter chocolate, mulberry wine

Fettercairn 30 YO
1978/2009 Rare Vintage
43.3°

Beeswax, lichen, pine resin, malted barley, benzoin, potpourri

Fettercairn 40 YO
1969/2009 Apostoles
40°

Orange jam, pine resin, oak, kumquat, mahogany, rancio

Glencadam
Distillery

Founded in 1825 by George Cooper.

Great vintages: 1974, 1977
2 Stills: 1 wash, 1 spirit – 1.3 million LPA

Park Road, Brechin, Angus DD9 7PA
Eastern Highlands
+44 (0) 1356 622 217
www.glencadamdistillery.co.uk
Owner: Angus Dundee Distillers Plc

| Glencadam | 10 YO | | 46° UN |

Pear, candlewax, malted milk, star anise, lemon, chervil

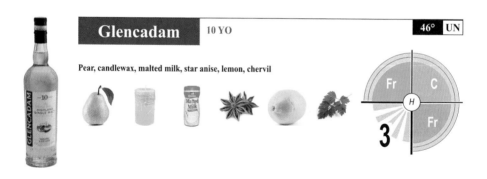

| Glencadam | 12 YO |
| | *Portwood Finish* | | 46° UN |

Raspberry, mown hay, barley malt syrup, star anise, rancio, ginger

Glencadam 14 YO
Oloroso Sherry Cask

46° UN

Orange peel, wild strawberry, chocolate malt, cranberry, ginger, hazelnut

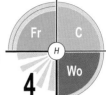

Fr | C
H
Wo
4

Glencadam 15 YO

46° UN

Beeswax, apple, barley malt syrup, eucalyptus, borage flower, lime tree

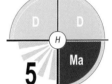

D | D
H
Ma
5

Glencadam 17 YO Triple Cask
2015 Bourbon Casks + Port Wood Finish

46° UN

Damson, peach, plum, geranium, mulberry wine, cinnamon

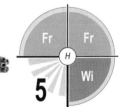

Fr | Fr
H
Wi
5

Glencadam 21 YO
Sherry Cask The Exceptional

46° UN

Lemon peel, nail polish, mirabelle, tonka bean, blackcurrant wine, lime tree

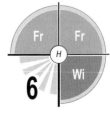

Fr | Fr
H
Wi
6

Glendronach
Distillery

Founded in 1826 by James Allardice.

Great vintages: 1968, 1972
4 Stills: 2 wash, 2 spirit – 1.4 million LPA

Forgue, Aberdeenshire AB54 6DB
Eastern Highlands
+44 (0) 1466 730 202
www.glendronachdistillery.com
Owner: Benriach Distillery Co. Ltd

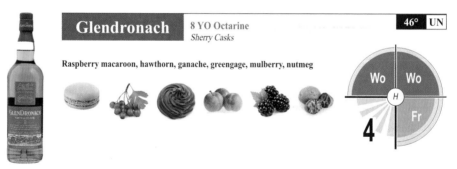

Glendronach 8 YO Octarine
Sherry Casks
46° UN

Raspberry macaroon, hawthorn, ganache, greengage, mulberry, nutmeg

Glendronach 8 YO The Hielan
2015 Bourbon & Sherry Casks
46° UN

Orange blossom, apricot jam, raisin, fruit cake, marzipan, plum

Glendronach

12 YO Original
PX & Oloroso Sherry Casks

43°

Rancio, fruit cake, dog-rose, sesame seed, milk chocolate, ginseng

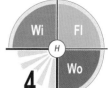

4

Glendronach

12 YO Sauternes
Sauternes Wine Barrels Finish

46°

Sultana, nectarine, freesia, quince jelly, vanilla, nutmeg

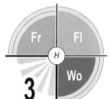

3

Glendronach

15 YO Revival
Oloroso Sherry Cask

46° UN

Cep, morello cherry in syrup, raisin, mocha, rancio, clove

6

Glendronach

18 YO Allardice
Oloroso Sherry Cask

46° UN

Morello cherry in syrup, walnut, raspberry wine, rancio, cigar box, blackcurrant

5

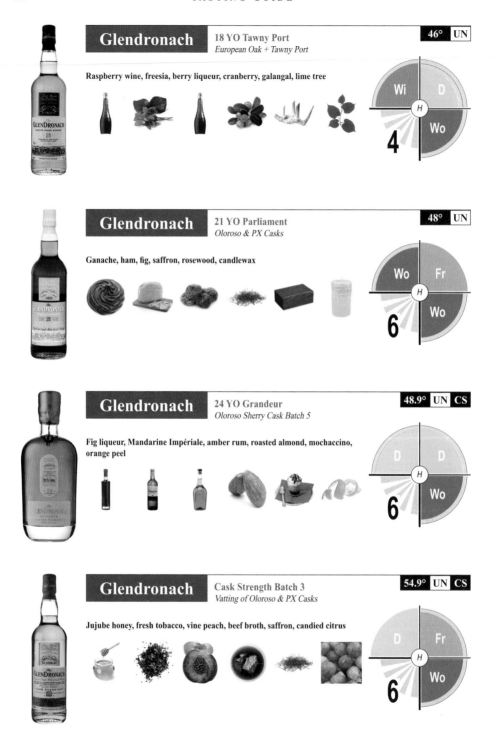

Glendronach — 18 YO Tawny Port
European Oak + Tawny Port

46° UN

Raspberry wine, freesia, berry liqueur, cranberry, galangal, lime tree

Wi / D / H / Wo

4

Glendronach — 21 YO Parliament
Oloroso & PX Casks

48° UN

Ganache, ham, fig, saffron, rosewood, candlewax

Wo / Fr / H / Wo

6

Glendronach — 24 YO Grandeur
Oloroso Sherry Cask Batch 5

48.9° UN CS

Fig liqueur, Mandarine Impériale, amber rum, roasted almond, mochaccino, orange peel

D / D / H / Wo

6

Glendronach — Cask Strength Batch 3
Vatting of Oloroso & PX Casks

54.9° UN CS

Jujube honey, fresh tobacco, vine peach, beef broth, saffron, candied citrus

D / Fr / H / Wo

6

Glen Garioch
Distillery

Founded in 1797 by Thomas Simpson.

Great vintages: 1968, 1971, 1972, 1975
3 Stills: 1 wash, 2 spirit – 1.370 million LPA

Oldmeldrum, Inverurie, Aberdeenshire AB51 0ES
Eastern Highlands
+44 (0) 1651 873 450
www.glengarioch.com
Owner: Morrison Bowmore Distillers Ltd (Beam Suntory Inc.)

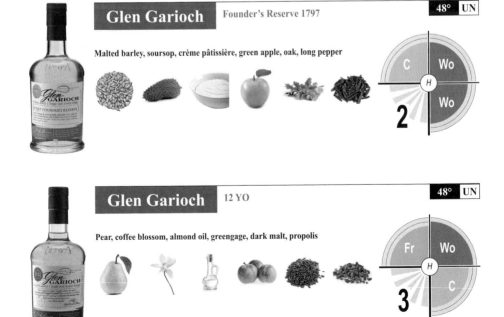

Glen Garioch Founder's Reserve 1797 — 48° UN

Malted barley, soursop, crème pâtissière, green apple, oak, long pepper

C — Wo — H — Wo
2

Glen Garioch 12 YO — 48° UN

Pear, coffee blossom, almond oil, greengage, dark malt, propolis

Fr — Wo — H — C
3

Glen Garioch — Virgin Oak
2013 Virgin Oak

48° UN

Apricot jam, cinnamon, ganache, dark malt, patchouli, Cayenne pepper

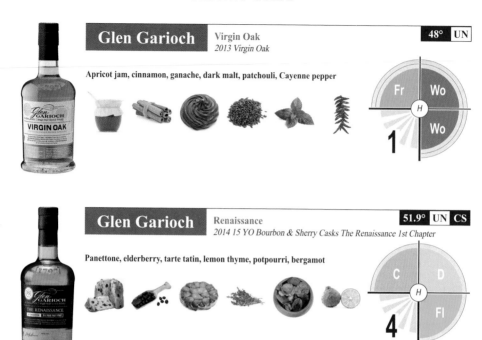

Glen Garioch — Renaissance
2014 15 YO Bourbon & Sherry Casks The Renaissance 1st Chapter

51.9° UN CS

Panettone, elderberry, tarte tatin, lemon thyme, potpourri, bergamot

Glen Garioch — Vintage 1999
1999/2013 Oloroso Sherry Cask Batch 30

56.3° UN CS

Menthol, elderberry, ginger, guava, liquorice, mugwort

Glenglassaugh
Distillery

Founded in 1875 by Glenglassaugh Distillery Co. (James Moir).
Closed from 1986 to 2008, operational since.

Great vintages: 1967, 1972
2 Stills: 1 wash, 1 spirit – 1.1 million LPA

Portsoy, Banffshire AB45 25Q
Eastern Highlands
+44 (0) 1261 842 367
www.glenglassaugh.com
Owner: Benriach Distillery Co. Ltd

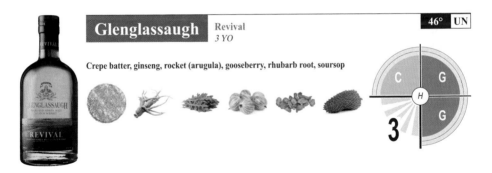

Glenglassaugh Revival
3 YO

46° UN

Crepe batter, ginseng, rocket (arugula), gooseberry, rhubarb root, soursop

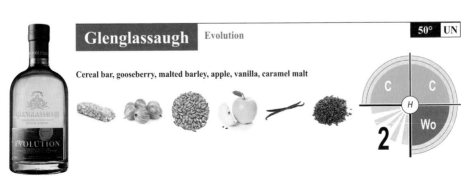

Glenglassaugh Evolution

50° UN

Cereal bar, gooseberry, malted barley, apple, vanilla, caramel malt

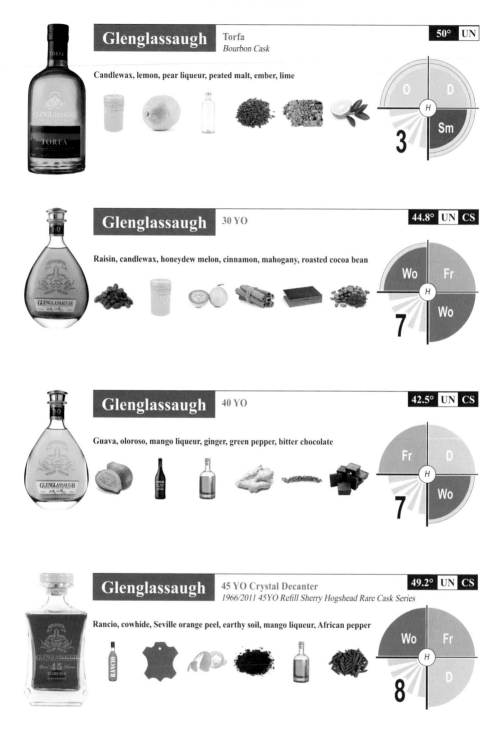

Glenglassaugh — Torfa
Bourbon Cask

50° UN

Candlewax, lemon, pear liqueur, peated malt, ember, lime

O | D
H
Sm

3

Glenglassaugh — 30 YO

44.8° UN CS

Raisin, candlewax, honeydew melon, cinnamon, mahogany, roasted cocoa bean

Wo | Fr
H
Wo

7

Glenglassaugh — 40 YO

42.5° UN CS

Guava, oloroso, mango liqueur, ginger, green pepper, bitter chocolate

Fr | D
H
Wo

7

Glenglassaugh — 45 YO Crystal Decanter
1966/2011 45YO Refill Sherry Hogshead Rare Cask Series

49.2° UN CS

Rancio, cowhide, Seville orange peel, earthy soil, mango liqueur, African pepper

Wo | Fr
H
D

8

Glengoyne
Distillery

Founded in 1833 by the Edmonstone family.
Formerly Burnfoot, then Glenguin Distillery.

Great vintages: 1967–1970, 1972
3 Stills: 1 wash, 2 spirit – 1.1 million LPA

Dumgoyne by Killearn, Glasgow, Lanarkshire G63 9LB
Western Highlands
+44 (0) 1360 550 254
www.glengoyne.com
Owner: Ian Macleod Distillers Ltd

Glengoyne   10 YO   40°

Green apple, macaroon, mown lawn, tarte tatin, linseed oil, caramel malt

Glengoyne   12 YO   43°

Lemon peel, malted milk, caramel malt, toffee apple, blood orange, cinnamon

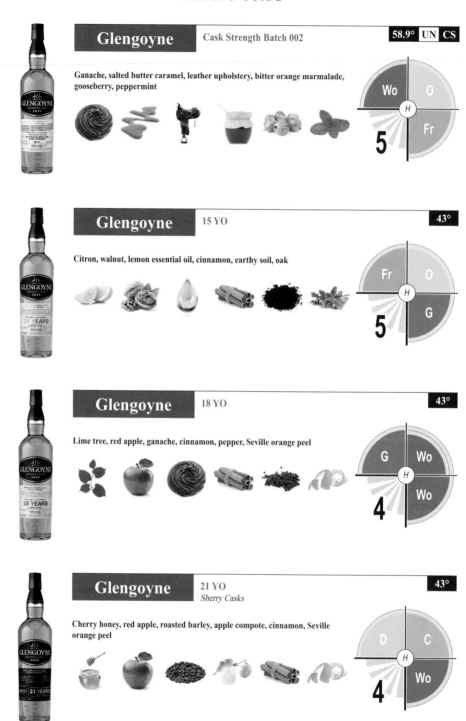

Glengoyne — Cask Strength Batch 002 — 58.9° UN CS

Ganache, salted butter caramel, leather upholstery, bitter orange marmalade, gooseberry, peppermint

Wo | O | H | Fr
5

Glengoyne — 15 YO — 43°

Citron, walnut, lemon essential oil, cinnamon, earthy soil, oak

Fr | O | H | G
5

Glengoyne — 18 YO — 43°

Lime tree, red apple, ganache, cinnamon, pepper, Seville orange peel

G | Wo | H | Wo
4

Glengoyne — 21 YO
Sherry Casks — 43°

Cherry honey, red apple, roasted barley, apple compote, cinnamon, Seville orange peel

D | C | H | Wo
4

Glenmorangie
Distillery

Founded in 1843 by William Matheson.
Closed from 1931 to 1936, operational since.

Great vintages: 1963, 1971
12 Stills (the tallest in Scotland at 5.14m/16ft): 6 wash, 6 spirit – 6 million LPA

Tain, Ross-shire, IV19 1PZ
Northern Highlands
+44 (0) 1862 892 477
www.glenmorangie.com
Owner: Glenmorangie Plc since 1997 (LVMH group)

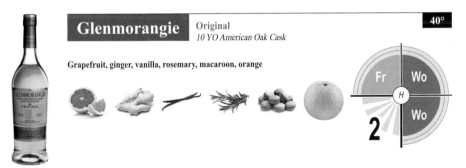

Glenmorangie — Original — *10 YO American Oak Cask* — 40°

Grapefruit, ginger, vanilla, rosemary, macaroon, orange

Fr | Wo | H | Wo — 2

Glenmorangie — Nectar d'Òr — *Sauternes Wine Cask* — 46° UN

Pineapple, buttercup, meringue, nutmeg, white chocolate, passion fruit/maracuja

Fr | Wo | H | Wo — 5

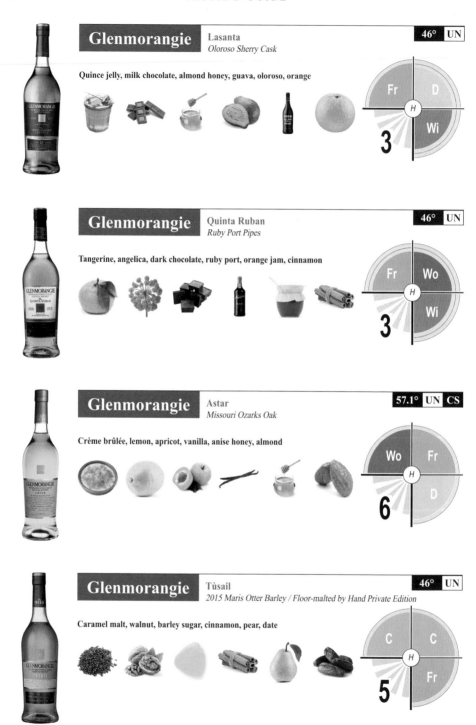

Glenmorangie — Lasanta
Oloroso Sherry Cask
46° UN

Quince jelly, milk chocolate, almond honey, guava, oloroso, orange

Fr / D / H / Wi — 3

Glenmorangie — Quinta Ruban
Ruby Port Pipes
46° UN

Tangerine, angelica, dark chocolate, ruby port, orange jam, cinnamon

Fr / Wo / H / Wi — 3

Glenmorangie — Astar
Missouri Ozarks Oak
57.1° UN CS

Crème brûlée, lemon, apricot, vanilla, anise honey, almond

Wo / Fr / H / D — 6

Glenmorangie — Tùsail
2015 Maris Otter Barley / Floor-malted by Hand Private Edition
46° UN

Caramel malt, walnut, barley sugar, cinnamon, pear, date

C / C / H / Fr — 5

Glenmorangie — Companta
Grand Cru Burgundy & Côtes du Rhône Casks Private Edition 46° UN

Cherry, peony, molasses/treacle, dark chocolate, liquorice cream, cranberry

Glenmorangie — Sonnalta PX
11 YO PX Sherry Cask Private Edition 46° UN

Milk chocolate, sultana, passion fruit/maracuja, vanilla, ginger, orange

      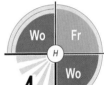

Glenmorangie — Finealta
American Oak + Oloroso Sherry Cask Private Edition 46° UN

Orange, nutmeg, almond, meringue, ginger, Parma violet

      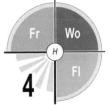

Glenmorangie — Artein
15 YO Super Tuscan Cask Private Edition 46° UN

Raspberry, radicchio, limestone, toffee apple, peppermint, ganache

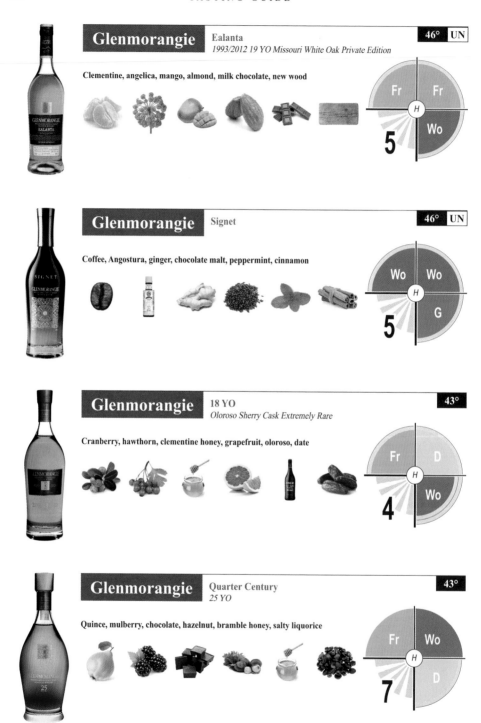

Glenmorangie — Ealanta
1993/2012 19 YO Missouri White Oak Private Edition

46° UN

Clementine, angelica, mango, almond, milk chocolate, new wood

Fr | Fr
H
Wo

5

Glenmorangie — Signet

46° UN

Coffee, Angostura, ginger, chocolate malt, peppermint, cinnamon

Wo | Wo
H
G

5

Glenmorangie — 18 YO
Oloroso Sherry Cask Extremely Rare

43°

Cranberry, hawthorn, clementine honey, grapefruit, oloroso, date

Fr | D
H
Wo

4

Glenmorangie — Quarter Century
25 YO

43°

Quince, mulberry, chocolate, hazelnut, bramble honey, salty liquorice

Fr | Wo
H
D

7

Glen Ord
Distillery

Founded in 1838 by Thomas Mackenzie.
Produces The Singleton for the Asian market
(Dufftown produces The Singleton for Europe and Africa,
Glendullan produces The Singleton for the US).

Great vintages: 1962, 1975
14 Stills: 7 wash, 7 spirit – 11 million LPA

Muir of Ord, Beauly, Ross-shire IV6 7UJ
Northern Highlands
+44 (0) 1463 872 004
www.malts.com
Owner: Diageo Plc

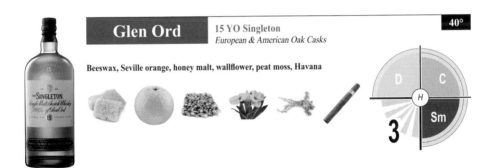

Glen Ord — 15 YO Singleton
European & American Oak Casks
40°

Beeswax, Seville orange, honey malt, wallflower, peat moss, Havana

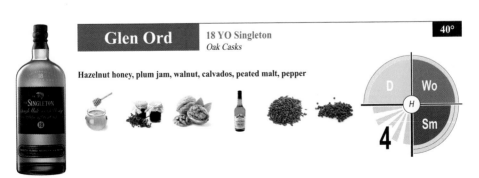

Glen Ord — 18 YO Singleton
Oak Casks
40°

Hazelnut honey, plum jam, walnut, calvados, peated malt, pepper

Glenturret
Distillery

Founded in 1775 (clandestine), 1818 (under licence), by John Drummon.
Closed in 1921, dismantled in 1929, restructured in 1959.

Great vintages: 1977, 1979
2 Stills: 1 wash, 1 spirit – 0.34 million LPA

The Host, Crieff, Perthhire PH7 4HA
Central Highlands
+44 (0) 1764 656 565
www.thefamousgrouse.com
Owner: The Edrington Group Ltd

Glenturret	10 YO	40°

Greengage, malted barley, green malt, juniper honey, mown hay, citrus peel

Glenturret	Sherry Edition *Sherry Butts*	40°

Fruit cake, acacia honey, fig wine, sandalwood, pepper, pink grapefruit

Highland Park
Distillery

Founded in 1798 by David Robertson.
Has its own malt houses.

Great vintages: 1955, 1956, 1962, 1964
4 Stills: 2 wash, 2 spirit – 2.5 million LPA

Holm Road, St. Ola, Kirkwall, Orkney KW15 1SU
Islands Highland
+44 (0) 1856 874 619
www.highlandpark.co.uk
Owner: The Edrington Group Ltd

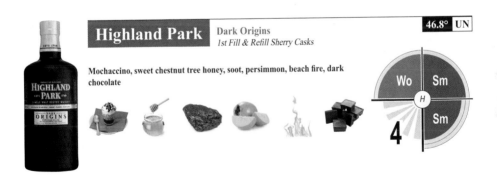

Highland Park Dark Origins
1st Fill & Refill Sherry Casks

46.8° UN

Mochaccino, sweet chestnut tree honey, soot, persimmon, beach fire, dark chocolate

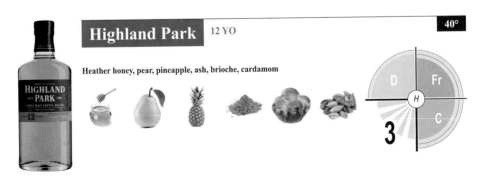

Highland Park 12 YO

40°

Heather honey, pear, pineapple, ash, brioche, cardamom

Highland Park   15 YO   40°

Heather honey, beach fire, ganache, candied citrus, orange, peated malt

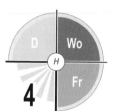

4

Highland Park   Odin   55.8°   UN   CS
2015 16 YO Valhalla Coll.

Nutmeg, coal, malted barley, walnut wine, umeshu, Seville orange

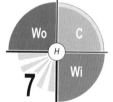

7

Highland Park   18 YO   43°

Lilac, libraries, acacia honey, nutmeg, marzipan, peated malt

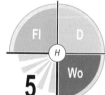

5

Highland Park   Einar   40°   TRE
2013 The Warrior Series

Heather honey, TCP antiseptic, gorse bush, myrtle, honey malt, ginger

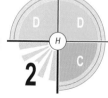

2

Highland Park — Harald
2013 The Warrior Series

40° TRE

Vanilla, peat smoke, fig, cinnamon, honey malt, clove

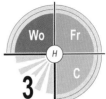

3

Highland Park — Ragnvald
2013 The Warrior Series

44.6° UN TRE

Beeswax, cedar, mango, lemon honey, peat smoke, libraries

7

Highland Park — Thorfinn
2013 The Warrior Series

45.1° UN TRE

Blueberry jam, camphor, ginger, beach fire, allspice, maple tree smoke

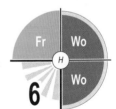

6

Highland Park — 21 YO

47.5° UN

Lilac, heather honey, ginger, libraries, pine tree smoke, green pepper

6

Highland Park 25 YO

48.1° UN

Mown hay, propolis, Seville orange peel, African pepper, peat smoke, blackberry jam

5

Highland Park 30 YO

48.1° UN

Sweet chestnut tree honey, morello cherry in syrup, dark chocolate, plum jam, Seville orange peel, liquorice

7

Highland Park 40 YO

48.1° UN

Propolis, beach fire, Papier d'Arménie, mate, Seville orange peel, camphor

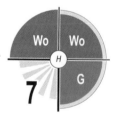

7

Highland Park 50 YO

44.8° UN CS

1960/2010 Sterling Silver Frame

Pine resin, libraries, propolis, Seville orange peel, liquorice, camphor

7

Isle of Jura
Distillery

Founded in 1810 by Archibald Campbell.

Great vintages: 1965, 1966, 1974–1976
4 Stills: 2 wash, 2 spirit – 2.2 million LPA

Craighouse, Jura, Argyllshire PA60 7XT
Islands Highland
+44 (0) 1496 820 240
www.isleofjura.com
Owner: Whyte & Mackay Ltd (Emperador Inc.)

Isle of Jura — Origin — *10 YO* — 40°

Malted barley, melon liqueur, oak moss, pear, caramel, salty liquorice

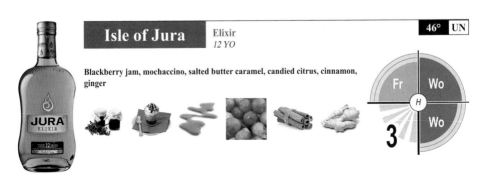

Isle of Jura — Elixir — *12 YO* — 46° — UN

Blackberry jam, mochaccino, salted butter caramel, candied citrus, cinnamon, ginger

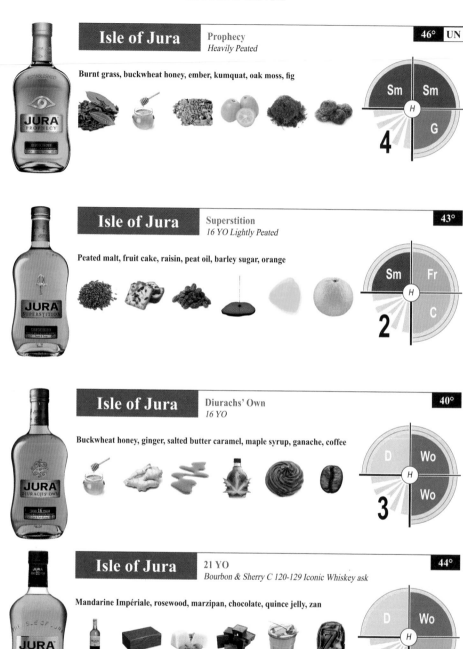

Isle of Jura — Prophecy
Heavily Peated

46° UN

Burnt grass, buckwheat honey, ember, kumquat, oak moss, fig

Sm | Sm
H
G

4

Isle of Jura — Superstition
16 YO Lightly Peated

43°

Peated malt, fruit cake, raisin, peat oil, barley sugar, orange

Sm | Fr
H
C

2

Isle of Jura — Diurachs' Own
16 YO

40°

Buckwheat honey, ginger, salted butter caramel, maple syrup, ganache, coffee

D | Wo
H
Wo

3

Isle of Jura — 21 YO
Bourbon & Sherry C 120-129 Iconic Whiskey ask

44°

Mandarine Impériale, rosewood, marzipan, chocolate, quince jelly, zan

D | Wo
H
Fr

5

Loch Lomond
Distillery

Founded in 1965 by Littlemill Distillery Co. Ltd.
(Duncan Thomas and American Barton Brands.)
30 km (18 miles) south of the old distillery (1814–17).

Great vintages: 1967, 1974, 1979
7 Stills: 1 wash, 1 spirit, 4 Lomond, 1 Coffey – 4 millions LPA

Lomond Estate, Alexandria, Dunbartonshire G83 0TL
Western Highlands
+44 (0) 1389 752 781
www.lochlomonddistillery.com
Owner: Loch Lomond Group (Exponent Private Equity)

Loch Lomond Original
Deer Label

40°

Dark malt, buckwheat honey, pineapple, malted barley, peated malt, fudge

3

Loch Lomond 12 YO
Islands – Inchmurrin

46° UN

Beeswax, lemon, brioche, galangal, citron, malted barley

4

Macduff / Glen Deveron
Distillery

Founded in 1962 by Marty Dyke, George Crawford and Brodie Hepburn.

Great vintages: 1964, 1969
6 Stills: 3 wash, 3 spirit – 3.34 million LPA

Banff, Aberdeenshire AB45 3JT
Eastern Highlands
+44 (0) 1261 812 612
www.glendeveron.com
Owner: John Dewar & Sons Ltd (Bacardi)

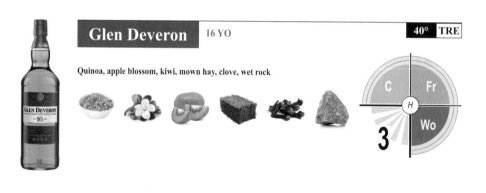

Glen Deveron   16 YO   40°   TRE

Quinoa, apple blossom, kiwi, mown hay, clove, wet rock

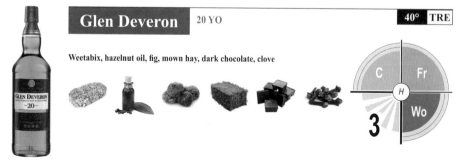

Glen Deveron   20 YO   40°   TRE

Weetabix, hazelnut oil, fig, mown hay, dark chocolate, clove

Oban
Distillery

Founded in 1794 by John and Hugh Stevenson.

Great vintages: 1963, 1969, 1984
2 Stills: 1 wash, 1 spirit – 0.87 million LPA

Stafford Street, Oban, Argyll PA34 5NH
Western Highlands
+44 (0) 1631 572 004
www.malts.com
Owner: Diageo Plc

Oban — 14 YO — 43°

Salt marsh, tangerine, fig, beach fire, coffee, Grand Marnier®

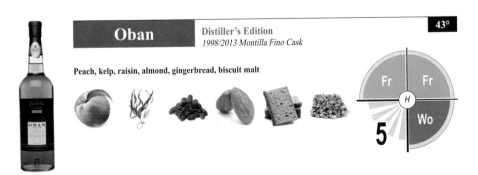

Oban — Distiller's Edition — 43°
1998/2013 Montilla Fino Cask

Peach, kelp, raisin, almond, gingerbread, biscuit malt

Old Pulteney
Distillery

Founded in 1826 by James Henderson.

Great vintages: 1964, 1972, 1977
2 Stills: 1 wash, 1 spirit – 1.8 million LPA

Huddart St, Wick, Caithness KW1 5BA
Northern Highlands
+44 (0) 1955 602 371
www.oldpulteney.com
Owner: Inver House Distillers Ltd (Thai Beverages Plc)

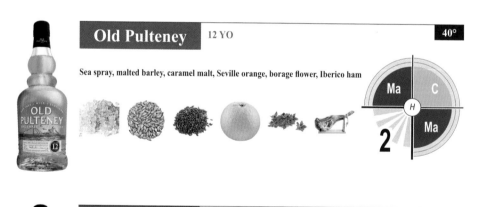

Old Pulteney   12 YO   **40°**

Sea spray, malted barley, caramel malt, Seville orange, borage flower, Iberico ham

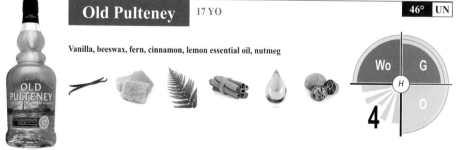

Old Pulteney   17 YO   **46°**   **UN**

Vanilla, beeswax, fern, cinnamon, lemon essential oil, nutmeg

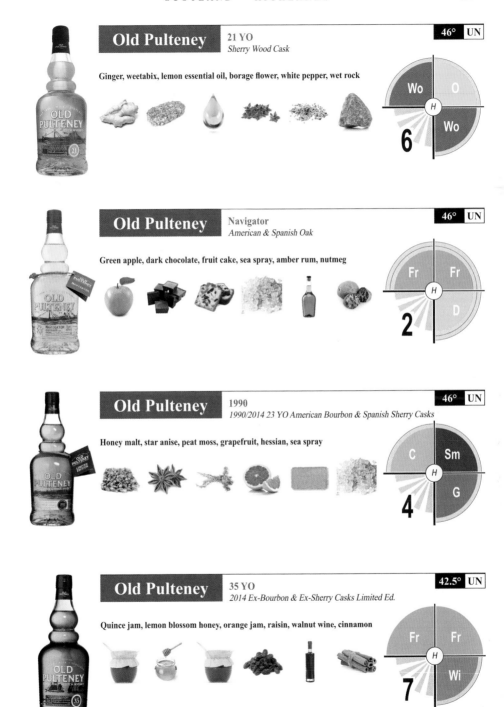

Old Pulteney 21 YO
Sherry Wood Cask
46° UN

Ginger, weetabix, lemon essential oil, borage flower, white pepper, wet rock

Wo | O
H
Wo
6

Old Pulteney Navigator
American & Spanish Oak
46° UN

Green apple, dark chocolate, fruit cake, sea spray, amber rum, nutmeg

Fr | Fr
H
D
2

Old Pulteney 1990
1990/2014 23 YO American Bourbon & Spanish Sherry Casks
46° UN

Honey malt, star anise, peat moss, grapefruit, hessian, sea spray

C | Sm
H
G
4

Old Pulteney 35 YO
2014 Ex-Bourbon & Ex-Sherry Casks Limited Ed.
42.5° UN

Quince jam, lemon blossom honey, orange jam, raisin, walnut wine, cinnamon

Fr | Fr
H
Wi
7

Royal Lochnagar
Distillery

Founded in 1845 by David Robertson.

Great vintages: 1969–1973, 1977
2 Stills: 1 wash, 1 spirit – 0.5 million LPA

Crathie, Ballater, Aberdeenshire AB35 5TB
Eastern Highlands
+44 (0) 1339 742 700
www.malts.com
Owner: Diageo Plc

Royal Lochnagar — 12 YO — 40°

Malted barley, crepe batter, molasses/treacle, greengage, peated malt, walnut

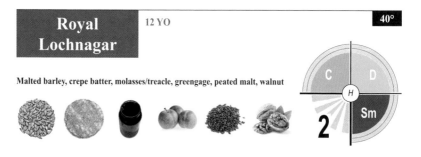

2

C | D
H
Sm

Royal Lochnagar — Selected Reserve — 43°

Parma violet, honey malt, molasses/treacle, beeswax, liquorice, malted barley

3

Fl | D
H
Wo

Scapa
Distillery

Founded in 1885 by Macfarlane & Townsend.

Great vintages: 1965, 1974, 1979
2 Stills: 1 wash, 1 spirit − 1.1 million LPA

Scapa, St Ola, Kirkwall, Orkney KW15 1SE
Islands Highland
+44 (0) 1856 876 585
www.scapamalt.com
Owner: Chivas Brothers Ltd (Pernod Ricard)

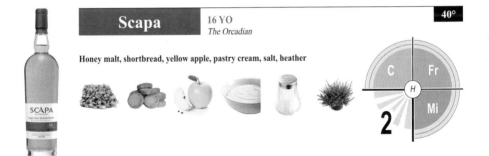

| Scapa | 16 YO
The Orcadian | 40° |

Honey malt, shortbread, yellow apple, pastry cream, salt, heather

Talisker
Distillery

Founded in 1830 by Hugh and Kenneth Macaskill.

Great vintages: 1955–1957, 1981
5 Stills: 2 wash, 3 spirit – 2.7 millions LPA

Carbost, Isle of Skye, Inverness-Shire IV47 8SR
Islands Highland
+44 (0) 1478 614 308
www.malts.com
Owner: Diageo Plc

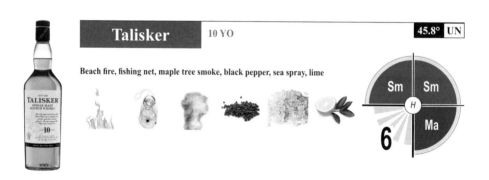

Talisker 10 YO 45.8° UN

Beach fire, fishing net, maple tree smoke, black pepper, sea spray, lime

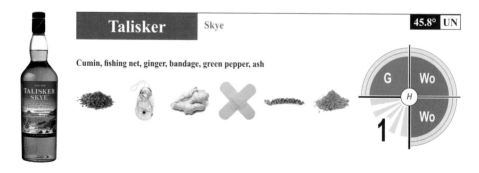

Talisker Skye 45.8° UN

Cumin, fishing net, ginger, bandage, green pepper, ash

Talisker — Storm

45.8° UN

Peat moss, sea spray, bandage, sweet pepper, oyster, white pepper

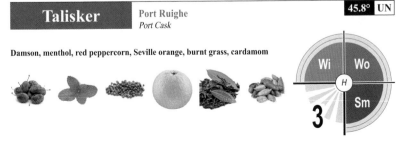

Sm | Sm
H
5 | Ma

Talisker — Dark Storm
2014 Heavily Charred Cask

45.8° UN TRE

Ember, bandage, peat smoke, vanilla, caramel, red apple

Sm | Sm
H
4 | Wo

Talisker — Distiller's Edition
2003/2014 Double Matured in Amoroso Cask Wood

45.8° UN

Dark chocolate, Seville orange, peat moss, blackberry jam, red peppercorn, fudge

Wo | Sm
H
5 | Wo

Talisker — Port Ruighe
Port Cask

45.8° UN

Damson, menthol, red peppercorn, Seville orange, burnt grass, cardamom

Wi | Wo
H
3 | Sm

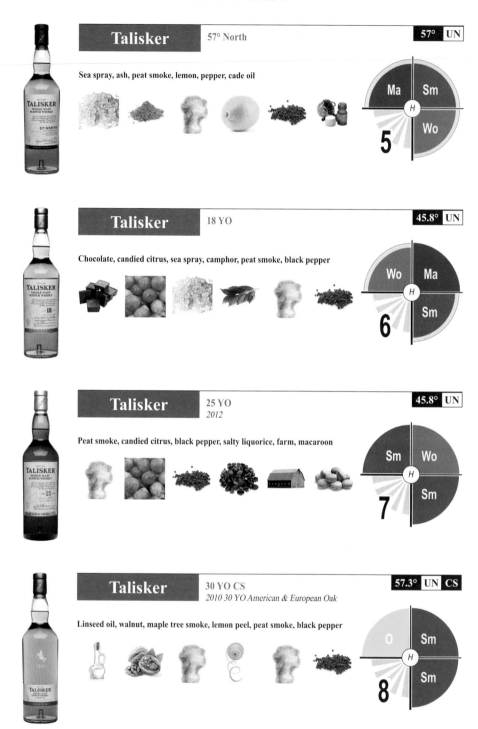

Talisker 57° North — 57° UN

Sea spray, ash, peat smoke, lemon, pepper, cade oil

Ma | Sm
H
Wo
5

Talisker 18 YO — 45.8° UN

Chocolate, candied citrus, sea spray, camphor, peat smoke, black pepper

Wo | Ma
H
Sm
6

Talisker 25 YO
2012 — 45.8° UN

Peat smoke, candied citrus, black pepper, salty liquorice, farm, macaroon

Sm | Wo
H
Sm
7

Talisker 30 YO CS
2010 30 YO American & European Oak — 57.3° UN CS

Linseed oil, walnut, maple tree smoke, lemon peel, peat smoke, black pepper

O | Sm
H
Sm
8

Tobermory / Ledaig
Distillery

Founded in 1798 by John Sinclair.

Great vintages: 1972, 1973
4 Stills: 2 wash, 2 spirit – 1 million LPA

Main Street, Tobermory, Isle of Mull, Argyllshire PA75 6NR
Islands Highland
+44 (0) 1688 302 647
www.tobermorydistillery.com
Owner: Burn Stewart Distillers Ltd (Distell Group Ltd)

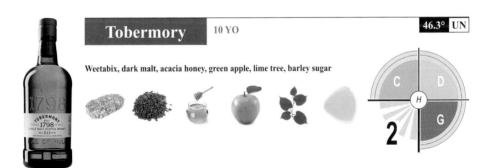

Tobermory 10 YO 46.3° UN

Weetabix, dark malt, acacia honey, green apple, lime tree, barley sugar

2

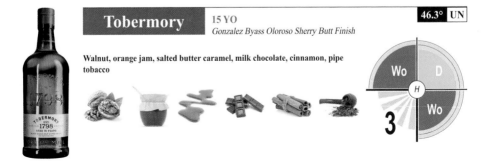

Tobermory 15 YO 46.3° UN
Gonzalez Byass Oloroso Sherry Butt Finish

Walnut, orange jam, salted butter caramel, milk chocolate, cinnamon, pipe tobacco

3

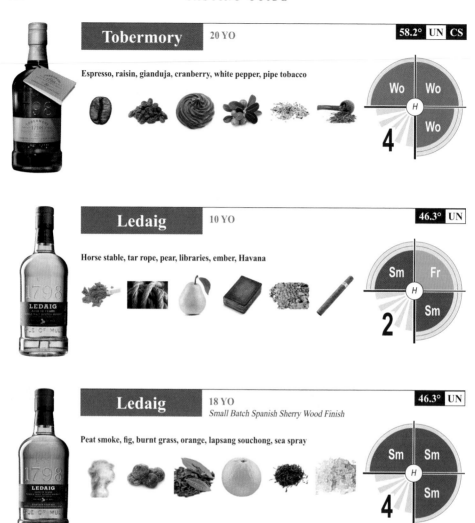

Tobermory 20 YO — 58.2° UN CS

Espresso, raisin, gianduja, cranberry, white pepper, pipe tobacco

Wo | Wo
H
Wo
4

Ledaig 10 YO — 46.3° UN

Horse stable, tar rope, pear, libraries, ember, Havana

Sm | Fr
H
Sm
2

Ledaig 18 YO — 46.3° UN
Small Batch Spanish Sherry Wood Finish

Peat smoke, fig, burnt grass, orange, lapsang souchong, sea spray

Sm | Sm
H
Sm
4

Tomatin
Distillery

**Founded in 1897 by The Tomatin Spey District Distillery Ltd.
(John MacDougall, John MacLeish and Alexander Allan.)
Part of its production is used in the Antiquary and Talisman blends.**

Great vintages: 1962, 1965, 1967, 1976
23 Stills: 12 wash, 11 spirit – 5.05 millions LPA

Tomatin, Inverness-shire IV13 7YT
Central Highlands
+44 (0) 1463 248 144
www.tomatin.com
Owner: The Tomatin Distillery Co. Ltd (Takara Shuzo Corp.)

Tomatin	Legacy	43°

NAS Bourbon & Virgin Oak

Panna cotta, pineapple, floral cream, soursop, lemon sorbet, cinnamon

Tomatin	12 YO	43°

2014 Bourbon Barrels + Sherry Casks

Grapefruit, biscuit malt, apple, walnut, floral cream, raisin

Tomatin — Cask Strength
Bourbon Barrels + Oloroso Sherry Casks
57.5° UN CS

Barley malt syrup, pear, caramel malt, walnut, gingerbread, fresh tobacco

D · C
H
Wo
3

Tomatin — 14 YO
Bourbon Barrel + Port Pipes
46° UN

Melon, pomegranate, white peach, walnut, apricot, cinnamon

Fr · Fr
H
Fr
3

Tomatin — 18 YO
Spanish Oloroso Sherry Cask
46° UN

Pomegranate, sugar apple, lemon tree honey, dark chocolate, rosewood, malted barley

Fr · D
H
Wo
4

Tomatin — Cù Bòcan
NAS Virgin & Bourbon & Sherry Casks
46° UN

Grapefruit, biscuit malt, maple tree smoke, cereal bar, espelette chilli, clove

Fr · Sm
H
Wo
3

Tullibardine
Distillery

Founded in 1949 by William Delmé-Evans.

Great vintages: 1964–1966, 1972
4 Stills: 2 wash, 2 spirit – 3 million LPA

Stirling St., Blackford, Perthshire PH4 1QG
Central Highlands
+44 (0) 1764 682 252
www.tullibardine.com
Owner: Terroirs Distillers (Picard Vins & Spiritueux)

Tullibardine	Sovereign	43°
	1st Fill Bourbon Barrel	

Malted barley, pear, chocolate malt, sugar apple, allspice, walnut

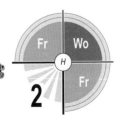

Tullibardine	225	43°
	Sauternes Finish	

Candied citrus, weetabix, vanilla cream, allspice, orange peel, cinnamon

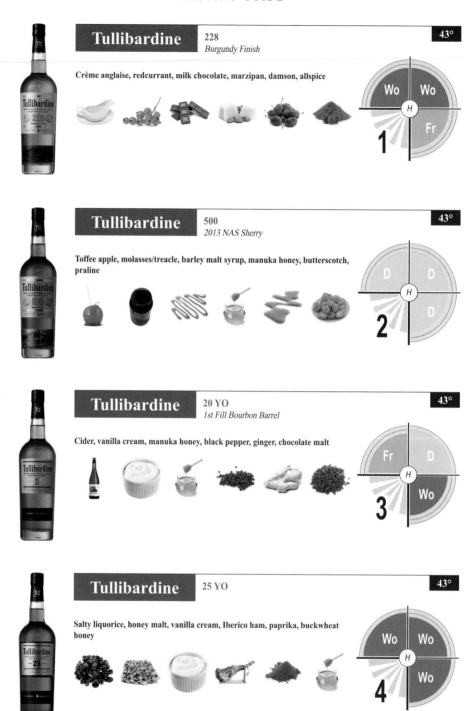

Tullibardine 228
Burgundy Finish
43°

Crème anglaise, redcurrant, milk chocolate, marzipan, damson, allspice

1

Tullibardine 500
2013 NAS Sherry
43°

Toffee apple, molasses/treacle, barley malt syrup, manuka honey, butterscotch, praline

2

Tullibardine 20 YO
1st Fill Bourbon Barrel
43°

Cider, vanilla cream, manuka honey, black pepper, ginger, chocolate malt

3

Tullibardine 25 YO
43°

Salty liquorice, honey malt, vanilla cream, Iberico ham, paprika, buckwheat honey

4

Aberlour
Distillery

Founded in 1825 by James Gordon and Peter Weir.
Rebuilt in 1879 and again in 1898 following fires.

---

4 Stills: 2 wash, 2 spirit – 3.8 million LPA

Aberlour, Banffshire AB38 9PJ
+44 (0) 1340 881 249
www.aberlour.com
Owner: Chivas Brothers Ltd (Pernod Ricard)

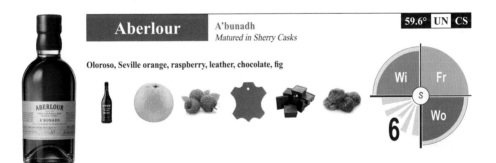

Aberlour — A'bunadh
Matured in Sherry Casks

59.6° UN CS

Oloroso, Seville orange, raspberry, leather, chocolate, fig

Wi | Fr
S
Wo
6

Aberlour — 10 YO Double Cask Matured
Matured in Sherry and Bourbon Casks

43°

Oloroso, marzipan, fruit cake, banana, malted barley, caramel

Wi | Fr
S
C
2

Aberlour   2005 White Oak   **40°**

Orange blossom honey, vanilla, white oak, malted barley, liquorice, caramel

3

Aberlour   12 YO Double Cask Matured   **40°**
Matured in Sherry & Bourbon Casks

Oloroso, lime tree honey, apricot, malted barley, oak, nutmeg

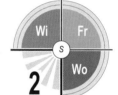

2

Aberlour   12 YO Sherry Cask Matured   **40°**
Matured in Sherry Casks

Oloroso, tarte tatin, almond honey, fresh tobacco, dark chocolate, ginger

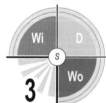

3

Aberlour   12 YO Non-chill-filtered   **46°** **UN**
Matured in Sherry & Bourbon Casks

Oloroso, apricot, mocha, chocolate, orange marmalade, star anise

4

Aberlour — 15 YO Double Cask Matured TRE
Matured in Sherry & Bourbon Casks

40°

Grapefruit, walnut, cream sherry, orange, cinnamon, oak smoke

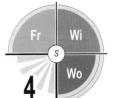

Fr Wi
S
Wo
4

Aberlour — 15 YO Select Cask Reserve
Matured in Sherry & Bourbon Casks

43°

Tonka bean, oloroso, buckwheat honey, peach, white pepper, orange

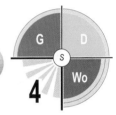

G D
S
Wo
4

Aberlour — 16 YO Double Cask Matured
Matured in Sherry & Bourbon Casks

40°

Raisin, milk chocolate, honeycomb, banana, hazelnut, lemon

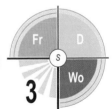

Fr D
S
Wo
3

Aberlour — 18 YO Double Cask Matured
Matured in Sherry & Bourbon Casks

43°

Oloroso, fruit cake, malted barley, nutmeg, liquorice, caramel

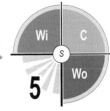

Wi C
S
Wo
5

AnCnoc / Knockdhu
Distillery

Founded in 1893 by John Morrison.
Closed from 1983 to 1989.
Its malt was named AnCnoc in 1993 to avoid confusion with Knockando.

2 Stills: 1 wash, 1 spirit – 1.7 million LPA

Knock, Huntly, AB54 7LJ
+44 1466 771 223
www.ancnoc.com
Owner: Inver House Distillers Ltd (Thai Beverages Plc)

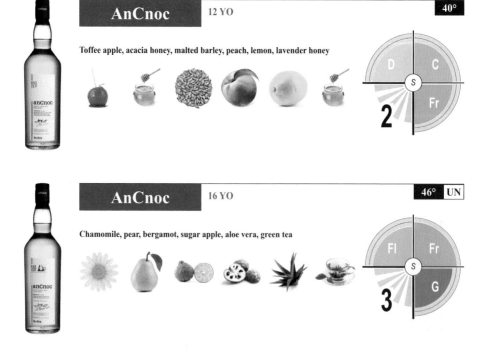

AnCnoc   12 YO   40°

Toffee apple, acacia honey, malted barley, peach, lemon, lavender honey

AnCnoc   16 YO   46°   UN

Chamomile, pear, bergamot, sugar apple, aloe vera, green tea

AnCnoc

18 YO
Matured in Sherry & Bourbon Casks

46° UN

Fudge, Seville orange marmalade, nutmeg, candied citrus, green pepper, walnut

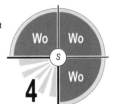

4

AnCnoc

22 YO
Matured in Sherry & Bourbon Casks

46° UN

Strawberry tree honey, tarte tatin, barley malt syrup, blood orange, roasted barley, green pepper

5

AnCnoc

2000
Matured in Sherry & Bourbon Casks

46° UN

Allspice, lemongrass, oloroso, crème brûlée, orange peel, praline

3

AnCnoc

Cutter

46° UN

Oak smoke, malted milk, peat oil, liquorice cream, walnut brandy, cocoa

3

Aultmore
Distillery

Founded in 1896 by Alexander Edward.
Bought by John Deware & Sons in 1923.
Rebuilt in the 1970s.

4 Stills: 2 wash, 2 spirit – 3 million LPA

Keith, Banffshire AB55 6QY
+44 (0) 1542 881 800
www.aultmore.com
Owner: John Dewar & Sons (Bacardi Martini)

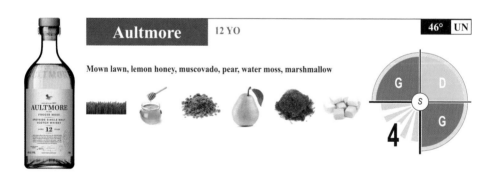

Aultmore 12 YO   46° UN

Mown lawn, lemon honey, muscovado, pear, water moss, marshmallow

Aultmore 25 YO   46° UN

Tonka bean, lemon honey, tarte tatin, fig liqueur, ganache, curaçao

Balvenie
Distillery

Founded in 1892 by William Grant.
Marketed as a single malt since 1973.
15% of its barley is always malted on the premises.

---

11 Stills: 5 wash, 6 spirit – 6.8 million LPA

Dufftown, Banffshire AB55 4DH
+44 (0) 1340 820 373
www.thebalvenie.com
Owner: William Grant & Sons

Balvenie 12 YO Double Wood — 40°
Matured in Sherry & Bourbon Casks

Orange blossom honey, coffee, malted barley, chocolate, raisin, ginger

3

Balvenie 12 YO Single Barrel First Fill — 47.8° UN
Matured in First Fill Bourbon Casks

Liquorice, malted barley, mirabelle, white pepper, crème anglaise, apricot

5

Balvenie

12 YO Triple Cask
Matured in Refill, First Fill Bourbon & Oloroso Sherry Casks

40°

Sandalwood, apple, sweet chestnut honey, cinnamon, oloroso, tonka bean

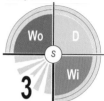

3

Balvenie

14 YO Caribbean Cask
Finished in Caribbean Rum Casks

43°

Passion fruit/maraca, fresh tobacco, orange peel, amber rum, vanilla, barley malt syrup

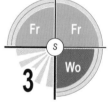

3

Balvenie

15 YO Single Barrel Sherry Cask
Matured in Sherry Cask

47.8° UN

Orange, oak, leather, roasted almond, oloroso, ginger

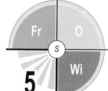

5

Balvenie

16 YO Triple Cask
Matured in Refill, First Fill Bourbon & Oloroso Sherry Casks

40°

Acacia honey, banana, crème brûlée, cinnamon, apricot, white pepper

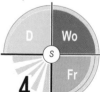

4

Balvenie

17 YO Double Wood
Matured in Sherry & Bourbon Casks

43°

Cherry blossom honey, green apple, cinnamon, honeysuckle, vanilla, almond

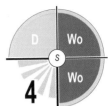

D | Wo
S
Wo

4

Balvenie

Tun 1509 Batch 1

47.1° UN

Orange blossom honey, apple, mango, quinine, orange peel, clove

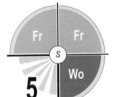

D | Fr
S
Fr

7

Balvenie

21 YO Port Wood
Finished in Port Casks

40°

Raspberry, beeswax, raisin, cherry blossom honey, ground pepper, cocoa

Fr | Fr
S
Wo

5

Balvenie

25 YO Triple Cask
Matured in Refill, First Fill Bourbon & Oloroso Sherry Casks

40°

Acacia honey, peach, lemon blossom honey, hazelnut, oak, malted barley

D | D
S
Wo

5

BenRiach
Distillery

**Founded in 1897 by John Duff & Co.
Closed from 1903 to 1965 and again from 2002 to 2004.
Acquired by the South African group Intra Trading in 2004.**

4 Stills: 2 wash, 2 spirit – 2.8 million LPA

Longmorn, Elgin, Morayshire IV30 8SJ
+44 (0) 1343 862 888
www.benriachdistillery.co.uk
Owner: Benriach Distillery Co

| BenRiach | Heart of Speyside | 40° |

Heather, farm, lemon marmalade, almond, acacia honey, white pepper

2

| BenRiach | 10 YO *Matured in Sherry & Bourbon Casks* | 43° |

Malted barley, greengage, apricot, lemon, white pepper, vanilla

3

BenRiach   12 YO

43°

Heather honey, reseda, peach liqueur, pastry cream, milk chocolate, nutmeg

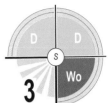

3

BenRiach   12 YO Sherry Matured
Matured in Sherry Casks

46° UN

Oloroso, leather, pedro ximénez, liquorice, walnut, chocolate

4

BenRiach   15 YO PX Finish
Finished in PX Sherry Casks

46° UN

Pedro ximénez, bergamot, eucalyptus honey, allspice, dark chocolate, molasses/treacle

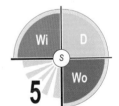

5

BenRiach   16 YO

43°

Heather honey, marzipan, barley sugar, apricot, vanilla cream, peat smoke

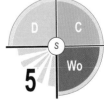

5

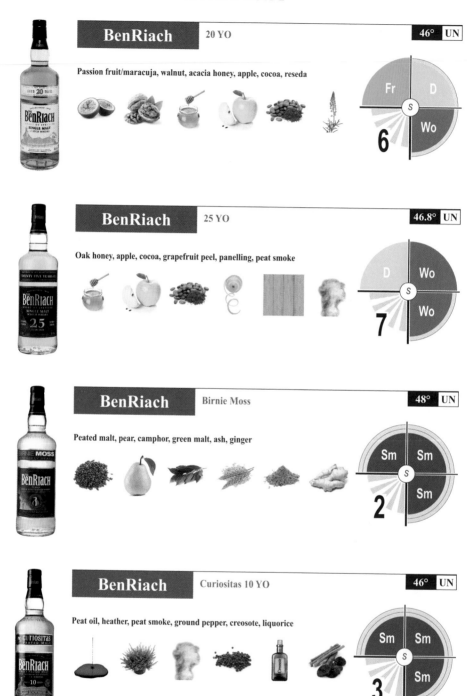

BenRiach 20 YO   46° UN

Passion fruit/maracuja, walnut, acacia honey, apple, cocoa, reseda

Fr | D
S
Wo

6

BenRiach 25 YO   46.8° UN

Oak honey, apple, cocoa, grapefruit peel, panelling, peat smoke

D | Wo
S
Wo

7

BenRiach Birnie Moss   48° UN

Peated malt, pear, camphor, green malt, ash, ginger

Sm | Sm
S
Sm

2

BenRiach Curiositas 10 YO   46° UN

Peat oil, heather, peat smoke, ground pepper, creosote, liquorice

Sm | Sm
S
Sm

3

Benromach
Distillery

Founded in 1898.
Closed from 1931 to 1937 and again from 1983 to 1998.
Bought by whisky merchant Gordon & MacPhail in 1993.
Sold in bulk as Glen Mosset.

2 Stills: 1 wash, 1 spirit – 0.5 million LPA

Invernes Road, Forres, Morayshire IV36 3EB
+44 (0) 1309 675 968
www.benromach.com
Owner: Gordon & MacPhail

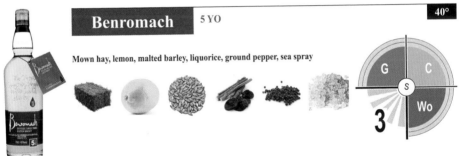

Benromach 5 YO

40°

Mown hay, lemon, malted barley, liquorice, ground pepper, sea spray

Benromach 10 YO
Finished in Oloroso Sherry Casks

43°

Oloroso, peated malt, kiwi, liquorice, arnica, cardamom

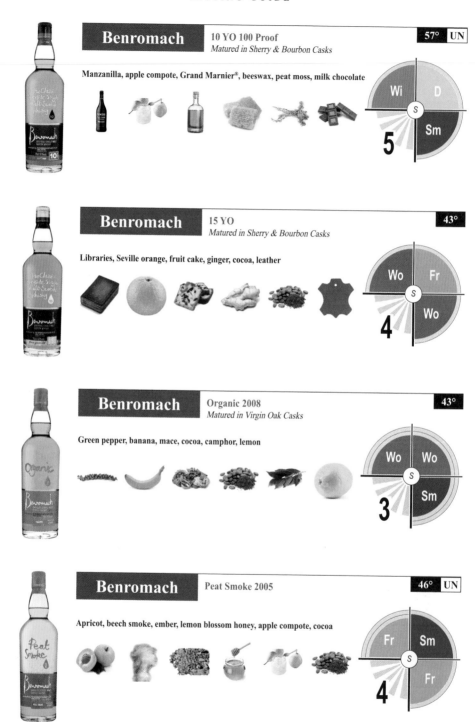

Benromach — 10 YO 100 Proof
Matured in Sherry & Bourbon Casks

57° UN

Manzanilla, apple compote, Grand Marnier®, beeswax, peat moss, milk chocolate

Wi · D · Sm · S

5

Benromach — 15 YO
Matured in Sherry & Bourbon Casks

43°

Libraries, Seville orange, fruit cake, ginger, cocoa, leather

Wo · Fr · Wo · S

4

Benromach — Organic 2008
Matured in Virgin Oak Casks

43°

Green pepper, banana, mace, cocoa, camphor, lemon

Wo · Wo · Sm · S

3

Benromach — Peat Smoke 2005

46° UN

Apricot, beech smoke, ember, lemon blossom honey, apple compote, cocoa

Fr · Sm · Fr · S

4

Cardhu
Distillery

Founded in 1824 by John Cumming.
Rebuilt in 1884 and again in 1960 to 1961.
Bought by John Deware & Sons in 1893.

6 Stills: 3 wash, 3 spirit – 3.4 million LPA

Knockando, Aberlour, Moray AB38 7RY
+44 (0) 1479 874 635
www.malts.com
Owner: Diageo

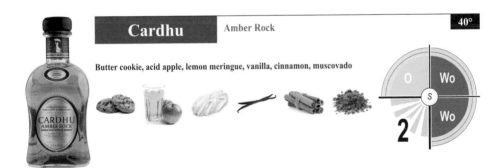

Cardhu Amber Rock 40°

Butter cookie, acid apple, lemon meringue, vanilla, cinnamon, muscovado

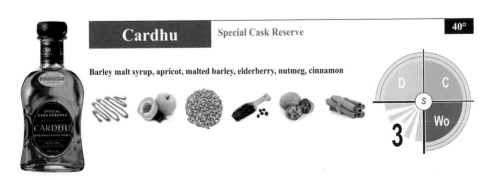

Cardhu Special Cask Reserve 40°

Barley malt syrup, apricot, malted barley, elderberry, nutmeg, cinnamon

Cardhu — Gold Reserve — 40°

Apple compote, toffee, malted barley, orange peel, black pepper, cocoa

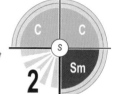

2

Cardhu — 12 YO — 40°

Bread, heather honey, panettone, apple compote, peated malt, milk chocolate

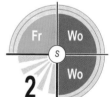

2

Cardhu — 15 YO — 40°

Fruit cake, almond, crème brûlée, apple compote, dark chocolate, oak

2

Cardhu — 18 YO — 40°

Greengage, leather, orange blossom honey, cocoa, hazelnut, pepper

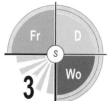

3

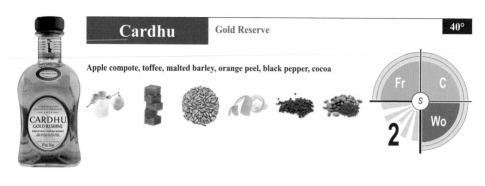

Cragganmore
Distillery

Founded in 1869 by John Smith.
Modernized in 1901 by the architect Charles Doig.
Closed from 1917 to 1918.

4 Stills: 2 wash, 2 spirit – 2.2 million LPA

Ballindalloch, Moray AB37 9AB
+44 (0) 1479 874 700
www.malts.com
Owner: Diageo

Cragganmore 12 YO   40°

Broom, grapefruit peel, mown lawn, sandalwood, malted barley, oak honey

Cragganmore Distiller's Edition 2001
Finished in Port Casks   40°

Fruit cake, oak smoke, orange blossom honey, chocolate malt, port wine, banana

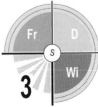

Craigellachie
Distillery

Founded in 1891 by Alexander Edward and Peter Mackie.
Production did not commence until 1898 and was taken over by John Dewar & Sons in 1923.
Modernized in 1964.

---

4 Stills: 2 wash, 2 spirit – 4 million LPA

Aberlour, Banffshire AB38 9ST
+44 (0) 1340 872 971
www.craigellachie.com
Owner: John Dewar & Sons (Bacardi Martini)

Craigellachie 13 YO   46° UN

Melon, cinnamon, lime tree honey, barley sugar, nutmeg, fresh tobacco

3

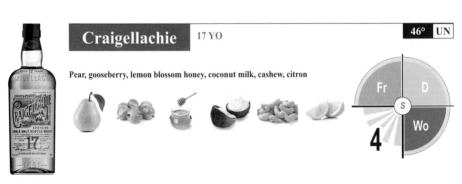

Craigellachie 17 YO   46° UN

Pear, gooseberry, lemon blossom honey, coconut milk, cashew, citron

4

Dufftown
Distillery

Founded in 1896 by Peter Mackenzie, Richard Stackpole, John Symon and Charles MacPherson.
Bought in 1933 by Arthur Bell & Sons.
Marketed since 2006 as a single malt under the name of Singleton.

6 Stills: 3 wash, 3 spirit – 6 million LPA

Dufftown, Keith, Banffshire AB55 4BR
+44 (0) 1340 822 100
www.malts.com
Owner: Diageo

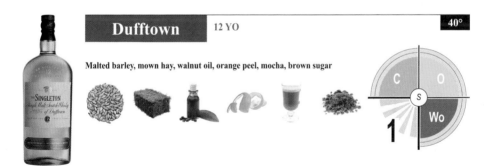

Dufftown 12 YO 40°

Malted barley, mown hay, walnut oil, orange peel, mocha, brown sugar

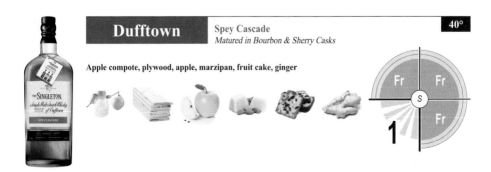

Dufftown Spey Cascade 40°
Matured in Bourbon & Sherry Casks

Apple compote, plywood, apple, marzipan, fruit cake, ginger

Glendullan
Distillery

Founded in 1897 by William Williams & Sons.
A second distillery was built next door in 1972.
The two distilleries produced together until 1985.

6 Stills: 3 wash, 3 spirit – 5 million LPA

Dufftown, Keith, Banffshire AB55 4BR
+44 (0) 1340 822 100
www.malts.com
Owner: Diageo

| Glendullan | 12 YO | | 40° |

Honey malt, fruit cake, leather, roasted almond, dark chocolate, pepper

      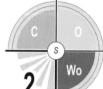

| Glendullan | Trinity | | 40° |

Honey malt, apricot, oak, peat smoke, allspice, liquorice

Glen Elgin
Distillery

Founded in 1898 by William Simpson and James Carle.
Closed from 1900 to 1906 and from 1992 to 1995.

---

6 Stills: 3 wash, 3 spirit – 2.7 million LPA

Longmorn Morayshire IV30 3SL
+44 (0) 1343 862 100
www.malts.com
Owner: Diageo

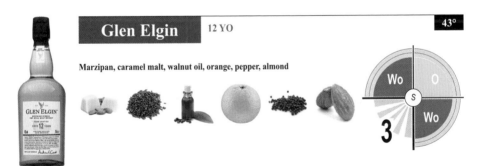

Glen Elgin — 12 YO — 43°

Marzipan, caramel malt, walnut oil, orange, pepper, almond

Wo | O | S | Wo — 3

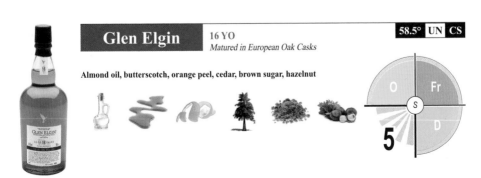

Glen Elgin — 16 YO — 58.5° UN CS
Matured in European Oak Casks

Almond oil, butterscotch, orange peel, cedar, brown sugar, hazelnut

O | Fr | S | D — 5

Glenfarclas
Distillery

Founded in 1836 par Robert Hay.
Bought by J. & G. Grant in 1870.
Direct-fired copper pot stills.

6 Stills: 3 wash, 3 spirit – 3.4 million LPA

Ballindalloch, Banffshire AB37 9BD
+44 (0) 1807 500 257
www.glenfarclas.co.uk
Owner: J. & G. Grant

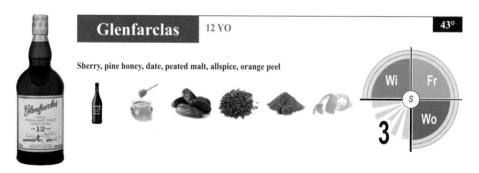

Glenfarclas 12 YO   43°

Sherry, pine honey, date, peated malt, allspice, orange peel

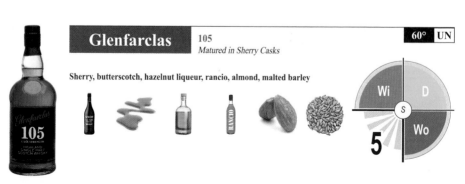

Glenfarclas 105   60° UN
Matured in Sherry Casks

Sherry, butterscotch, hazelnut liqueur, rancio, almond, malted barley

Glenfarclas 15 YO

46° UN

Cream sherry, peated malt, raisin, toffee, walnut, coffee

Wi | Fr
S
Wo

5

Glenfarclas 17 YO

43°

Butterscotch, bergamot, oak, nutmeg, chocolate, peated malt

D | Wo
S
Wo

4

Glenfarclas 21 YO

43°

Mango, roasted almond, brioche, liquorice cream, milk chocolate, malted barley

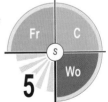

Fr | C
S
Wo

5

Glenfarclas 25 YO

43°

Oloroso, walnut honey, orange, fresh walnut, oak, chocolate

Wi | Fr
S
Wo

5

Glenfiddich
Distillery

Founded in 1886 by William Grant.
Marketed since 1957 as a single malt in a triangular-shaped bottle.

28 Stills: 10 wash, 18 spirit – 14 million LPA

Dufftown, Banffshire AB55 4DH
+44 (0) 1340 820 373
www.glenfiddich.com
Owner: William Grant & Sons

| Glenfiddich | 12 YO
Matured in Bourbon & Sherry Casks | 40° |

Honeysuckle, pear, lemon blossom honey, oak, apple, bison grass

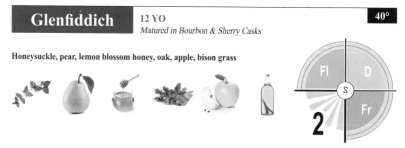

| Glenfiddich | Vintage Cask | 40° |

Tonka bean, bonfires, peated malt, crème brûlée, oak smoke, vanilla

Glenfiddich

Rich Oak
Finished in Virgin Spanish & American Casks

40°

Oak, almond, vanilla, apple, hazelnut, oak smoke

Wo | Wo
S
Wo

4

Glenfiddich

Malt Master's Edition
Finished in Sherry Casks

43°

Roasted almond, chocolate malt, plum, orange peel, walnut, malted barley

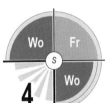

Wo | Fr
S
Wo

4

Glenfiddich

15 YO Solera
Matured in European & New American Oak Casks

40°

Orange blossom honey, raisin, sherry, marzipan, cinnamon, vanilla

D | Wi
S
Wo

4

Glenfiddich

15 YO Distillery Edition
Matured in Bourbon & Sherry Casks

51° UN

Floral cream, oak, pear, allspice, malted barley, liquorice

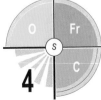

O | Fr
S
C

4

Glenfiddich — 18 YO
Matured in Bourbon & Sherry Casks

40°

Apple, oak honey, almond, orange peel, cinnamon, liquorice

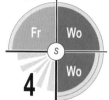

4

Glenfiddich — 21 YO Gran Reserva
Finished in Caribbean Rum Casks

40°

Muscovado, leather, allspice, lemon peel, coffee, orange marmelade

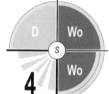

4

Glenfiddich — 30 YO
Matured in Bourbon & Sherry Casks

43°

Cocoa, oak, oloroso, vanilla, orange blossom honey, walnut

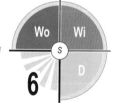

6

Glenfiddich — 40 YO

44.5° **UN**

Mahogany, leather, fruit cake, chocolate, mango, mace

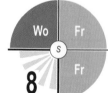

8

Glen Grant
Distillery

Founded in 1840 by brothers John and James Chivas.
The famous Major Grant managed the distillery from 1872 until 1931.

8 Stills: 4 wash, 4 spirit − 6.2 million LPA

Elgin Road, Rothes, Banffshire AB38 7BS
+44 (0) 1340 820 373
www.glengrant.com
Owner: Campari Group

Glen Grant	The Major's Reserve	40°

Malted barley, apple, new wood, lemon, hazelnut, caramel

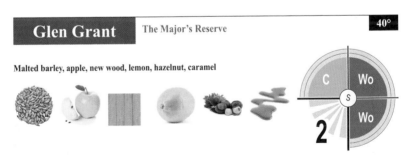

Glen Grant	10 YO	40°

Honeysuckle, toffee, pear, malted barley, walnut, orange

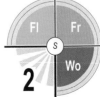

Glen Grant 16 YO   43°

Apple, coumarin, pear, vanilla cream, hazelnut, coffee

3

Glen Grant 1992 Cellar Reserve   46° UN

Pear, grape, pear compote, lime tree honey, pear, liquorice

4

Glen Grant Five Decades   46° UN

Almond honey, peach, apple, orange blossom honey, acid apple, crème anglaise

4

Glen Grant 25 YO
Matured in Sherry Casks   43°

Oloroso, eucalyptus honey, raisin, apple compote, liquorice, coffee

5

Glenlivet
Distillery

Founded in 1824 by George Smith.
His father had already owned a farm and distillery on the site since 1774.

14 Stills: 7 wash, 7 spirit – 10.5 million LPA

Ballindalloch, Banffshire AB37 9DB
+44 (0) 1340 821 720
www.theglenlivet.com
Owner: Chivas Brothers Ltd (Pernod Ricard)

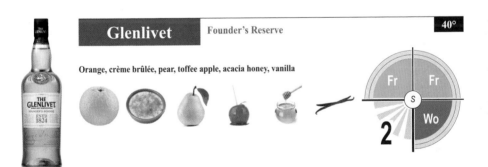

Glenlivet — Founder's Reserve — 40°

Orange, crème brûlée, pear, toffee apple, acacia honey, vanilla

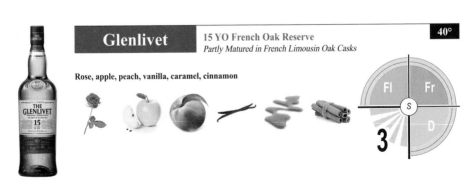

Glenlivet — 15 YO French Oak Reserve
Partly Matured in French Limousin Oak Casks — 40°

Rose, apple, peach, vanilla, caramel, cinnamon

Glenlivet — 18 YO — 43°
Matured in Bourbon & Sherry Casks

Almond honey, apple, orange peel, maple syrup, liquorice, raisin

D / Fr / S / Wo — 4

Glenlivet — 21 YO Archive — 43°
Matured in Bourbon & Sherry Casks

Sandalwood, pine honey, walnut oil, fruit cake, hazelnut, ginger

Wo / O / S / Wo — 5

Glenlivet — XXV 25 YO — 43°
Matured in Sherry Casks

Oloroso, raisin, cinnamon, chocolate, walnut, orange peel

Wi / Wo / S / Wo — 5

Glenlivet — Nàdurra Oloroso — 48° UN
Matured in First Fill Oloroso Casks

Walnut, apricot, orange marmalade, liquorice, raisin, ginger

Wo / Fr / S / Fr — 4

Glen Moray
Distillery

Founded in 1897.
Closed from 1910 to 1923.
Bought by Macdonald & Muir (now Glenmorangie Plc) in 1920.
Then sold to LVMH in 2004 and again to La Martiniquaise in 2008.

6 Stills: 3 wash, 3 spirit – 3.3 million LPA

Bruceland Road, Elgin, Morayshire IV30 1YE
+44 (0) 1343 542 577
www.glenmoray.com
Owner: La Martiniquaise

Glen Moray — Classic — 40°

Malted barley, mown hay, barley malt syrup, lemongrass, cereal bar, ginger

1

Glen Moray — Classic Port Cask
Finished in Port Casks — 40°

Vanilla cream, chocolate, caramel, port wine, cinnamon, acacia honey

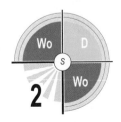

2

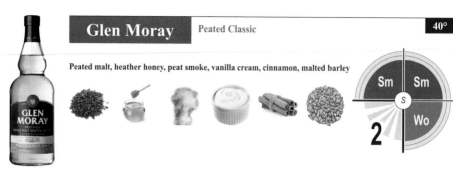

Glen Moray   Peated Classic   40°

Peated malt, heather honey, peat smoke, vanilla cream, cinnamon, malted barley

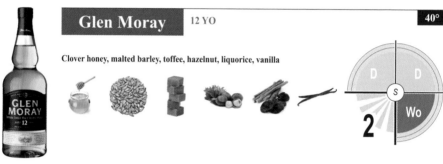

Glen Moray   12 YO   40°

Clover honey, malted barley, toffee, hazelnut, liquorice, vanilla

Glen Moray   16 YO   40°

Fig, vanilla cream, apple compote, chocolate, barley sugar, hazelnut

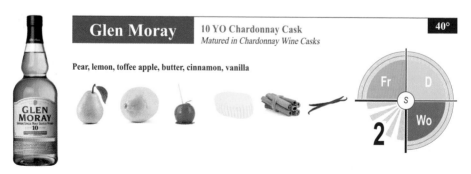

Glen Moray   10 YO Chardonnay Cask
Matured in Chardonnay Wine Casks   40°

Pear, lemon, toffee apple, butter, cinnamon, vanilla

Glenrothes
Distillery

Founded in 1878 by James Stuart & Co.
Previously known by the name of Glenrothes-Glenlivet.
Bought by Edrington in 1999.

---

10 Stills: 5 wash, 5 spirit – 5.6 million LPA

Rothes, Morayshire AB38 7AA
+44 (0) 1340 872 300
www.theglenrothes.com
Owners: Edrington Group, the distillery;
Berry Bros & Rudd, the brand

Glenrothes — Select Reserve — 43°

Malted barley, crème brûlée, pear, acacia honey, mocha, lemon

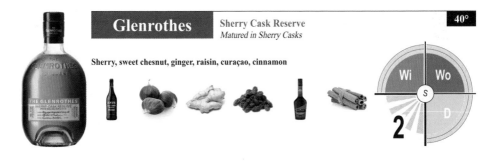

Glenrothes — Sherry Cask Reserve — 40°
Matured in Sherry Casks

Sherry, sweet chesnut, ginger, raisin, curaçao, cinnamon

Glenrothes 2001

43°

Barley malt syrup, pastry cream, orange blossom honey, toffee apple, cinnamon, orange peel

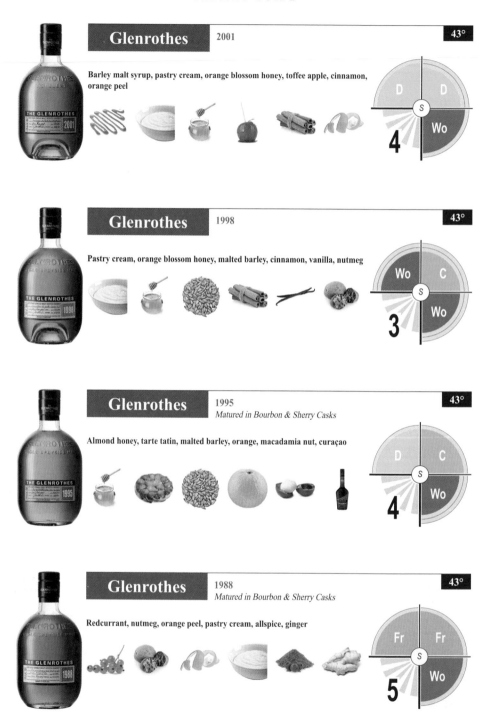

Glenrothes 1998

43°

Pastry cream, orange blossom honey, malted barley, cinnamon, vanilla, nutmeg

Glenrothes 1995
Matured in Bourbon & Sherry Casks

43°

Almond honey, tarte tatin, malted barley, orange, macadamia nut, curaçao

Glenrothes 1988
Matured in Bourbon & Sherry Casks

43°

Redcurrant, nutmeg, orange peel, pastry cream, allspice, ginger

Knockando
Distillery

Founded in 1898 by John Thompson, designed by the architect Charles Doig.
Closed from 1900 to 1903.
Emblem of the J&B blend and its Ultima Vault warehouse, which assembles
all Scotch malts and grain whiskies.

---

4 Stills: 2 wash, 2 spirit – 1.4 million LPA

Knockando, Morayshire AB38 7RT
+44 (0) 1340 882 000
www.malts.com
Owner: Diageo

Knockando   12 YO Season   43°

Barley malt syrup, almond, hazelnut oil, lemon, malted barley, chocolate

D | O
S
C

2

Knockando   15 YO Richly Matured
Matured in Bourbon & Sherry Casks   43°

Brioche, dark chocolate, mochaccino, cinnamon, acacia honey, malted barley

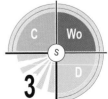

C | Wo
S
D

3

Knockando

18 YO Slow Matured
Matured in Sherry Casks

43°

Mangosteen, crème brûlée, sherry, malted barley, oak, cherry

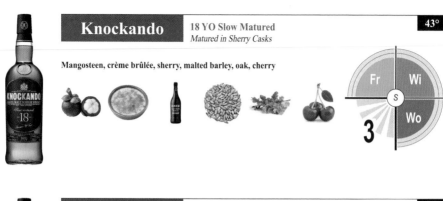

3

Knockando

21 YO Master Reserve
Matured in Bourbon & Sherry Casks

43°

Oak, praline, plum, almond, walnut, liquorice

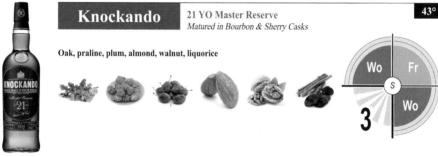

3

Knockando

25 YO
Matured in Sherry Casks

43°

Oloroso, oak smoke, strawberry, orange, cedar, cardamom

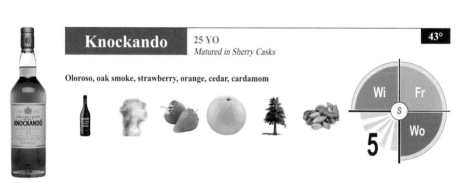

5

Longmorn
Distillery

Founded in 1894 by John Duff & Co.
The neighbouring and related Benriach Distillery was for a long time known as Longmorn 2.
At the heart of the Chivas Regal 18 Year Old blend.

---

8 Stills: 4 wash, 4 spirit – 4.5 million LPA

Longmorn Morayshire IV30 8SJ
+44 (0) 1343 554 139
www.maltwhiskydistilleries.com
Owner: Chivas Brothers Ltd (Pernod Ricard)

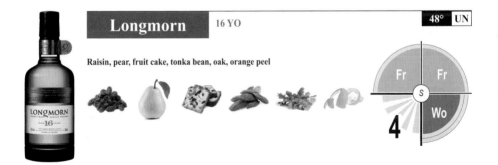

Longmorn 16 YO 48° UN

Raisin, pear, fruit cake, tonka bean, oak, orange peel

Fr Fr
S
4 Wo

Macallan
Distillery

Founded in 1824 by Alexander Reid under the name of Elchies.
Renamed Macallan-Glenlivet in 1892.

---

21 Stills: 7 wash, 14 spirit – 9.8 million LPA

Easter Elchies, Craigellachie, Morayshire AB38 9RX
+44 (0) 1340 812 471
www.themacallan.com
Owner: Edrington Group

Macallan — Gold
Matured in Sherry Casks   40°

Lemon peel, chocolate, orange, toffee apple, barley malt syrup, ginger

Macallan — Amber
Matured in Sherry Casks   40°

Raisin, praline, lemon, vanilla, cinnamon, orange blossom honey

Macallan — Sienna
Matured in Sherry Casks

43°

Fruit cake, chocolate, date, sandalwood, allspice, orange blossom honey

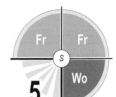

5

Macallan — Ruby
Matured in Sherry Casks

43°

Pedro ximénez, oak, raisin, Seville orange, nutmeg, clove

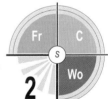

4

Macallan — 12 YO Fine Oak
Matured in Bourbon & Sherry Casks

40°

Peach, porridge (oatmeal), malted barley, orange peel, roasted almond, raisin

2

Macallan — 15 YO Fine Oak
Matured in Bourbon & Sherry Casks

43°

Acid apple, mace, milk chocolate, soursop, oak, orange peel

5

Macallan — 18 YO Fine Oak
Matured in Bourbon & Sherry Casks

43°

Cocoa, jasmine, orange, oak smoke, cinnamon, raisin

Macallan — 12 YO Sherry Oak
Matured in Sherry Casks

43°

Date, vanilla, oloroso, cinnamon, butterscotch, oak smoke

Macallan — 18 YO Sherry Oak 1995
Matured in Sherry Casks

43°

Fruit cake, leatherwood honey, raisin, mocha, dark chocolate, ginger

Mortlach
Distillery

Founded in 1823 by James Findlater.
Triple and even quadruple partial distillations (distilled 2.81 times).

6 Stills: 3 wash, 3 spirit – 3.8 million LPA

Dufftown, Keith, Banffshire AB55 4AQ
+44 (0) 1340 822 100
www.malts.com
Owner: Diageo

Mortlach Rare Old 43.4°

Malted barley, loam, chocolate, fruit cake, cherry blossom honey, cinnamon

Mortlach 18 YO 43.4°

Loam, lemon peel, gamey, prune, mocha, fresh tobacco

Speyburn
Distillery

Founded in 1897 by John Hopkin Co.
Closed from 1930 to 1934.
Bought by Inver House Distilleries in 1991.

---

3 Stills: 1 wash, 2 spirit – 4.2 million LPA

Rothes, Morayshire AB38 7AG
+44 (0) 1479 872 569
www.speyburn.com
Owner: Inver House Distillers (Thai Beverage)

Speyburn	Bradan Orach	40°

Crepe batter, pineapple, pear, barley, oak, ginger

Speyburn	10 YO	40°

Orange, almond, barley malt syrup, wintergreen, liquorice, malted barley

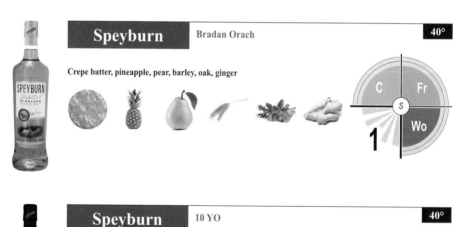

Strathisla
Distillery

Founded in 1786 by Alexander Milne and George Taylor under the name Milltown then Milton.
Bought by the Chivas Brothers in 1950.
At the heart of the Chivas Regal 12 Year Old blend.

---

4 Stills: 2 wash, 2 spirit – 2.5 million LPA

Seafield Avenue, Keith, Banffshire, AB55 5BS
+44 (0) 1542 783 044
www.maltwhiskydistilleries.com
Owner: Chivas Brothers Ltd (Pernod Ricard)

Strathisla 12 YO 40°

Freesia, pear, panetone, coffee, apricot, butter cookie

Fl C
S
Fr
2

Tamdhu
Distillery

Founded in 1896 by a consortium led by William Grant.
Designed by the architect Charles Doig.
Closed from 1911 to 1913 then from 1928 to 1948.
Bought by the Chivas Brothers in 1950.

6 Stills: 3 wash, 3 spirit – 4 million LPA

Knockando, Aberlour, Moray AB38 7RP
+44 (0) 1340 872 200
www.tamdhu.com
Owner: Ian Macleod Distillers

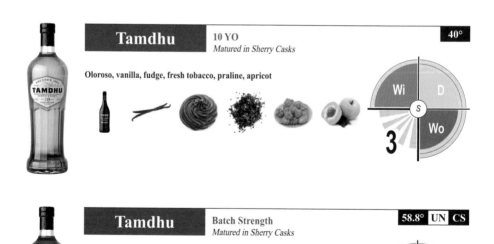

Tamdhu — 10 YO — 40°
Matured in Sherry Casks

Oloroso, vanilla, fudge, fresh tobacco, praline, apricot

Wi | D
S
Wo
3

Tamdhu — Batch Strength — 58.8° UN CS
Matured in Sherry Casks

Oloroso, dark chocolate, cherry, allspice, oak, orange marmalade

Wi | Fr
S
Wo
5

Tomintoul
Distillery

Founded in 1964.
Bought in 2000 by Angus Dundee at Whyte & Mackay.

4 Stills: 2 wash, 2 spirit – 3.3 million LPA

Ballindalloch, Banffshire AB37 9AQ
+44 (0) 1807 590 274
www.tomintouldistillery.co.uk
Owner: Angus Dundee Distillers

Tomintoul 10 YO 40°

Caramel, lemon, roasted barley, acacia honey, green malt, liquorice

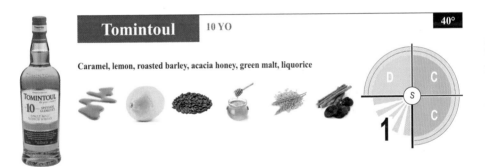

1

Tomintoul 12 YO Oloroso Cask Finish 40°
Finish in Oloroso Sherry Casks

Malted barley, oloroso, praline, mulberry, walnut, pepper

     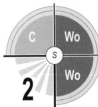

2

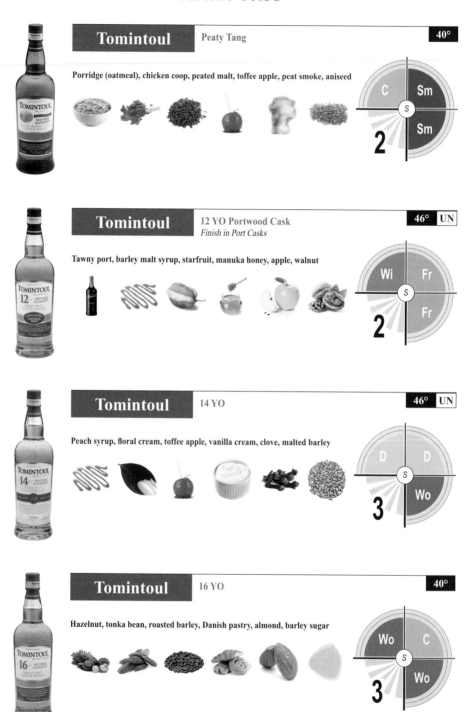

Tomintoul — Peaty Tang
40°

Porridge (oatmeal), chicken coop, peated malt, toffee apple, peat smoke, aniseed

Tomintoul — 12 YO Portwood Cask
Finish in Port Casks
46° UN

Tawny port, barley malt syrup, starfruit, manuka honey, apple, walnut

Tomintoul — 14 YO
46° UN

Peach syrup, floral cream, toffee apple, vanilla cream, clove, malted barley

Tomintoul — 16 YO
40°

Hazelnut, tonka bean, roasted barley, Danish pastry, almond, barley sugar

Tormore
Distillery

Founded in 1958 by Schenley International, owner of the Long John brand. Bought by Allied Lyons, now Allied Domecq, in 1989 then by the Chivas Brothers in 2005.

8 Stills: 4 wash, 4 spirit – 4.4 million LPA

Tormore, Advie, Grantown-on-Spey, Morayshire PH26 3LR
+44 (0) 1807 510 244
www.tormoredistillery.com
Owner: Chivas Brothers Ltd (Pernod Ricard)

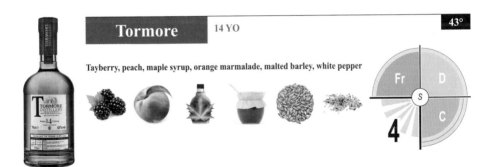

Tormore 14 YO — 43°

Tayberry, peach, maple syrup, orange marmalade, malted barley, white pepper

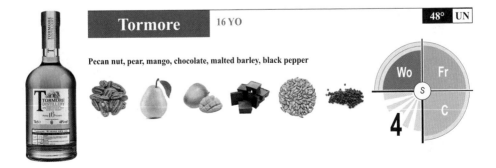

Tormore 16 YO — 48° UN

Pecan nut, pear, mango, chocolate, malted barley, black pepper

Ardbeg
Distillery

Founded in 1815 by John MacDougall
Closed from 1981 to 1989, operational since.

Great vintages: 1967, 1972, 1974–1976
2 Stills: 2 wash, 2 spirit – 1.3 million LPA

Port Ellen, Isle of Islay, PA42 7EA
Islay South Shore
+44 (0) 1496 302 244
www.ardbeg.com
Owner: Glenmorangie Plc since 1997 (LVMH Group)

Ardbeg	Ten	46° UN
	10 YO	

Tar, cocoa, smoked herring, pineapple, molasses/treacle, salty liquorice

5

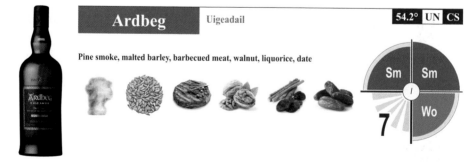

Ardbeg	Uigeadail	54.2° UN CS

Pine smoke, malted barley, barbecued meat, walnut, liquorice, date

7

Ardbeg — Corryvreckan

57.1° UN CS

Tar, cedar, pine smoke, pepper steak, coffee, camphor

Sm	Sm
7	Wo

Ardbeg — Blasda

40°

Milk jam, clove, pine, muscovado, Parma violet, vanilla

O	Wo
2	Wo

Ardbeg — Kildalton
Bourbon & Refill Sherry

46° UN

Lichen, peat moss, charcoal, panna cotta, coal, Angostura

G	Sm
4	Sm

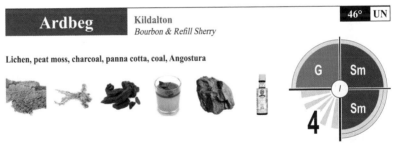

Ardbeg — Supernova SN2014
Bourbon & Sherry Casks Ardbeg Committee Exclusive

55° UN CS

Smoky mezcal, pine resin, peat smoke, lemon liqueur, molasses/treacle, barbecued meat

Sm	Sm
7	Wo

Bowmore
Distillery

Founded in 1779 by David Simpson.
The main warehouse (No. 1 Vaults) is situated below sea level.

Great vintages: 1955, 1961, 1964–1969
4 Stills: 2 wash, 2 spirit – 2 million LPA

School Street, Isle of Islay PA43 7GS
Islay Loch Indaal
+44 (0) 1496 810 441
www.bowmore.com
Owner: Morrison Bowmore Distillers Ltd (Beam Suntory Inc.)

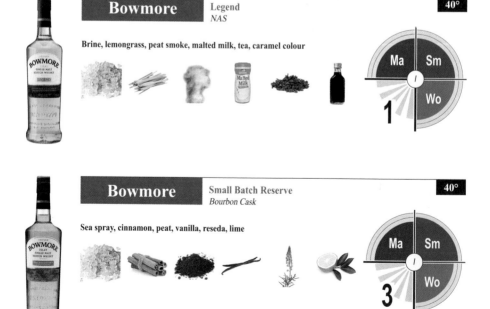

Bowmore	Legend	40°
	NAS	

Brine, lemongrass, peat smoke, malted milk, tea, caramel colour

Ma | Sm | Wo
1

Bowmore	Small Batch Reserve	40°
	Bourbon Cask	

Sea spray, cinnamon, peat, vanilla, reseda, lime

Ma | Sm | Wo
3

Bowmore — Black Rock
Predominately Spanish Sherry

40° TRE

Peat smoke, Seville orange, charcoal, blackcurrant wine, molasses/treacle, salt marsh

Sm | Sm

D

2

Bowmore — Gold Reef
2014 Bourbon & Sherry Casks

43° TRE

Kelp, lemon, peat smoke, kaffir lime, pencil-lead, cinnamon

Ma | Sm

Sm

3

Bowmore — 10 YO Tempest
2014 1st Fill Bourbon Barrel

55.9° UN CS SB Release 5

Peat oil, pineapple, sea spray, green tea, ginger, liquorice cream

Sm | Ma

Wo

4

Bowmore — 10 YO Devil's Casks II
2014 1st Fill Sherry Cask

56.3° UN CS SB

Peat oil, blackcurrant liqueur, maple tree smoke, pineapple, tar, liquorice cream

Sm | Sm

Sm

6

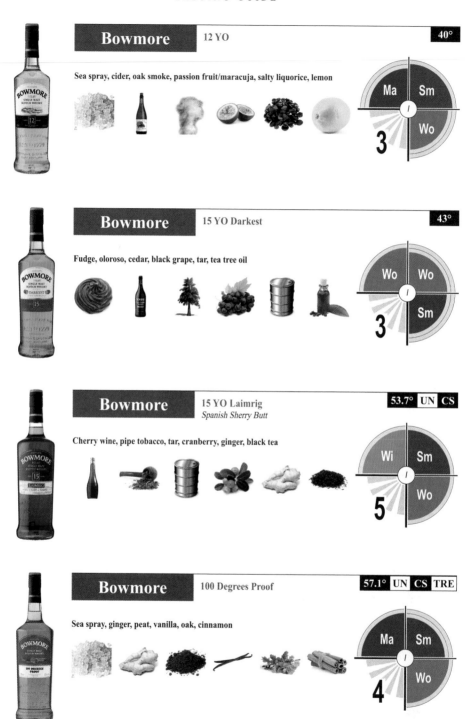

Bowmore — 12 YO — 40°

Sea spray, cider, oak smoke, passion fruit/maracuja, salty liquorice, lemon

Ma | Sm
Wo

3

Bowmore — 15 YO Darkest — 43°

Fudge, oloroso, cedar, black grape, tar, tea tree oil

Wo | Wo
Sm

3

Bowmore — 15 YO Laimrig — 53.7° UN CS
Spanish Sherry Butt

Cherry wine, pipe tobacco, tar, cranberry, ginger, black tea

Wi | Sm
Wo

5

Bowmore — 100 Degrees Proof — 57.1° UN CS TRE

Sea spray, ginger, peat, vanilla, oak, cinnamon

Ma | Sm
Wo

4

Bruichladdich
Distillery

Founded in 1881 by the Harvey brothers.
Closed from 1995 to 2001.
The original Octomore Distillery was closed in 1852.

Great vintages: 1964, 1970, 1986
4 Stills: 2 wash, 2 spirit – 1.5 million LPA

Bruichladdich, Isle of Islay, PA49 7UN
Islay Loch Indaal
+44 (0) 1496 850 221
www.bruichladdich.com
Owner: Bruichladdich Distillery Co. (Rémy Cointreau)

Bruichladdich Islay Barley 07-14
2007/2014 Rockside Farm Bourbon Cask

50° UN

Honey malt, lime tree, barley malt syrup, green apple, honeysuckle, malted milk

Bruichladdich Scottish Barley
2013 The Classic Laddie

50° UN

Barley sugar, vetiver, oak honey, greengage, honey malt, myrtle

Bruichladdich
Organic Scottish Barley
2013

50° | UN | TRE

Weetabix, guava, barley sugar, acid pear, calamus, manzana verde

C | C
I |
| G

3

Port Charlotte
PC Islay Barley HP
2008/2014 6 YO

50° | UN

Peated malt, black bread, tar rope, farmyard, graphite, salt marsh

Sm | Sm
I |
| Mi

5

Port Charlotte
PC Scottish Barley HP

50° | UN

Peat smoke, barley, peat oil, lemon, graphite, sea spray

     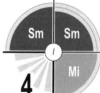

Sm | Sm
I |
| Mi

4

Octomore
10 YO
2012 1st Limited Release

50° | UN | CS

Incense, lemon thyme, lapsang souchong, sugar apple, Havana tobacco ash, juniper berry

Sm | Sm
I |
| Sm

6

Bunnahabhain
Distillery

Founded in 1881 by William Robertson and the brothers William and James Greenless. Used in the Black Bottle and Famous Grouse blends.

Great vintages: 1960, 1968, 1976, 1979
4 Stills: 2 wash, 2 spirit – 2.7 million LPA

Port Askaig, Isle of Islay, PA46 7RP
Islay East Shore
+44 (0) 1496 840 646
www.bunnahabhain.com
Owner: Burn Stewart Distillers Ltd (Distell Group Ltd)

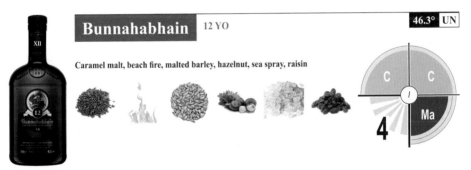

Bunnahabhain 12 YO   46.3° UN

Caramel malt, beach fire, malted barley, hazelnut, sea spray, raisin

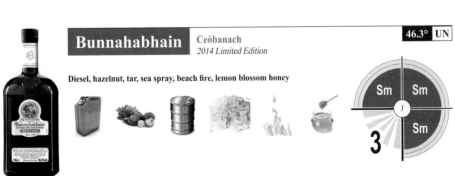

Bunnahabhain Ceòbanach
                  2014 Limited Edition   46.3° UN

Diesel, hazelnut, tar, sea spray, beach fire, lemon blossom honey

Bunnahabhain Toiteach 46° UN

Liquid smoke, dry hay, mulch, pear compote, creosote, red peppercorn

Sm | G
Sm
2

Bunnahabhain Darach Ùr
2013 Fresh American Oak 46.3° UN TRE

Cress, dog-rose, ginger, walnut, oak, white pepper

G | Wo
Wo
4

Bunnahabhain 18 YO 46.3° UN

Dark malt, chestnut honey, leather upholstery, morello cherry in syrup, panelling, white pepper

C | O
Wo
4

Bunnahabhain 25 YO 46.3° UN

Brown sherry, caramel, leather upholstery, roasted barley, panelling, fig

Wi | O
Wo
6

Caol Ila
Distillery

**Founded in 1846 by Hector Henderson.
Part of its production is used in Johnnie Walker blends.**

Great vintages: 1966–1969, 1974–1976, 1979, 1984
6 Stills: 3 wash, 3 spirit − 3 warehouses − 6.5 millions LPA

Port Askaig, Isle of Islay, PA46 7RL
Islay East Shore
+44 (0) 1496 302 760
www.malts.com
Owner: Diageo Plc

Caol Ila	12 YO	43°

Peat oil, salty liquorice, coal smoke, apple, dry seaweed, lemon

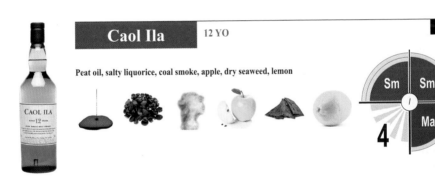

Caol Ila	Moch	43°

Sea spray, oilskin, burning pine needles, preserved lemon, coal smoke, gentian

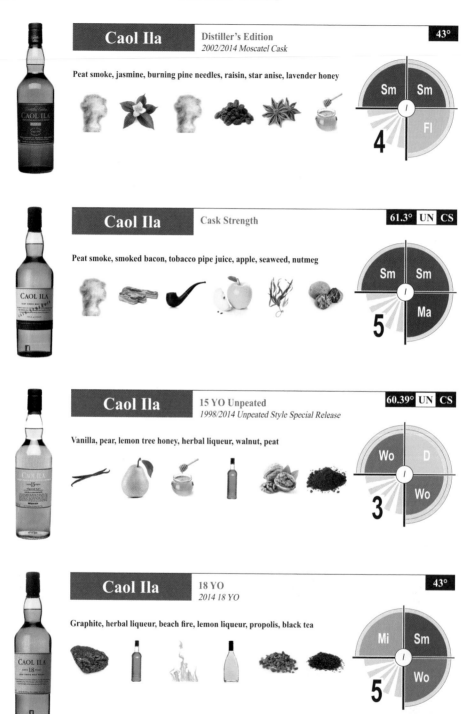

Caol Ila — Distiller's Edition
2002/2014 Moscatel Cask
43°

Peat smoke, jasmine, burning pine needles, raisin, star anise, lavender honey

Sm | Sm
Fl
4

Caol Ila — Cask Strength
61.3° UN CS

Peat smoke, smoked bacon, tobacco pipe juice, apple, seaweed, nutmeg

Sm | Sm
Ma
5

Caol Ila — 15 YO Unpeated
1998/2014 Unpeated Style Special Release
60.39° UN CS

Vanilla, pear, lemon tree honey, herbal liqueur, walnut, peat

Wo | D
Wo
3

Caol Ila — 18 YO
2014 18 YO
43°

Graphite, herbal liqueur, beach fire, lemon liqueur, propolis, black tea

Mi | Sm
Wo
5

Kilchoman
Distillery

Founded in 2005 by Anthony Wills, the first distillery created on Islay for more than a century. All stages of production are carried out on site.

---

2 Stills: 1 wash, 1 spirit − 3 warehouses − 0.15 million LPA

Rockside Farm, Bruichladdich, Isle of Islay, PA49 7UT
Islay Loch Indaal
+44 (0) 1496 850 011
www.kilchomandistillery.com
Owner: Kilchoman Distillery Co. Ltd

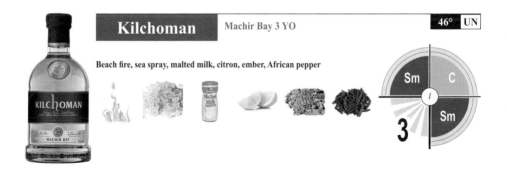

Kilchoman — Machir Bay 3 YO — 46° UN

Beach fire, sea spray, malted milk, citron, ember, African pepper

Sm / C / Sm — 3

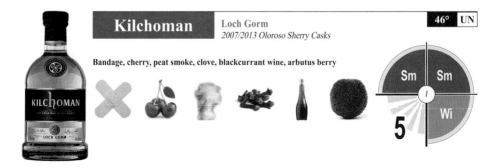

Kilchoman — Loch Gorm
2007/2013 Oloroso Sherry Casks — 46° UN

Bandage, cherry, peat smoke, clove, blackcurrant wine, arbutus berry

Sm / Sm / Wi — 5

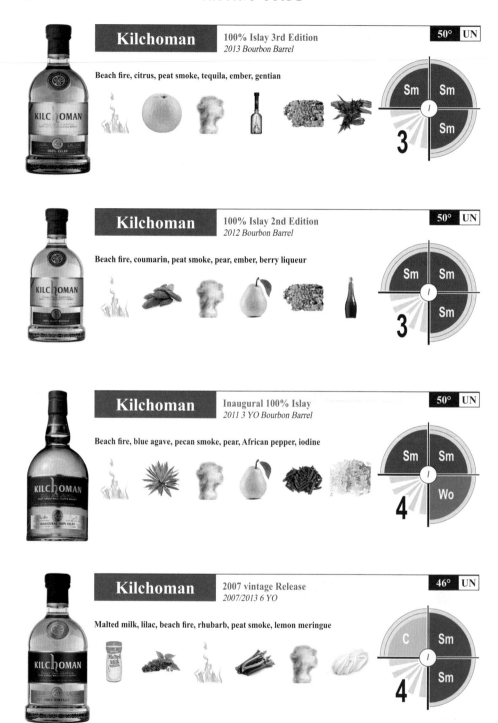

Kilchoman 100% Islay 3rd Edition
2013 Bourbon Barrel
50° UN

Beach fire, citrus, peat smoke, tequila, ember, gentian

Sm | Sm
Sm
3

Kilchoman 100% Islay 2nd Edition
2012 Bourbon Barrel
50° UN

Beach fire, coumarin, peat smoke, pear, ember, berry liqueur

Sm | Sm
Sm
3

Kilchoman Inaugural 100% Islay
2011 3 YO Bourbon Barrel
50° UN

Beach fire, blue agave, pecan smoke, pear, African pepper, iodine

Sm | Sm
Wo
4

Kilchoman 2007 vintage Release
2007/2013 6 YO
46° UN

Malted milk, lilac, beach fire, rhubarb, peat smoke, lemon meringue

C | Sm
Sm
4

Lagavulin
Distillery

Founded in 1816 by John Johnston.
Part of its production is used in the White Horse blend.

Great vintages: 1973, 1979, 1981, 1985, 1993
4 Stills: 2 wash, 2 spirit − 2.45 million LPA

Port Ellen, Isle of Islay, PA42 7DZ
Islay South Shore
+44 (0) 1496 302 749
www.malts.com
Owner: Diageo Plc

Lagavulin	12 YO CS 14th Release	54.4° UN CS
	2014 Special Release	

Arnica, burnt grass, peat oil, pink grapefruit, wormwood, salt

Sm | Sm
G
7

Lagavulin	16 YO	43°

Peated malt, cocoa, peat oil, kelp, liquorice, rosewood

Sm | Sm
Wo
5

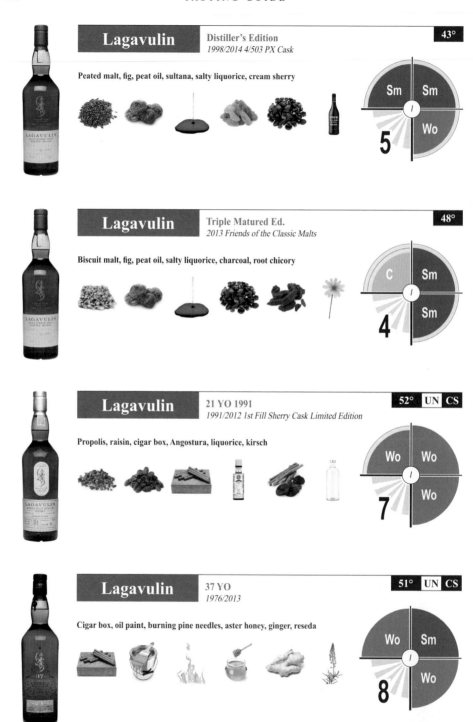

Lagavulin
Distiller's Edition
1998/2014 4/503 PX Cask

43°

Peated malt, fig, peat oil, sultana, salty liquorice, cream sherry

Sm | Sm
Wo

5

Lagavulin
Triple Matured Ed.
2013 Friends of the Classic Malts

48°

Biscuit malt, fig, peat oil, salty liquorice, charcoal, root chicory

C | Sm
Sm

4

Lagavulin
21 YO 1991
1991/2012 1st Fill Sherry Cask Limited Edition

52° UN CS

Propolis, raisin, cigar box, Angostura, liquorice, kirsch

Wo | Wo
Wo

7

Lagavulin
37 YO
1976/2013

51° UN CS

Cigar box, oil paint, burning pine needles, aster honey, ginger, reseda

Wo | Sm
Wo

8

Laphroaig
Distillery

Founded in 1815 by Donald & Alexander Johnstons.
90% of its production is used in the Islay Mist,
Black Bottle and Long John blends.

Great vintages: 1967, 1970, 1974, 1978, 1980
7 Stills: 3 wash, 4 spirit – 3.3 million LPA

Port Ellen, Isle of Islay, PA42 7DU
Islay South Shore
+44 (0) 1496 302 418
www.laphroaig.com
Owner: Beam Suntory Inc.

Laphroaig Select 40°

Bandage, water mint, peated malt, lemon, green tea, coconut milk

Sm	Sm
1	G

Laphroaig 10 YO 40°

Bandage, seaweed, peated malt, eucalyptus, beach fire, brine

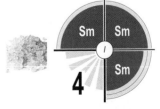

Sm	Sm
4	Sm

Laphroaig — 10 YO Cask Strength

58° | UN | CS

Arnica, fishing net, peat oil, grapefruit, beach fire, gingerbread

Sm | Sm
Sm

6

Laphroaig — Quarter Cask

48° | UN

Gorse, smoky sauna, wormwood, black olive, reseda, white pepper

Wo | G
Sm

5

Laphroaig — Triple Wood
Bourbon, Quarter, Oloroso Sherry

48° | UN

TCP antiseptic, apricot, cream liquorice, raisin, burnt grass, cream liqueur

Sm | Wo
Sm

4

Laphroaig — An Cuan Mòr

48° | UN | TRE

Camphor, calamus, cream liquorice, curaçao, peat, marron glacé

Sm | Wo
Sm

4

Laphroaig — PX Cask

48° UN TRE

Brown sherry, seaweed, smoky sauna, lavender, embers, cranberry

Wi | Sm
Sm

3

Laphroaig — QA Cask
Un-Charred American Oak

40° TRE

Brine, lava stone, vanilla, maple honey, burnt leave, amber rum

Ma | Wo
Sm

2

Laphroaig — 18 YO

48° UN

Peated malt, Seville orange, beach fire, sea spray, tar rope, salty liquorice

Sm | Sm
Sm

6

Laphroaig — 25 YO
Bourbon & Oloroso Sherry Barrels

45.1° UN CS

Raspberry wine, beach fire, peat moss, red apple, tar rope, liquorice cream

Wi | Sm
Sm

8

Port Ellen†
Distillery

Founded in 1825 by Alexander Kerr Mackay, closed since 1983, partially demolished.

Great vintages: 1969, 1973, 1978–1979
4 Stills: 2 wash, 2 spirit

Port Ellen, Isle of Islay, PA42 7AH
Islay South Shore
Owner: Diageo Plc

Port Ellen   14th Release   56.5° UN CS
1978/2014 35 YO

Creosote, hessian, beach fire, lemon liqueur, smoked shellfish, peppermint

Sm   Sm
Sm
8

Port Ellen   13th Release   55° UN CS
1978/2013 34 YO

Tobacco pipe juice, propolis, mahogany, lemon liqueur, salty liquorice, smoked herring

Sm   Wo
Wo
9

Auchentoshan
Distillery

Founded in 1823 by John Bulloch.
One of the few Scotch distilleries, with Hazelburn (Springbank),
to produce a triple distilled single malt.

Great vintages: 1957, 1965–1967, 1975, 1977, 1979
3 Stills: 1 wash, 1 middle, 1 spirit – 1.65 million LPA

Dalmuir, Clydebank, Dunbartonshire G81 4SG
+44 (0) 1389 878 561
www.auchentoshan.com
Owner: Morrison Bowmore Distillers Ltd (Beam Suntory Inc.)

Auchentoshan	American Oak	40°	3D

Matured in First Fill North American Bourbon Casks

Lemon meringue, mown lawn, vanilla cream, white peach, grapefruit, cardamom

Auchentoshan	Three Wood	43°	3D

Fresh tobacco, blackcurrant, walnut honey, toffee, rosewood, lemongrass

Auchentoshan — Valinch
57.2° UN CS 3D

Crème brûlée, orange peel, lemon meringue, lavender honey, peony, nutmeg

Wo | Fr
L
Fl
5

Auchentoshan — 12 YO
40° 3D

Crème brûlée, hazelnut, lime tree, Parma violet, Earl Grey tea, ginger

Wo | G
L
Fl
2

Auchentoshan — 18 YO
43° 3D

Fresh tobacco, green tea, lime tree, barley sugar, tangerine, roasted almond

G | G
L
Fr
3

Auchentoshan — 21 YO
43° 3D

Bergamot, gooseberry, ginger, chocolate malt, mahogany, tonka bean

Fr | Wo
L
Wo
5

Bladnoch
Distillery

Founded in 1825 by Thomas McClelland.
The northernmost distillery in Scotland.

Great vintages: 1957, 1958, 1964, 1966, 1972
2 Stills: 1 wash, 1 spirit − 11 warehouses − 0.25 million LPA

Bladnoch, Newton Stewart, Wigtownshire DG8 9AB
+44 (0) 1988 402 605
www.bladnoch.co.uk
Owner: David Prior

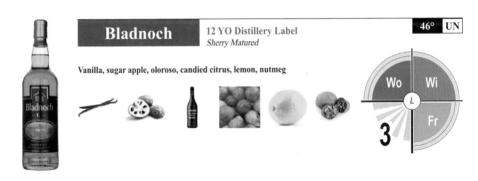

Bladnoch | 12 YO Distillery Label | 46° UN
Sherry Matured

Vanilla, sugar apple, oloroso, candied citrus, lemon, nutmeg

Wo | Wi
Fr
3

Bladnoch | 13 YO Beltie Label | 55° UN CS

Wet sand, scented verbena, lemon liqueur, pink peppercorn, cereal bar, guarana

Ma | D
C
4

Glenkinchie
Distillery

Founded in 1837 by John & George Rate.
One of six top distilleries chosen as Classic Malts of Scotland in 1988.

Great vintages: 1975, 1986, 1992
2 Stills: 1 wash, 1 spirit – 2.5 million LPA

Pencaitland, Tranent, East Lothian EH34 5ET
+44 (0) 1875 342 004
www.malts.com
Owner: Diageo Plc

Glenkinchie	12 YO		43°

Broom, quince jelly, floral cream, malted barley, rhubarb sorbet, slate

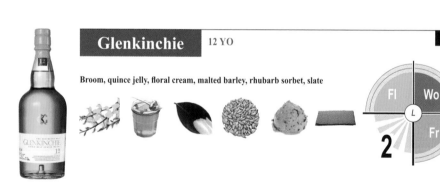

Glenkinchie	Distiller's Edition 2000/2013 Amontillado		43°

Amontillado, hazelnut, biscuit malt, raisin, fresh tobacco, caramel malt

Littlemill†
Distillery

Founded in 1772, closed in 1994,
partially demolished in 1996, destroyed by fire in 2004.

Great vintages: 1965, 1985, 1990, 1992
3 Stills: 1 wash, 2 spirit

Bowling, Dumbartonshire G60 5BG
www.lochlomondgroup.com
Owner: Loch Lomond Distillery Co. Ltd (Exponent)

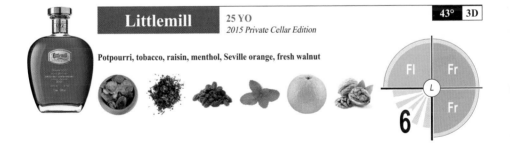

Littlemill	25 YO	43°	3D
	2015 Private Cellar Edition		

Potpourri, tobacco, raisin, menthol, Seville orange, fresh walnut

Rosebank†
Distillery

Founded in 1798, closed in 1993, partially demolished in 2010.

Great vintages: 1973, 1974, 1991, 1992
3 Stills: 1 wash, 1 spirit, 1 feints

Falkirk, Stirlingshire FK1 5BW
www.malts.com
Owner: Diageo Plc

Rosebank	21 YO	55.3° UN CS
	1990/2011 Special Release Refill American Oak	

Orange, buttercup, lemon liqueur, barley sugar, candied citrus, ginseng

Rosebank	25 YO	61.4° UN CS
	1981/2007	

Reseda, compost, lemon liqueur, green pepper, candied citrus, green tea

Glengyle / Kilkerran
Distillery

Founded in 1872 by William Mitchell and closed in 1925.
Rebuilt in 2004 under the instigation of Hedley Wright
on the site of the former Glengyle Distillery.

---

2 Stills: 1 wash, 1 spirit – 0.75 million LPA

Glengyle Road, Campbeltown, PA28 6LR
+44 (0) 1586 552 009
www.kilkerran.com
Owner: Mitchell's Glengyle Ltd. (J & A Mitchell & Co. Ltd)

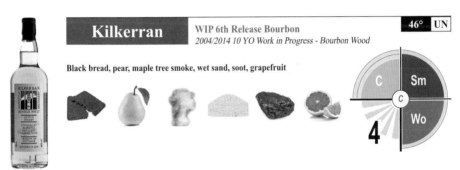

Kilkerran — WIP 6th Release Bourbon
2004/2014 10 YO Work in Progress - Bourbon Wood
46° UN

Black bread, pear, maple tree smoke, wet sand, soot, grapefruit

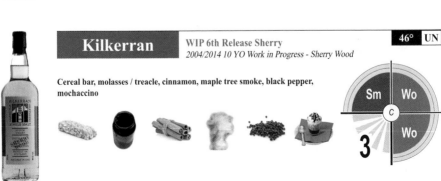

Kilkerran — WIP 6th Release Sherry
2004/2014 10 YO Work in Progress - Sherry Wood
46° UN

Cereal bar, molasses / treacle, cinnamon, maple tree smoke, black pepper,
mochaccino

Glen Scotia
Distillery

Founded in 1832 by the Galbraith family.
Closed from 1994 to 1999, operational since.

Great vintages: 1972, 1975, 1977, 1991, 1999
2 Stills: 1 wash, 1 spirit – 0.75 million LPA

12 High Street, Campbeltown, PA28 6DS
+44 (0) 1586 552 288
www.glenscotia-distillery.co.uk
Owner: Loch Lomond Group (Exponent Private Equity)

Glen Scotia   15 YO   46° UN
Matured in American Oak Barrels

Orange blossom honey, vanilla cream, galangal, sea spray, agarwood, pomelo

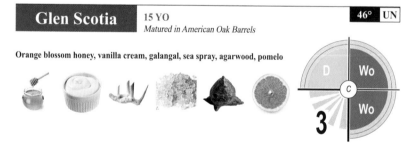

Glen Scotia   Victoriana   51.5° UN
Finished in Deep Charred Oak Casks

Prune, cubeb (Java pepper), root chicory, orange, burnt toast, peppermint

Springbank
Distillery

Founded in 1828 by the Reid family. Bought by John & William Mitchell in 1837. Springbank produces two other whiskies on its site: Hazelburn and Longrow.

Great vintages: 1958, 1965–1969, 1972–1975
4 Stills: 2 wash, 2 spirit – 0.75 million LPA

Well Close, Campbeltown, PA28 6ET
+44 (0) 1586 551 710
www.springbankdistillers.com
Owner: Springbank Distillers Ltd (J. & A. Mitchell & Co. Ltd)

Springbank — 10 YO — 46° UN

Salt marsh, pear, linseed oil, honey malt, beach fire, citrus

Springbank — 12 YO CS Batch 9
60% Fresh + 40% Refill Sherry Hogsheads — 54.3° UN CS

Peat moss, yuzu, rooibos, Seville orange, soot, ginger

Springbank 15 YO

46° UN

Butterscotch, graphite, coffee, mandarine, dark chocolate, juniper berry

Wo | Wo
C
Wo

4

Springbank 18 YO
2014

46° UN

Blueberry, reseda, linseed oil, raisin, dark chocolate, juniper berry

Fr | O
C
Wo

5

Springbank 21 YO

46° UN

Rhubarb, Banyuls, reseda, blackcurrant, star anise, raisin

Fr | Wo
C
G

6

Longrow Peated

46° UN

Peat smoke, oilskin, arnica, floral cream, salty liquorice, quinine

Sm | Sm
C
Ma

5

Longrow — 11 YO Red
2014 Fresh Port Casks

51.8° UN CS

Cigar box, ginger, farm, cranberry liqueur, cherry wine, African pepper

Wo | Sm
Wi
4

Longrow — 18 YO

46° UN

Wet sand, pear, peat moss, mandarine, African pepper, bergamot

Mi | Sm
Wo
6

Hazelburn — 10 YO
Matured in Bourbon Barrels

46° UN 3D

White peach, thatch, rhubarb, white chocolate, dried hops, slate

Fr | Fr
G
3

Hazelburn — 12 YO

46° UN 3D

Kumquat, amoroso, bitter orange marmalade, Sichuan pepper, white chocolate, Angostura

Fr | Fr
Wo
4

Ballantine's

Founded in 1827 by George Ballantine.
Finest is its oldest recipe, created in 1910.

The second bestselling Scotch whisky brand,
with more than 50 million litres (13.2 million gallons) sold per year

Visitor centre at the Glenburgie Distillery, Forres (Speyside)
+44 (0) 1343 850 258
www.ballantines.com
Owner: Pernod Ricard

Ballantine's   Finest   40°

Barley sugar, lemon, apple, milk chocolate, vanilla, caramel

1

Ballantine's   12 YO   40°

Vanilla, barley sugar, acacia honey, apple, caramel malt, wood smoke

2

Ballantine's 17 YO

43°

Elderflower, peach, beeswax, apple, crème brûlée, liquorice

Fl | D
B
Wo

4

Ballantine's Limited

43°

Pear, peat smoke, chocolate, orange, nutmeg, clove

Fr | Wo
B
Wo

3

Ballantine's 21 YO

43°

Marmalade, peat smoke, hazel honey, orange, liquorice, date

Fr | D
B
Wo

4

Ballantine's 30 YO

43°

Mango, rose, acacia honey, cocoa, peat smoke, Seville orange

Fr | D
B
Sm

7

Chivas Regal

Founded in 1801 by brothers John and James Chivas.

The 25 Year Old was first created in 1909 and was the first luxury Scotch whisky.
The third bestselling Scotch whisky brand, with more than
40 million litres (10.6 million gallons) sold per year.

Visitor centre at the Strathisla Distillery, Keith (Speyside)
www.chivas.com
Owner: Pernod Ricard

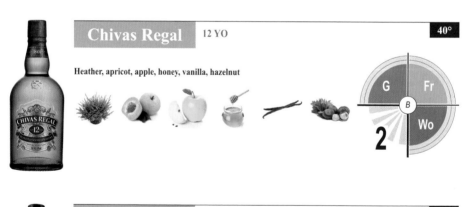

Chivas Regal 12 YO   40°

Heather, apricot, apple, honey, vanilla, hazelnut

2

Chivas Regal Brother's Blend 12 YO   40°

Peach, honeycomb, pear, cinnamon, liquorice, marmalade

3

Chivas Regal Extra

40°

Date, cinnamon, pear, caramel, almond, ginger

2

Chivas Regal 18 YO

40°

Caramel, fruit cake, malted barley, dark chocolate, nutmeg, orange peel

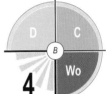

4

Chivas Regal 25 YO

40°

Almond, iris, orange, honey malt, sweet chestnut honey, tobacco

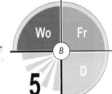

5

Cutty Sark

Founded in 1923 by Francis Berry and Hugh Rudd.
Named after one of the last British clippers that was then converted
into a training ship.

Once in the top ten of bestselling Scotch whiskies, with more than
20 million litres (5.3 million gallons) sold per year, it is currently being relaunched,
with more than 7 million litres (1.8 million gallons) sold.

Visitor centre at the Glenrothes Distillery, Rothes (Speyside)
www.cutty-sark.com
Owner: Edrington

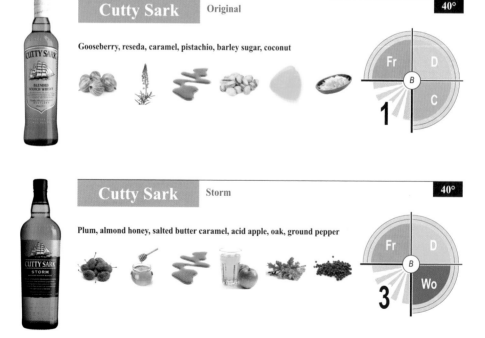

Cutty Sark Original 40°

Gooseberry, reseda, caramel, pistachio, barley sugar, coconut

Cutty Sark Storm 40°

Plum, almond honey, salted butter caramel, acid apple, oak, ground pepper

Cutty Sark — Prohibition Edition

50°

Malted milk, orange, butterscotch, vanilla, barley malt syrup, allspice

3

Cutty Sark — Tam o' Shanter 25 YO

46.5°

Panelling, cherry, leather, fig, ginger, dark chocolate

5

Cutty Sark — 33 YO

41.7°

Orange blossom honey, mahogany, pineapple, liquorice, walnut, tobacco

6

Dewar's

Founded in 1846 by John Dewar.
The White Label recipe was created in 1899.

In the top ten of Scotch whisky brands with nearly
30 million litres (7.9 million gallons) sold per year

Visitor centre at the Aberfeldy Distillery (Highlands)
www.dewars.com
Owner: Bacardi

Dewar's White Label   40°

Heather honey, pear, caramel, smoke, vanilla, lemon

D | D
B
Wo
1

Dewar's White Label Scratched Cask   40°

White oak, roasted barley, salted butter caramel, vanilla, orange, cinnamon

Wo | D
B
Fr
3

Dewar's — 12 YO The Ancestor

40°

Cherry blossom honey, butterscotch, orange, coumarin, nutmeg, crème anglaise

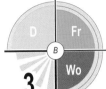

3

Dewar's — 15 YO The Monarch

40°

Pine honey, crème caramel, oak, pineapple, walnut, milk chocolate

4

Dewar's — 18 YO The Vintage

40°

Fruit cake, chocolate, apricot, ginger, malted barley, peat smoke

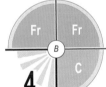

4

Dewar's — Signature

40°

White currant, vanilla, orange blossom honey, walnut, gentian, peat smoke

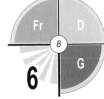

6

The Famous Grouse

Founded in 1896 by Matthew Gloag.
It is named after the famous Scottish bird.

In the top ten of Scotch whisky brands with nearly
30 million litres (7.9 million gallons) sold per year

Visitor centre at the Glenturret Distillery, Crieff (Highlands)
www.thefamousgrouse.com
Owner: Edrington

The Famous Grouse

The Famous Grouse — 40°

Potpourri, almond honey, plum, toffee, malted barley, lemon

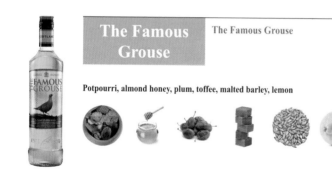

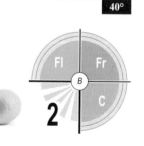

Fl / Fr / B / C

2

The Famous Grouse

The Black Grouse — 40°

Bonfires, malted barley, oak, almond, peat smoke, liquorice

Sm / Wo / B / Sm

3

The Famous Grouse

The Black Grouse Alpha Edition

40°

Orange peel, dark chocolate, peated malt, vanilla, liquorice, tar

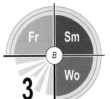

3

The Famous Grouse

The Naked Grouse

40°

Cherry, roasted almond, leather, fig, cinnamon, tobacco

4

The Famous Grouse

16 YO
Double Matured

40°

Butterscotch, pear, nutmeg, cherry, cinnamon, vanilla

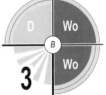

3

The Famous Grouse

40 YO
Blended Malt

47°

Mango, cardamom, mandarine, cinnamon, ginger, peat smoke

6

Grant's

**Founded in 1898 by William Grant.
Marketed in its triangular bottle since 1957.**

In the top ten of Scotch whisky brands, with more than
40 million litres (10.5 million gallons) sold per year

Visitor centre at the Glenfiddich Distillery, Dufftown (Speyside)
www.grantswhisky.com
Owner: William Grant & Sons

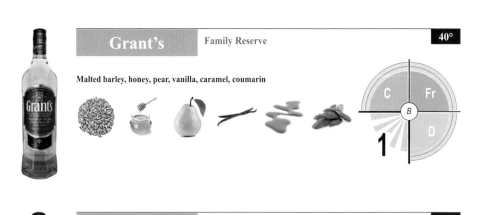

Grant's — Family Reserve — 40°

Malted barley, honey, pear, vanilla, caramel, coumarin

Grant's — Ale Cask Finish — 40°

Malted barley, heather, apple, dried hops, oak, lemon blossom honey

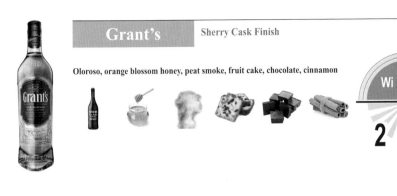

Grant's — Sherry Cask Finish

40°

Oloroso, orange blossom honey, peat smoke, fruit cake, chocolate, cinnamon

Wi | Sm
B
Wo

2

Grant's — Signature

40°

Malted barley, caramel, cinnamon, vanilla, roasted almond, honey

C | Wo
B
Wo

1

Grant's — 25 YO

40°

Cigar box, peach, thyme honey, ginger, dark chocolate, cinnamon

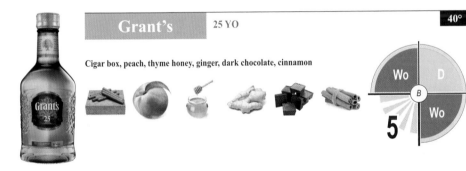

Wo | D
B
Wo

5

Hankey Bannister

Founded in 1757 by Beaumont Hankey and Hugh Bannister.
A blended whisky favoured by kings and by Winston Churchill.

www.hankeybannister.com
Owner: Inver House Distillers (Thai Beverage)

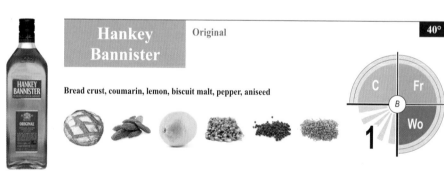

Hankey Bannister Original   40°

Bread crust, coumarin, lemon, biscuit malt, pepper, aniseed

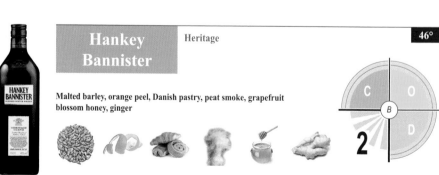

Hankey Bannister Heritage   46°

Malted barley, orange peel, Danish pastry, peat smoke, grapefruit
blossom honey, ginger

Hankey Bannister
12 YO Old Regency

40°

Orange peel, roasted almond, ganache, raisin, acacia honey, vanilla

Fr Wo
B
D

3

Hankey Bannister
21 YO Partners Reserve

40°

Nectarine, malted barley, mango, ginger, liquorice, turmeric

Fr Fr
B
Wo

5

Hankey Bannister
25 YO

40°

Lemon, vanilla, clementine blossom honey, barley malt syrup, allspice, leather

Fr D
B
Wo

6

Hankey Bannister
40 YO

44.3° UN CS

Rancio, rose, peach, walnut wine, eucalyptus honey, orange liqueur

Wo Fr
B
D

9

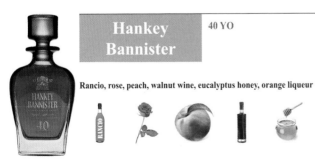

Johnnie Walker

Founded in 1923 by John Walker.
Its iconic square bottle dates from the 19th century.

The world's bestselling Scotch whisky brand, with more than
180 million litres (47.6 million gallons) sold per year.

Visitor centre at the Cardhu Distillery, Aberlour (Speyside)
www.johnniewalker.com
Owner: Diageo

Johnnie Walker Red Label   40°

Orange peel, peat smoke, pine honey, coumarin, malted barley, ginger

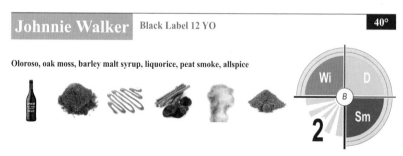

1

Johnnie Walker Black Label 12 YO   40°

Oloroso, oak moss, barley malt syrup, liquorice, peat smoke, allspice

2

Johnnie Walker — Double Black

40°

Charcoal, citron, vanilla, black pepper, peat smoke, malted barley

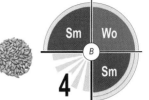

Sm | Wo
B
Sm

4

Johnnie Walker — Gold Label Reserve

40°

Lemon blossom honey, chocolate, mango, peat smoke, pepper, beeswax

D | Fr
B
Wo

4

Johnnie Walker — Platinum Label 18 YO

40°

Almond honey, raisin, apricot, peat smoke, liquorice, vanilla

D | Fr
B
Wo

4

Johnnie Walker — Blue Label

40°

Hazelnut honey, rose, liquorice, peated malt, fig, tobacco

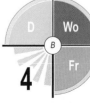

D | Wo
B
Fr

4

Royal Salute

**Founded in 1953 by the master blender Charles Julian
to commemorate the coronation of Queen Elizabeth II.**

More than 1.5 million litres (0.4 million gallons)
of whisky aged for at least 21 years are sold per year

Visitor centre at the Strathisla distillery, Keith (Speyside)
www.royalsalute.com
Owner: Pernod Ricard

Royal Salute 21 YO   40°

Oloroso, blueberry, peach, walnut, liquorice, caramel

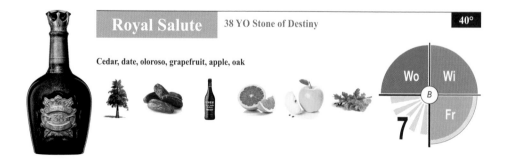

Royal Salute 38 YO Stone of Destiny   40°

Cedar, date, oloroso, grapefruit, apple, oak

Irish distilleries

West Cork	Operational distillery
Burren	Proposed distillery
Coleraine	Closed distillery

Sliabh Liag □

Connacht □

Nephin □

Clare

Lough Corrib

Irish Fiddler □ Galway

Atlantic.
Ocean

Burren □

Limerick

IRISH

Dingle
□

Watercourse
(Hewitt's)
□
C

West Cork □ Dúchas
□

Horse Island □

SCOTLAND

Islay

Kintyre

Bushmills

St Brendan's

Coleraine

North
Channel

NORTHERN
IRELAND

Belfast

The Echlinville

Belfast

Portaferry

Lough Allen

Great Northern

Cooley

The Shed

Dublin Distilleries

Slane Castle

☐ Teeling   ☐ Jones' Road

☐ Dublin   ☐ Old Jameson

☐ Alltech   ☐ John's Lane
Dublin

Lough Ree

Boyne

Kilbeggan

D.E. Williams

Dublin

Tullamore D.E.W.

Nore

Glendalough

Alltech
Carlow

Walsh

Irish Sea

EPUBLIC

Slaney

perary   Suir

Kilkenny

Waterford

Blackwater

Waterford

Kilmacthomas

New Midleton

Old Midleton

Celtic Sea

IRISH REP.

Europe

1000 km

Bushmills
Distillery

Founded in 1784 by Hugh Anderson.
1608 refers to the year of allocation of a distillation licence in County Antrim.
Bought by Diageo in 2005 then acquired by José Cuervo in 2015.

10 Stills: 5 wash, 5 spirit – 4.5 million LPA

2 Distillery Rd, Bushmills, County Antrim BT57 8XH
+44 (0) 28 2073 3218
www.bushmills.com
Owner: José Cuervo

Bushmills	Original	40°	3D
	Matured in Bourbon, Virgin Oak & Sherry Casks		

Bread, hay, cereal bar, hazelnut tree honey, crème brûlée, spices

Bushmills	Black Bush	40°	3D
	Mainly Matured in Oloroso Sherry Casks		

Blackcurrant, coconut, oloroso, chocolate, barley malt syrup, liquorice

Bushmills	10 YO
	Mainly matured in Bourbon Casks

40° 3D

Pear, vanilla, lemon, malted barley, oak honey, nutmeg

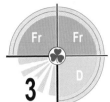

3

Bushmills	16 YO
	Matured in Bourbon & Sherry Casks, finished in Port Casks

40° 3D

Banana, almond, port wine, apricot, cinnamon, milk chocolate

4

Bushmills	21 YO
	Matured in Bourbon & Sherry Casks, finished in Madeira Casks

40° 3D

Chocolate, greengage, date, tobacco, vanilla, malted barley

4

Cooley
Distillery

Founded in 1987 by John Teeling.
Bought by Beam in 2012.

Production of grain and malt whiskey
4 Stills: 2 copper pot stills, 2 column stills
0.65 million LPA (malt spirit) + 2.6 million LPA (grain spirit)

Dundalk Rd, Dundalk, Co. Louth
+353 (0) 42 937 6102
www.kilbeggandistillingcompany.com
Owner: Kilbeggan Distilling Co. (Beam Suntory Inc.)

Connemara   Original   **40°**
Matured in Bourbon Casks

Peated malt, lime, barley sugar, roasted almond, manuka honey, ash

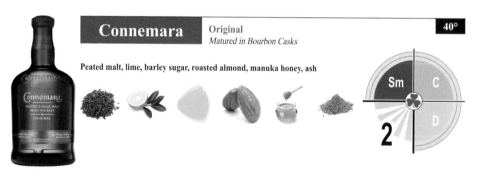

Connemara   Cask Strength   **58.5°** **UN** **CS**
Matured in Bourbon Casks

Bonfires, mown lawn, grapefruit peel, peat smoke, peated malt, dark chocolate

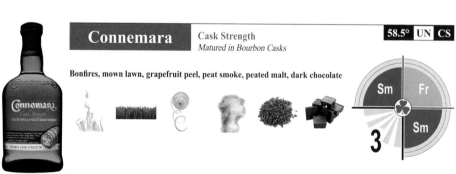

Connemara

12 YO
Matured in Bourbon Casks

40°

Burnt leave, lemon peel, pear, soot, burnt wood, ginger

2

Connemara

22 YO
Matured in First Fill Bourbon Barrels

46° UN

Oak smoke, white currant, peach, peat smoke, ginger, leather

      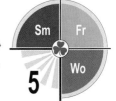

5

Greenore

8 YO Small Batch
Matured in Bourbon Barrels

40°

Lemon blossom honey, banana, corn oil, almond, nutmeg, pecan nut

2

Greenore

18 YO Special Edition
Matured in Bourbon Barrels

46° UN

Vanilla, corn, butterscotch, banana, liquorice, orange

3

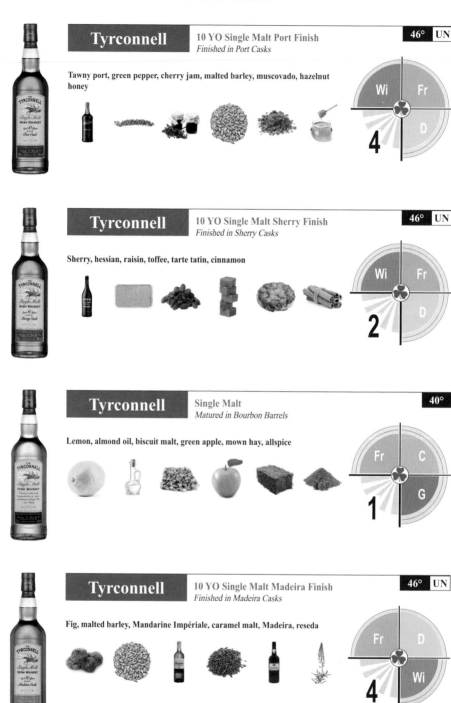

Tyrconnell — 10 YO Single Malt Port Finish — 46° UN
Finished in Port Casks

Tawny port, green pepper, cherry jam, malted barley, muscovado, hazelnut honey

Wi / Fr / D — 4

Tyrconnell — 10 YO Single Malt Sherry Finish — 46° UN
Finished in Sherry Casks

Sherry, hessian, raisin, toffee, tarte tatin, cinnamon

Wi / Fr / D — 2

Tyrconnell — Single Malt — 40°
Matured in Bourbon Barrels

Lemon, almond oil, biscuit malt, green apple, mown hay, allspice

Fr / C / G — 1

Tyrconnell — 10 YO Single Malt Madeira Finish — 46° UN
Finished in Madeira Casks

Fig, malted barley, Mandarine Impériale, caramel malt, Madeira, reseda

Fr / D / Wi — 4

Kilbeggan

Founded in 1757, closed in 1954,
then rebuilt in 2007 for its 250th anniversary.

The brand is used as blended whiskey
2 Stills: 1 wash, 1 spirit – 0.2 million LPA

Lower Main St, Kilbeggan, Co. Weastmeath
+353 (0) 57 933 2134
www.kilbeggandistillery.com
Owner: Kilbeggan Distilling Co. (Beam Suntory Inc.)

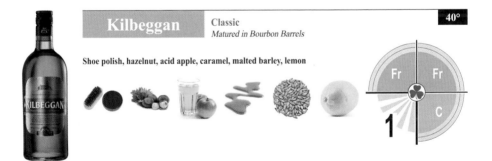

Kilbeggan — Classic — *Matured in Bourbon Barrels* — 40°

Shoe polish, hazelnut, acid apple, caramel, malted barley, lemon

Fr | Fr
C

1

Kilbeggan — 21 YO — *Matured in Bourbon, Sherry, Port & Madeira Casks* — 40°

Apple compote, cedar, eucalyptus honey, bran, liquorice, mint

Fr | D
Wo

3

Midleton / Jameson
Distillery

The Jameson brand dates back to 1780 and alone represents 65% of Irish whiskey sales,
with more than 40 million litres (10.6 million gallons) sold per year.
New distillery built in 1975.

---

13 Stills: 7 copper pot stills, 6 column stills – 64 million LPA

Old distillery Walk, Midleton, Co. Cork
+353 (0) 21 461 3594
www.irishdistillers.ie
Owner: Irish Distillers (Pernod Ricard)

Jameson	Jameson	40° 3D
	Matured in Bourbon & Sherry Casks	

Blackcurrant bud, copper, linseed oil, barley sugar, oloroso, pepper

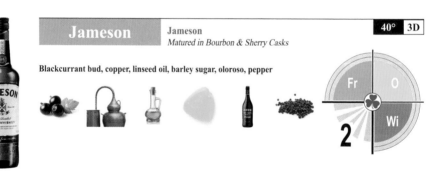

Jameson	Crested Ten	40° 3D
	Matured in Bourbon & Sherry Casks	

Blackcurrant bud, copper, oloroso, coffee, butterscotch, apple

Jameson	Caskmates	40° 3D
	Finish in Stout Casks	

Green apple, hazelnut, prune, dried hops, marzipan, cocoa

2

Jameson	12 YO Special Reserve	40° 3D
	Matured in Bourbon & Sherry Casks	

Caramel, blackcurrant, oloroso, hazelnut, apple, oak

3

Jameson	Select Reserve Black barrel	40° 3D
	Matured in Bourbon & Sherry Casks	

Nectarine, cereal bar, oak honey, apricot, nutmeg, cocoa

4

Jameson	Signature Reserve	40° 3D
	Matured in Bourbon & Sherry Casks	

Walnut honey, apple, heather honey, vanilla cream, beeswax, almond

4

Jameson — Gold Reserve
Matured in Bourbon & Sherry Casks
40° 3D

Cedar, fruit cake, gorse bush, apple, liquorice, vanilla

Wo | D
Wo
4

Jameson — 18 YO Limited Release
Matured in Bourbon & Sherry Casks
40° 3D

Peach, marzipan, butterscotch, gooseberry, mocha, tobacco

Fr | D
Wo
5

Jameson — Rarest Vintage Reserve
Matured in Bourbon & Port Casks
46° UN 3D

Damson, banana, molasses/treacle, mango, toffee apple, long pepper

Fr | D
D
7

Paddy — Paddy
Matured in Bourbon Barrels
40° 3D

Biscuit malt, oak, orange tree honey, cinnamon, sweet almond, vanilla cream

C | D
Wo
2

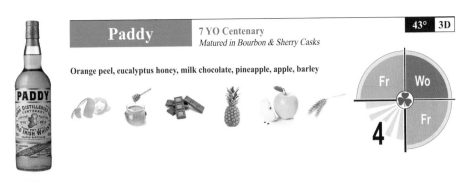

Paddy

7 YO Centenary
Matured in Bourbon & Sherry Casks

43° 3D

Orange peel, eucalyptus honey, milk chocolate, pineapple, apple, barley

Fr | Wo
Fr
4

Green Spot

Green Spot
Matured in Bourbon & Sherry Casks

40° 3D

Walnut oil, white peach, pineapple, vanilla, almond, barley

O | Fr
Wo
3

Yellow Spot

12 YO
Matured in Bourbon, Sherry & Malaga Casks

46° UN 3D

Mown hay, clove, coffee bush honey, apple, barley malt syrup, pineapple

G | D
D
4

Power's

Gold Label
Matured in Bourbon Barrels

40° 3D

Apple, orange peel, acacia honey, barley, pepper, pear

Fr | D
Wo
2

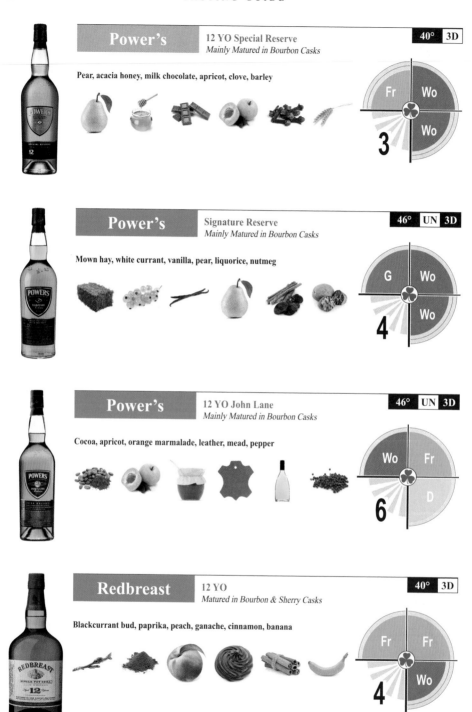

Power's — 12 YO Special Reserve — 40° 3D
Mainly Matured in Bourbon Casks

Pear, acacia honey, milk chocolate, apricot, clove, barley

Fr | Wo | Wo — 3

Power's — Signature Reserve — 46° UN 3D
Mainly Matured in Bourbon Casks

Mown hay, white currant, vanilla, pear, liquorice, nutmeg

G | Wo | Wo — 4

Power's — 12 YO John Lane — 46° UN 3D
Mainly Matured in Bourbon Casks

Cocoa, apricot, orange marmalade, leather, mead, pepper

Wo | Fr | D — 6

Redbreast — 12 YO — 40° 3D
Matured in Bourbon & Sherry Casks

Blackcurrant bud, paprika, peach, ganache, cinnamon, banana

Fr | Fr | Wo — 4

Redbreast

12 YO Cask Strength
Matured in Bourbon & Sherry Casks

59.9° UN CS 3D

Fig, marzipan, orange, pepper, vanilla, barley sugar

6

Redbreast

15 YO
Matured in Bourbon & Sherry Casks

46° UN 3D

Roasted almond, apricot, orange peel, date, milk chocolate, gooseberry

5

Redbreast

21 YO
Matured in Bourbon & Sherry Casks

46° UN 3D

Blackcurrant, passion fruit / maracuja, nutmeg, mango, blood orange, ginger

7

Midleton

Barry Crocket Legacy
Matured in Bourbon & Virgin Oak Casks

46° UN 3D

Mango, oak, lime, acacia honey, ginger, barley sugar

7

Teeling

Founded in 2012 by John Teeling.
His ancestor Walter Teeling was already distilling in Dublin in 1782.
New distillery opened in 2015.

13–17 Newmarket, Dublin 8
+353 (0) 1 531 0888
www.teelingwhiskey.com
Owner: Teeling Whiskey Co.

Teeling — Small Batch
Finished in Nicaraguan Rum Casks — 46° UN

Nutmeg, pear, apricot, lemon, chocolate, caramel

Teeling — Single Grain
Matured in Californian Red Wine Casks — 46° UN

Broom, brown sugar, butter, vanilla, Cabernet Sauvignon, toffee

Teeling

Single Malt
Finished in Sherry, Madeira, Port, White Burgundy & Cabernet Sauvignon Casks

46° UN

Pineapple, reseda, salted butter caramel, acid apple, lemon peel, almond

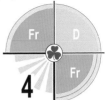

4

Teeling

21 YO Single Malt
Finished in Sauternes Casks

46° UN

Acacia honey, mown lawn, Sauternes, quince, apricot, white chocolate

6

Teeling

26 YO Single Malt 1987
Finished in White Burgundy Casks

46° UN

Plum, linseed oil, shortbread, raisin, apple, white pepper

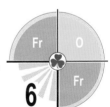

6

Teeling

30 YO Single Malt 1983
Matured in Bourbon Barrels

46° UN

Mango, clementine blossom honey, guava, cinnamon, papaya, oak

7

The Irishman

Founded in 1999 by Bernard and Rosemary Walsh.
Whiskey merchants since 2007.
Distillery under construction at Carlow.

+353 (0) 59 913 3232
www.theirishmanwhiskey.com
Owner: The Irishman Whiskey

The Irishman Founder's Reserve   40° 3D
Matured in Bourbon Barrels

Orange marmalade, ginger, barley malt syrup, cinnamon, barley, hazelnut

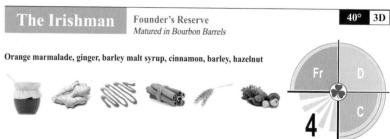

The Irishman Single Malt   40° 3D
Matured in Bourbon & Sherry Casks

Peach, roasted almond, pastry cream, biscuit malt, dark chocolate, coconut

The Irishman Single Malt 12 YO   40° 3D
Matured in Bourbon Barrels

Reseda, clove, pear, barley sugar, dark chocolate, caramel

Tullamore D.E.W.

Founded in 1829 at Tullamore by Michael Molloy.
Bought around 1873 by Daniel E. Williams.
The distillery was closed in 1950 and a new distillery was opened in 2014
by William Grant & Sons, who has owned the brand since 2010.

Visitor Centre at Bury Quay, Tullamore, Co. Offaly
+353 (0) 57 932 5015
www.tullamoredew.com
Owner: William Grant & Sons

Tullawmore DEW — Original
Matured in Bourbon & Sherry Casks

40° 3D

Lemon blossom honey, cereal bar, acid apple, reseda, marzipan, vanilla

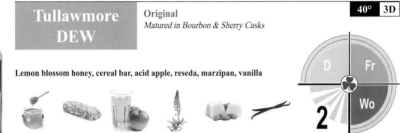

2

Tullawmore DEW — 10 YO Single Malt
Matured in Bourbon, Dry Oloroso, Port & Madeira Casks

40° 3D

Pineapple, coumarin, walnut, fig, rancio, malted barley

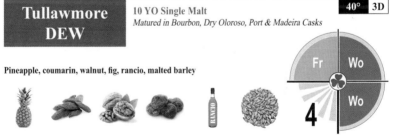

4

Tullawmore DEW — 12 YO Special Reserve
Matured in Bourbon & Sherry Casks

40° 3D

Blackcurrant, oloroso, linseed oil, peach, roasted almond, cream sherry

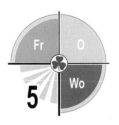

5

Japanese distilleries

Malt distilleries

Chichibu	Operational distillery
Akkeshi	Proposed distillery
Karuizawa	Closed distillery

Grain distilleries

Miyagikyo	Operational distillery
Nishinomiya	Closed distillery

NORTH KOREA

SOUTH KOREA

Sea of Japan

Eigashima
White Oak

Sanraku Ocea

Shinsh

Miyashita

Kyoto

Osaka   Nagoya

Hiroshima

Yamazaki

Fukuoka

Chita

Nagasaki   *Kyushu*   *Shikoku*

Nishinomiya

Kagoshima

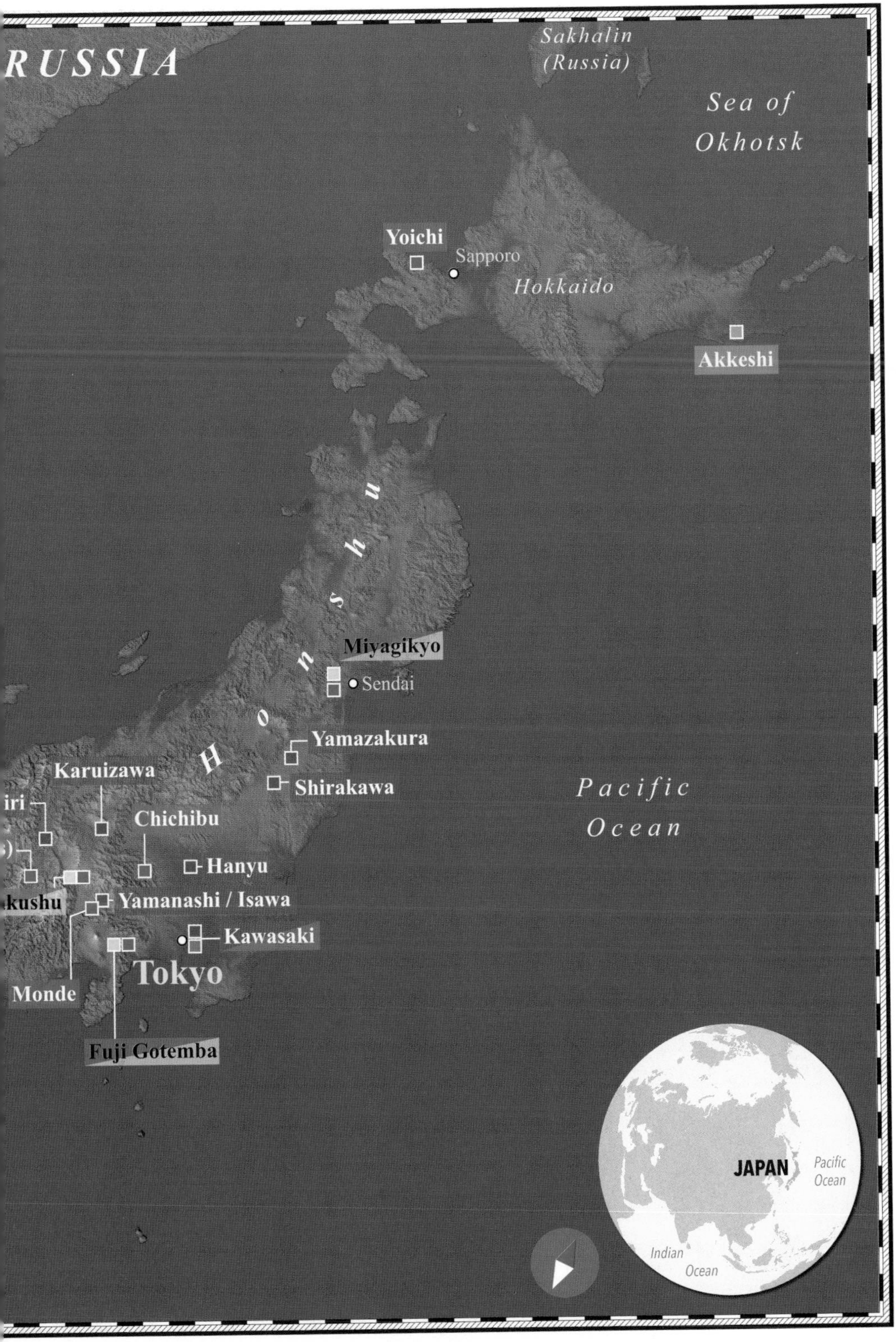

RUSSIA

Sakhalin
(Russia)

Sea of
Okhotsk

Yoichi
Sapporo

Hokkaido

Akkeshi

H
o
n
s
h
u

Miyagikyo
Sendai

Yamazakura

Karuizawa

Shirakawa

iri

Chichibu

Hanyu

kushu

Yamanashi / Isawa

Kawasaki

Monde

Tokyo

Fuji Gotemba

Pacific
Ocean

JAPAN

Pacific
Ocean

Indian
Ocean

Chichibu 秩父蒸留所
Distillery

Founded in 2008 by Ichiro Akuto.

---

2 Stills: 1 wash, 1 spirit – 0.08 million LPA

Midorigaoka 49, Chichibu-shi, Saitama 368-0067
+81 494 62 4601
Owner: Venture Whisky Ltd

Chichibu	The First	61.8° UN CS
	2008/2011 3 YO Bourbon Barrel	

Malted barley, persimmon, barley sugar, quince jelly, candied citrus, white pepper

      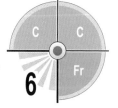

Chichibu	Floor Malted	50.5° UN CS
	2009/2012 Bourbon Barrel	

Kernel, cherry, malted barley, pineapple, greengage, apple

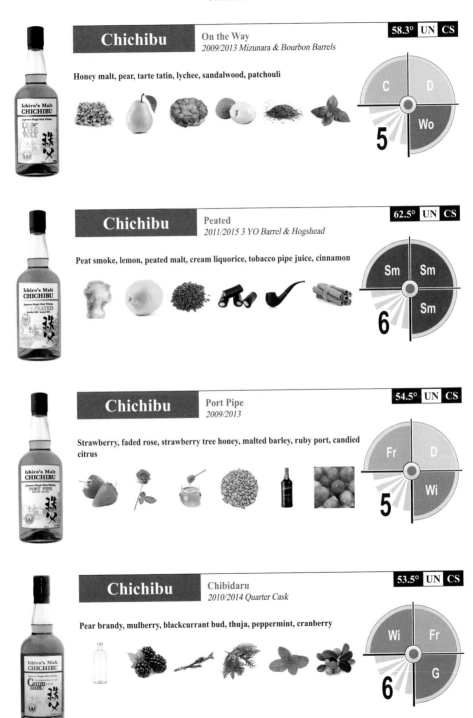

Chichibu
On the Way
2009/2013 Mizunara & Bourbon Barrels

58.3° UN CS

Honey malt, pear, tarte tatin, lychee, sandalwood, patchouli

Chichibu
Peated
2011/2015 3 YO Barrel & Hogshead

62.5° UN CS

Peat smoke, lemon, peated malt, cream liquorice, tobacco pipe juice, cinnamon

Chichibu
Port Pipe
2009/2013

54.5° UN CS

Strawberry, faded rose, strawberry tree honey, malted barley, ruby port, candied citrus

Chichibu
Chibidaru
2010/2014 Quarter Cask

53.5° UN CS

Pear brandy, mulberry, blackcurrant bud, thuja, peppermint, cranberry

Hakushu 白州蒸留所
Distillery

Founded in 1973 by Suntory Ltd.
Direct-fired stills.
Benefits from the pure waters of the Ojira River (Minami Alps Tennensui).

Great vintages: 1981, 1982, 1989
16 Stills: 8 wash, 8 spirit – 4 million LPA

Torihara 2913-1, Hakushu-cho, Hokuto-shi, Yamanashi-ken, 408-0316
+81 551 35 2211
www.suntory.com
Owner: Beam Suntory Inc.

Hakushu	Distiller's Reserve	43°

Honeydew melon, spearmint, lime tree, black tea, kaffir lime, salt

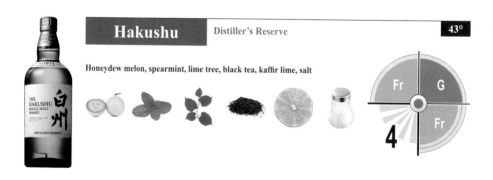

4

Hakushu	12 YO	43°

Kumquat, ash, mochaccino, longan, mown lawn, beach fire

3

Hakushu   18 YO

43°

Floral cream, vanilla, tarte tatin, lapsang souchong, cinnamon, vine peach

Wo | D

Wo

5

Hakushu   25 YO

43°

Lapsang souchong, rhubarb wine, peat moss, spearmint, graphite, Angostura

Sm | Sm

Mi

6

Hakushu   Sherry Cask

48° UN

Coffee ground, red apple, blackcurrant wine, dark chocolate, rosewood, menthol

Wo | Wi

Wo

6

Hibiki 響

Blended whisky (including Hakushu and Yamazaki) – Hibiki means resonance, harmony.
Bottles have 24 facets, symbolizing the 24 seasons of the Japanese lunar calendar,
with the exception of the 30 Year Old, which has 30.
Aged in different types of casks,
which may include Mizunara or Umeshu (plum liqueur) casks.

www.suntory.com
Owner: Beam Suntory Inc.

| Hibiki | Japanese Harmony | 43° |
| | *Matured in American oak, Sherry & Mizunara Casks* | |

Rose, sandalwood, orange blossom honey, rosemary, white chocolate, Japanese oak

| Hibiki | 12 YO | 43° |
| | *Finished in Umeshu Plum Liqueur Casks* | |

Pineapple, almond blossom honey, greengage, double cream, jasmine, barley sugar

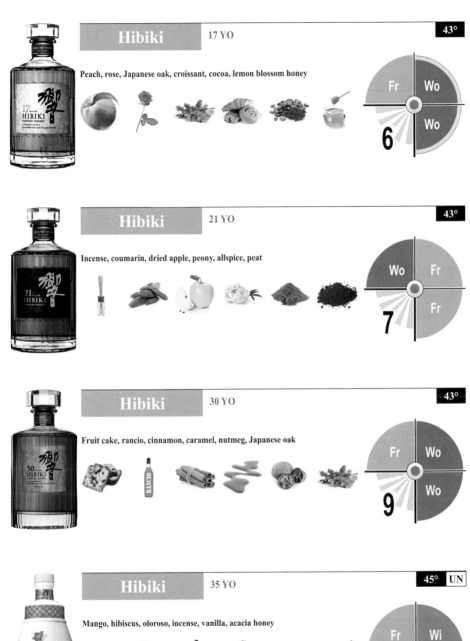

Hibiki 17 YO 43°

Peach, rose, Japanese oak, croissant, cocoa, lemon blossom honey

Fr Wo
Wo
6

Hibiki 21 YO 43°

Incense, coumarin, dried apple, peony, allspice, peat

Wo Fr
Fr
7

Hibiki 30 YO 43°

Fruit cake, rancio, cinnamon, caramel, nutmeg, Japanese oak

Fr Wo
Wo
9

Hibiki 35 YO 45° UN

Mango, hibiscus, oloroso, incense, vanilla, acacia honey

Fr Wi
Wo
9

Karuizawa† 軽井沢蒸留所
Distillery

**Founded in 1955 by Mercian Wine Co., ceased operations in 2000,
definitively closed in 2011.
Remaining stocks were bought by Number One Drinks Company in 2011.**

Oaza Maseguchi 1795-2, Miyota-machi, Kitasaku-gun, Nagano-ken, 389-0207
Owner: Kirin Brewery Co. Ltd

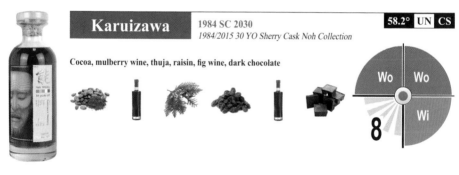

Karuizawa   1984 SC 2030   58.2° UN CS
1984/2015 30 YO Sherry Cask Noh Collection

Cocoa, mulberry wine, thuja, raisin, fig wine, dark chocolate

Karuizawa   1984 SC 8173   58.5° UN CS
1984/2014 Bourbon Cask LMDW

Papier d'Arménie, fresh tobacco, mandarine, black tea, rosewood, clove

Miyagikyo 宮城峡蒸留所
Distillery

Founded in 1969 by Masataka Taketsuru.

10 Stills: 4 wash, 4 spirit, 2 Coffey – 3 millions LPA

Nikka Ichiban-chi, Aoba-ku, Sendai-shi, Miyagi-ken, 989-3433
+81 223 95 2111
www.nikka.com
Owner: Nikka Whisky Distilling Co. (Asahi Breweries Ltd)

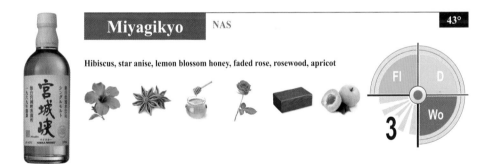

Miyagikyo   NAS   43°

Hibiscus, star anise, lemon blossom honey, faded rose, rosewood, apricot

3

Miyagikyo   10 YO   45°

Lavender honey, citron, oak, salty liquorice, Angostura, ginger

4

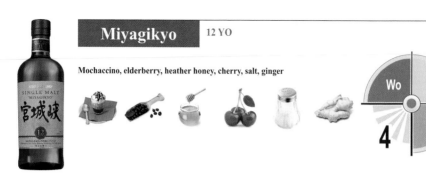

Miyagikyo 12 YO — 45°

Mochaccino, elderberry, heather honey, cherry, salt, ginger

Wo | D
Mi
4

Miyagikyo 15 YO — 45°

Walnut wine, poppy, oak, gingerbread, raisin, salty liquorice

Wi | Wo
Fr
6

Nikka Whisky Distilling Co.
ニッカウヰスキー

Founded in 1934 by Masataka Taketsuru. The second largest whisky producer in Japan with around 20 million litres (5.3 million gallons) sold every year.

www.nikka.com
Owner: Ashari Breweries Ltd

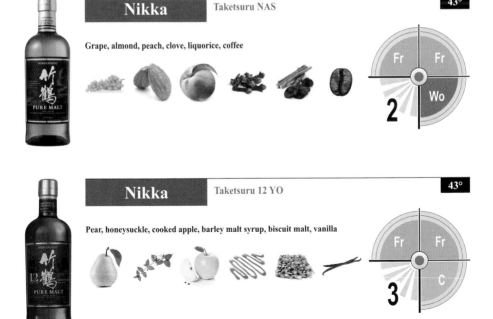

Nikka   Taketsuru NAS   43°

Grape, almond, peach, clove, liquorice, coffee

2

Nikka   Taketsuru 12 YO   43°

Pear, honeysuckle, cooked apple, barley malt syrup, biscuit malt, vanilla

3

Nikka — Taketsuru 17 YO — 43°

Pine, peach, Seville orange peel, cinnamon, quinine, peat smoke

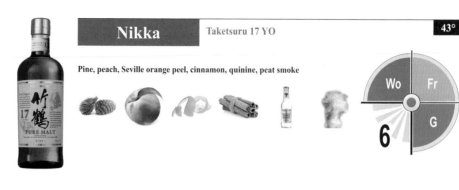

6 — Wo | Fr | G

Nikka — Taketsuru 21 YO — 43°

Magnolia, prune, pineapple, cigar box, coconut, turmeric

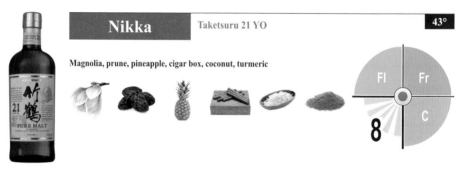

8 — Fl | Fr | C

Nikka — Pure Malt Red — 43°

Tangerine, herb, quince, walnut, malted barley, chocolate

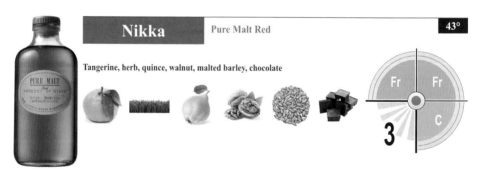

3 — Fr | Fr | C

Nikka — Pure Malt Black — 43°

Orange blossom honey, pepper, plum, peat smoke, liquorice, chocolate

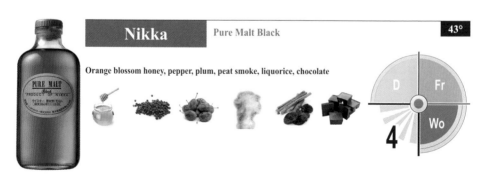

4 — D | Fr | Wo

Nikka — Pure Malt White — 43°

Camphor, pear, pine honey, peated malt, sea spray, walnut

Sm / D / Ma — 3

Nikka — Blended — 40°

Pear, almond, orange blossom honey, malted barley, grape, coconut

Fr / D / Fr — 1

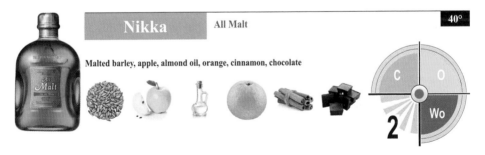

Nikka — All Malt — 40°

Malted barley, apple, almond oil, orange, cinnamon, chocolate

C / O / Wo — 2

Nikka — Black Nikka 8 YO — 40°

Malted barley, orange, manuka honey, cardamom, pine, lemon

C / D / Wo — 2

Nikka — From the Barrel   51.4°

Sesame oil, clove, peach, vanilla, oak, spices

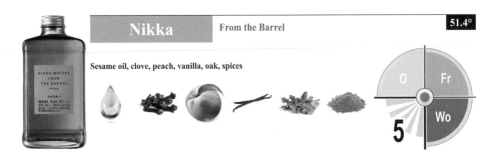

O   Fr   Wo   **5**

Nikka — 40 YO   43°

Panelling, mango, bergamot, chocolate, roasted sesame, camphor

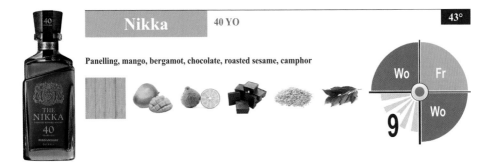

Wo   Fr   Wo   **9**

Nikka — Coffey Malt   45°

Panetone, vanilla, cinnamon, orange, pear, caramel

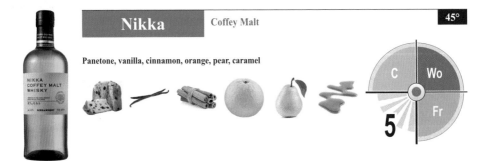

C   Wo   Fr   **5**

Nikka — Coffey Grain   45°

White oak, pear, orange blossom honey, corn, coconut, grapefruit

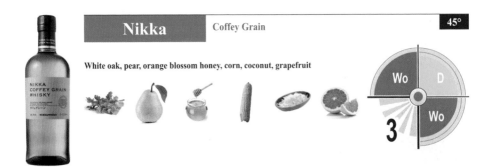

Wo   D   Wo   **3**

White Oak
ホワイトオーク蒸留所
Distillery

Founded in 1919 beside the Seto Inland Sea.
The oldest whisky distillery in Japan.

2 Stills: 1 wash, 1 spirit – 0.06 million LPA

Nishijma 919, Okubo-machi, Akashi-shi, Hyogo-ken, 674-0065
+81 789 46 1001
www.ei-sake.jp
Owner: Eigashima Shuzo

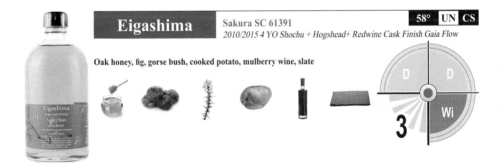

Eigashima | Sakura SC 61391 | 58° UN CS
2010/2015 4 YO Shochu + Hogshead+ Redwine Cask Finish Gaia Flow

Oak honey, fig, gorse bush, cooked potato, mulberry wine, slate

3

White Oak | Akashi | 46° UN

Peach, malted barley, rooibos, pale cream sherry, oak honey, peat

2

Yamazaki 山崎蒸溜所
Distillery

Founded in 1923 by Shinjirō Torii.
The first distillery in Japan to produce single malt.

---

12 Stills: 6 wash, 6 spirit – 6 million LPA

Yamazaki 5-2-1, Shimamoto-cho, Mishima-gun, 618-0001
+81 759 62 1423
www.suntory.com
Owner: Beam Suntory Inc.

Yamazaki   Distiller's Reserve   43°

Strawberry, vanilla cream, sandalwood, cinnamon, lemon blossom honey, redcurrant

Fr | Wo | D — 4

Yamazaki   12 YO   43°
American, Spanish & Mizunara Oaks

Peach, peat moss, red apple, peated malt, cinnamon, plum

Fr | Fr | Wo — 4

Yamazaki — 18 YO
Sherry, Bourbon & Mizunara Casks

43°

Fig wine, ganache, date, sandalwood, mochaccino, pipe tobacco

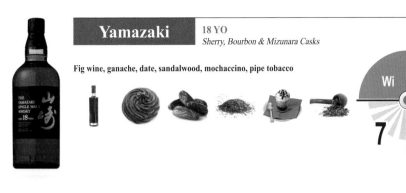

Wi | Fr
Wo

7

Yamazaki — Sherry Cask

48° UN

Umeshu, sandalwood, oloroso, blackcurrant jam, balsamic vinegar, quince jelly

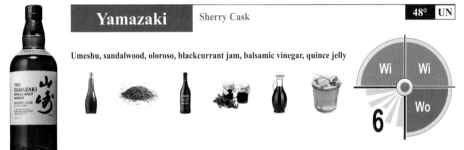

Wi | Wi
Wo

6

Yamazaki — Puncheon

48° UN

Pear, vanilla, malted barley, plum, gooseberry, ginger

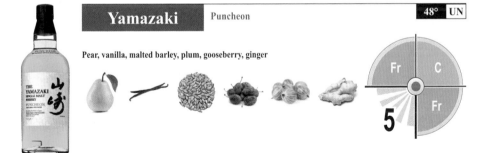

Fr | C
Fr

5

Yamazaki — Mizunara

48° UN

Cardamom, aloe vera, sandalwood, persimmon, tamarind, incense

Wo | Wo
Fr

7

Yoichi 余市蒸留所
Distillery

Founded in 1934 by Masataka Taketsuru.

***

Direct coal-fired stills
6 Stills: 3 wash, 3 spirit – 2 million LPA

Kurokawa-cho 7-6, Yoichi-gun, Shiribeshi, Hokkaidō 046-0003
+81 135 23 3131
www.nikka.com
Owner: Nikka Whisky Distilling Co. (Asahi Breweries Ltd)

Yoichi	NAS	43°

Tayberry, marzipan, walnut liqueur, peat moss, oak, beach fire

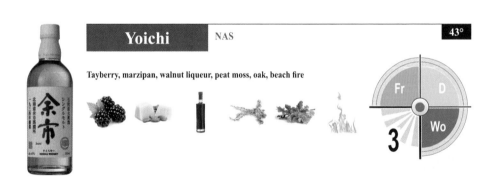

Yoichi	10 YO	45°

Apricot, burnt stick, peated malt, iris, ginger, lavender

Yoichi — 12 YO — 45°

Calamus, apricot, burnt stick, red apple, cinnamon, black tea

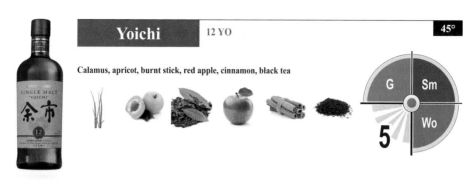

G | Sm
Wo

5

Yoichi — 15 YO — 45°

White peach, walnut wine, peat oil, star anise, mochaccino, tobacco

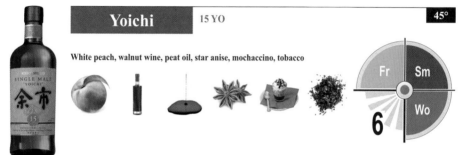

Fr | Sm
Wo

6

Yoichi — 20 YO — 52° UN

Encaustic, candied citrus, peat smoke, quince, leather upholstery, cigar box

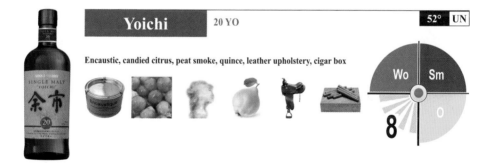

Wo | Sm
O

8

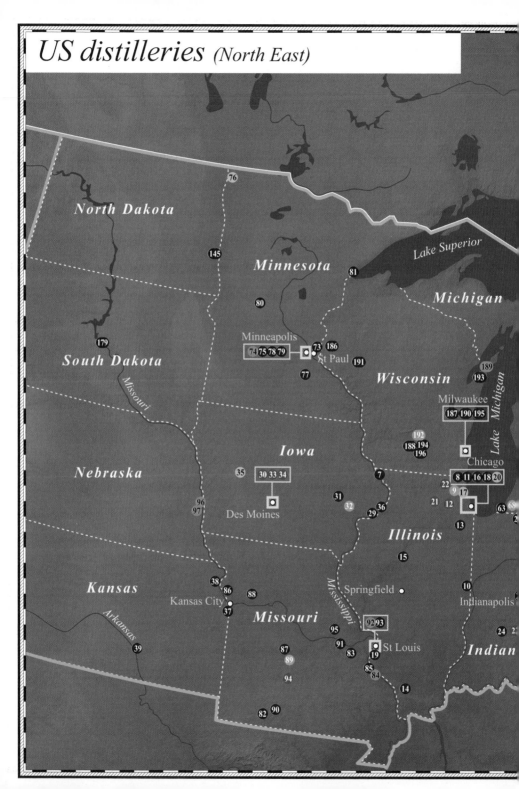

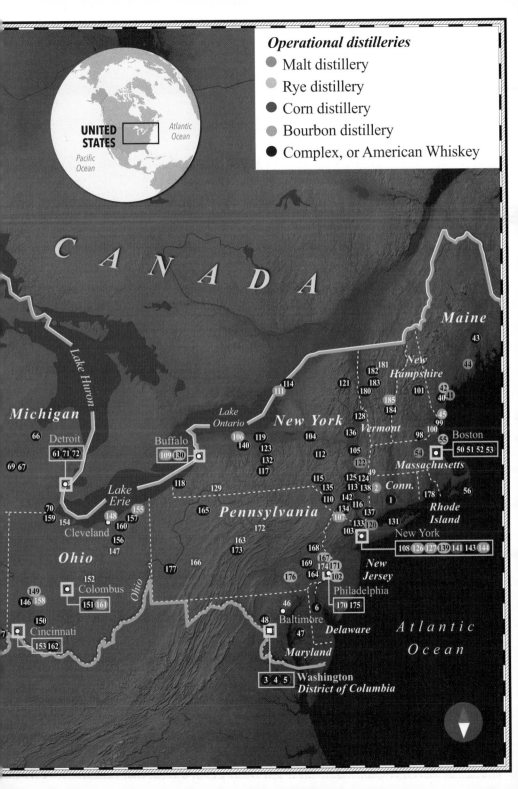

US distilleries (South East)

Oklahoma

Arkansas

3

5

2

□ 67 68
Oklahoma City

Arkansas

4

109

117

106 105
Dallas 107

110

Texas

101
Brazos

Louisiana

M

Mississippi

108 115

102

114

112 113 □

111 104

103

116 118 Houston

53

Baton Rouge ●

New Orleans

San Antonio

MEXICO

Gulf of Mexico

Operational distilleries

● Malt distillery   ● Tennessee Whiskey distillery

● Rye distillery   ● Bourbon distillery

● Corn distillery   ● Complex, or American Whiskey

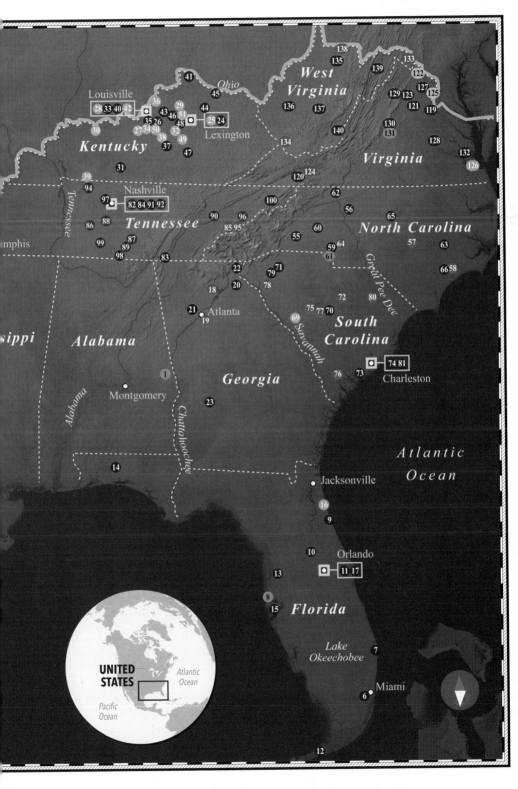

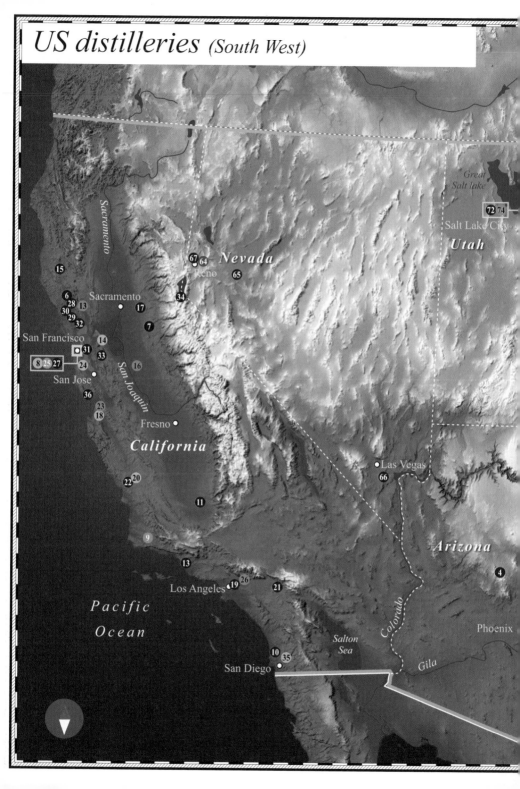

US distilleries (South West)

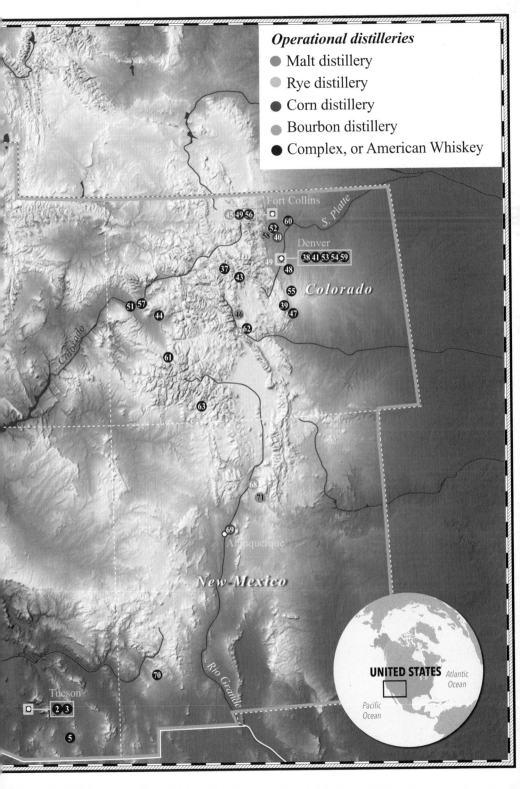

Operational distilleries

- Malt distillery
- Rye distillery
- Corn distillery
- Bourbon distillery
- Complex, or American Whiskey

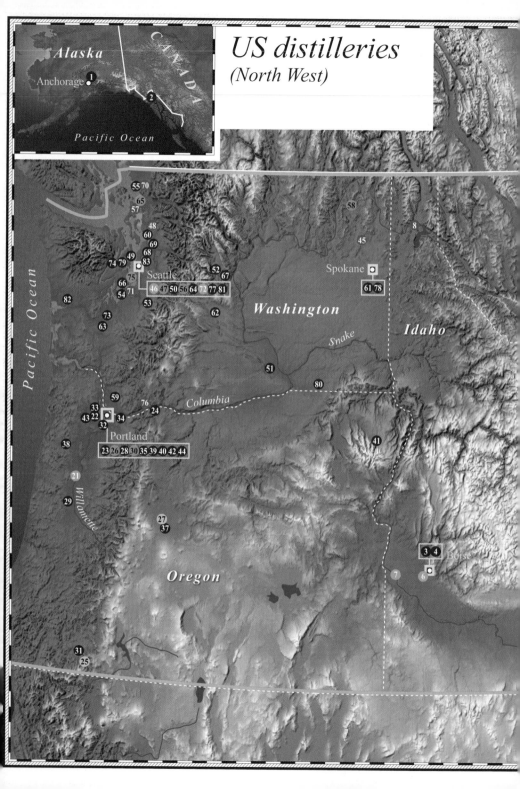

US distilleries
(North West)

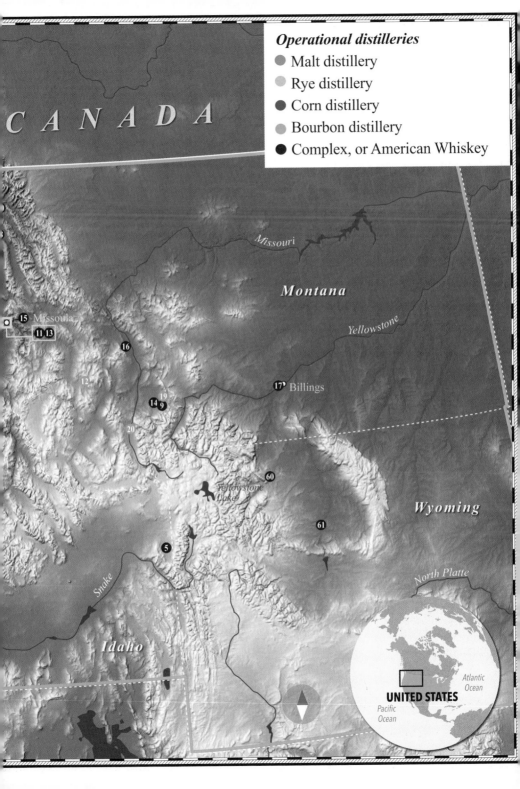

Operational distilleries
- Malt distillery
- Rye distillery
- Corn distillery
- Bourbon distillery
- Complex, or American Whiskey

The names in italics relate to proposed distilleries or those under construction.

NORTH EAST

US DISTILLERIES	STATE		US DISTILLERIES	STATE	
Elm City	Connecticut	1	Sweetgrass Farm	Maine	44
Litchfield	Connecticut	2	Wiggly Bridge	Maine	45
Filibuster	DC	3	Louthan	Maryland	46
Georgetown	DC	4	Lyon	Maryland	47
One Eight	DC	5	Twin Valley Distillers	Maryland	48
Painted Stave Distilling	Delaware	6	Berkshire Mountain	Massachussets	49
Blaum Bros. Distilling	Illinois	7	Boston Harbor	Massachussets	50
Chicago Distilling	Illinois	8	Bully Boy Distillers	Massachussets	51
Copper Fiddle Distillery	Illinois	9	Damnation Alley	Massachussets	52
Copper Ridge	Illinois	10	GrandTen	Massachussets	53
FEW Spirits	Illinois	11	Nashoba	Massachussets	54
Fox River Distilling	Illinois	12	Ryan & Wood	Massachussets	55
Frankfort Spirits	Illinois	13	Triple Eight	Massachussets	56
Grand River Spirits	Illinois	14	Artesian Distillers	Michigan	57
JK Williams Distilling	Illinois	15	Big Cedar Distilling.	Michigan	58
Koval Distillery	Illinois	16	Civilized Spirits	Michigan	59
Oppidan	Illinois	17	Coppercraft Distillery	Michigan	60
Quincy Street Distillery	Illinois	18	Detroit City Distillery	Michigan	61
Stumpy's Spirits	Illinois	19	Grand Traverse Distillery	Michigan	62
Three Rangers	Illinois	20	Journeyman	Michigan	63
Whiskey Acres	Illinois	21	Long Road Distillers	Michigan	64
Wondertucky	Illinois	22	New Holland Brewing	Michigan	65
Bear Wallow Distillery	Indiana	23	Old Town Distillery	Michigan	66
Cardinal Spirits	Indiana	24	Red Cedar Spirits	Michigan	67
Hotel Tango Artisan Distillery	Indiana	25	Round Barn	Michigan	68
Indiana Whiskey	Indiana	26	Sanctuary Spirits	Michigan	69
MGPI of Indiana	Indiana	27	Temperance Distilling	Michigan	70
Starlight Distillery	Indiana	28	Two James Spirits	Michigan	71
Artisan Grain	Iowa	29	Valentine Distilling.	Michigan	72
Broadbent Distillery	Iowa	30	11 Wells	Minnesota	73
Cedar Ridge	Iowa	31	Bent Brewstillery	Minnesota	74
Copper Moon Distillery	Iowa	32	Du Nord Craft Spirits	Minnesota	75
Dehner	Iowa	33	Far North Spirits	Minnesota	76
Iowa Distilling Company	Iowa	34	Loon Liquors	Minnesota	77
Iowa Legendary Rye	Iowa	35	Millers and Saints	Minnesota	78
Mississippi River Distilling	Iowa	36	Norseman Distillery	Minnesota	79
Dark Horse Distillery	Kansas	37	Panther Distillery	Minnesota	80
High Plains	Kansas	38	Vikre Distillery	Minnesota	81
Wheat State	Kansas	39	Copper Run Distillery	Missouri	82
Liquid Riot	Maine	40	Coulter & Payne	Missouri	83
Maine Craft	Maine	41	Crown Valley	Missouri	84
New England	Maine	42	*Defiant Spirits*	Missouri	85
Penobscot Bay	Maine	43	McCormick Distilling	Missouri	86

Mid-Best	Missouri	87	Orange County	New York	134
Of the Earth	Missouri	88	Prohibition Distillery	New York	135
Ozark	Missouri	89	Saratoga	New York	136
Ozark Hills Moonshine	Missouri	90	Still the One	New York	137
Pinckney Bend Distillery	Missouri	91	Taconic	New York	138
Square One	Missouri	92	The New York Distilling	New York	139
Still 630 Distillery	Missouri	93	The O'Begley Distillery	New York	140
T's Redneck	Missouri	94	Tirado	New York	141
Wood Hat Spirits	Missouri	95	Tuthilltown	New York	142
Brickway	Nebraska	96	Van Brunt	New York	143
Cut Spike	Nebraska	97	Widow Jane /		
Djinn Spirits	New Hampshire	98	Cacao Prieto Distillery	New York	144
Sea Hagg Distillery	New Hampshire	99	Proof	North Dakota	145
Smoky Quartz Distillery	New Hampshire	100	Belle of Dayton Distillery	Ohio	146
Tamworth	New Hampshire	101	Canal Spirits	Ohio	147
Cooper River	New Jersey	102	Cleveland Whiskey	Ohio	148
Jersey Artisan	New Jersey	103	Indian Creek Distillery	Ohio	149
Adirondack Distilling	New York	104	John McCulloch	Ohio	150
Albany	New York	105	Middle West Spirits	Ohio	151
Black Button	New York	106	Mill Street	Ohio	152
Black Dirt Distillery	New York	107	Northside	Ohio	153
Breuckelen	New York	108	Oak N' Harbor	Ohio	154
Buffalo Distillery	New York	109	Red Eagle Distillery	Ohio	155
Catskill	New York	110	Renaissance Artisan	Ohio	156
Clayton	New York	111	Seven Brothers	Ohio	157
Cooperstown Distillery	New York	112	Stillwrights Distillery	Ohio	158
Coppersea Distillery	New York	113	Toledo Spirits	Ohio	159
Dark Island	New York	114	Tom's Foolery	Ohio	160
Delaware Phoenix	New York	115	Watershed Distillery	Ohio	161
Denning's Point Distillery	New York	116	Woodstone Creek	Ohio	162
Finger Lakes	New York	117	Big Spring Spirits	Pennsylvania	163
Five & 20	New York	118	Bluebird	Pennsylvania	164
Glenrose Spirits	New York	119	CJ Spirits	Pennsylvania	165
Good Shepherd	New York	120	Disobedient Spirits	Pennsylvania	166
Gristmill	New York	121	Hewn	Pennsylvania	167
Harvest Spirits	New York	122	Lehigh Valley Social Still	Pennsylvania	168
Hidden Marsh	New York	123	Manatawny Still Works	Pennsylvania	169
Hillrock Estate Distillery	New York	124	Millstone Spirits Group	Pennsylvania	170
Hudson Valley Distillers	New York	125	Mountain Laurel / Dad's Hat	Pennsylvania	171
JW Overbey	New York	126	Mountain Top	Pennsylvania	172
Kings County	New York	127	Nittany Mountain	Pennsylvania	173
Lake George Distilling	New York	128	Philadelphia	Pennsylvania	174
Little Chicago	New York	129	Rowhouse Spirits	Pennsylvania	175
Lockhouse	New York	130	Thistle Finch	Pennsylvania	176
Long Island	New York	131	Wigle	Pennsylvania	177
Myer Farm	New York	132	Sons of Liberty Spirits	Rhode Island	178
Nahmias et Fils	New York	133	Dakota Spirits	South Dakota	179

Appalachian Gap Distillery	Vermont	180	Door County Distillery	Wisconsin	189
Caledonia Spirits	Vermont	181	Great Lakes Distillery	Wisconsin	190
Green Mountain	Vermont	182	Infinity Beverages	Wisconsin	191
Mad River	Vermont	183	*J. Henry & Sons*	Wisconsin	192
SILO	Vermont	184	Lo Artisan /		
Vermont Spirits	Vermont	185	Hmong Rice Spirits	Wisconsin	193
45th Parallel	Wisconsin	186	Old Sugar Distillery	Wisconsin	194
Central Standard	Wisconsin	187	Sammleton / Shypoke	Wisconsin	195
Death's Door Spirits	Wisconsin	188	Yahara Bay Distillers	Wisconsin	196

SOUTH EAST

US DISTILLERIES	STATE		US DISTILLERIES	STATE	
John Emerald Distilling	Alabama	1	Kentucky Artisan	Kentucky	36
Arkansas Moonshine	Arkansas	2	Limestone Branch Distillery	Kentucky	37
Core / Harvest Spirits	Arkansas	3	Maker's Mark Distillery	Kentucky	38
Rock Town Distillery	Arkansas	4	MB Roland Distillery	Kentucky	39
White River Distillery	Arkansas	5	Michters Distillery	Kentucky	40
Alchemist	Florida	6	New Riff Distilling	Kentucky	41
Citrus Distillers	Florida	7	Stitzel-Weller Distillery	Kentucky	42
Cotherman Distilling	Florida	8	*The Bulleit Distilling*	Kentucky	43
Flagler Spirits	Florida	9	The Gentleman Distillery	Kentucky	44
Florida Farm Distillers	Florida	10	The Old Pogue Distillery	Kentucky	45
JLA Distillery	Florida	11	Three Boys Farm Distillery	Kentucky	46
Key West Distilling	Florida	12	Wadelyn Ranch	Kentucky	47
NJoy Spirits	Florida	13	Wild Turkey Distillery	Kentucky	48
Peaden Brothers Distillery	Florida	14	Wilderness Trail Distillery	Kentucky	49
St. Petersburg	Florida	15	Willett Distillery	Kentucky	50
St. Augustine	Florida	16	Woodford Reserve Distillery	Kentucky	51
Winter Park	Florida	17	Atelier Vie	Louisiana	52
Dawsonville Moonshine	Georgia	18	Louisiana Lightning	Louisiana	53
Independent Distilling	Georgia	19	Cathead Distillery	Mississippi	54
Ivy Mountain Distillery	Georgia	20	Blue Ridge Distilling	North Carolina	55
Lazy Guy	Georgia	21	Broad Branch	North Carolina	56
Moonrise	Georgia	22	Broadslab Distillery	North Carolina	57
Thirteenth Colony	Georgia	23	Diablo	North Carolina	58
Alltech Lexington	Kentucky	24	Doc Porter's Distillery	North Carolina	59
Barrel House	Kentucky	25	Foothills Distillery	North Carolina	60
Barton 1792 Distillery	Kentucky	26	Great Wagon Road	North Carolina	61
Boundary Oak	Kentucky	27	Mayberry Spirits	North Carolina	62
Brown Forman	Kentucky	28	Mother Earth	North Carolina	63
Buffalo Trace Distillery	Kentucky	29	Southern Grace	North Carolina	64
Charles Medley Distillery-KY	Kentucky	30	TOPO Distillery	North Carolina	65
Corsair Bowling Green	Kentucky	31	Walton's	North Carolina	66
Four Roses Distillery	Kentucky	32	Scissortail Distillery	Oklahoma	67
Heaven Hill Bernheim Distillery	Kentucky	33	Twister	Oklahoma	68
Jim Beam Boston	Kentucky	34	Carolina Moon	South Carolina	69
Jim Beam Clermont	Kentucky	35	Crouch	South Carolina	70

Dark Corner	South Carolina	71	Garrison Brothers	Texas	108
Dark Water	South Carolina	72	Ironroot Republic Distilling	Texas	109
Firefly Distillery	South Carolina	73	Kiepersol Estates	Texas	110
High Wire Distilling	South Carolina	74	Loblolly Spirits	Texas	111
Hollow Creek	South Carolina	75	Ranger Creek	Texas	112
Lucky Duck	South Carolina	76	Rebecca Creek Distillery	Texas	113
Moonlight / Yesternight	South Carolina	77	Rio Brazos Distillery	Texas	114
Palmetto Moonshine	South Carolina	78	Swift	Texas	115
Six and Twenty	South Carolina	79	Whitmeyer's Distilling	Texas	116
Straw Hat	South Carolina	80	Witherspoon Distillery	Texas	117
Striped Pig Distillery	South Carolina	81	Yellow Rose Distilling	Texas	118
Beechtree	Tennessee	82	A. Smith Bowman Distillery	Virginia	119
Chattanooga	Tennessee	83	Appalachian Mountain Spirits /		
Corsair Nashville	Tennessee	84	Sweetwater Distillery	Virginia	120
Doc Collier Moonshine	Tennessee	85	Belmont Farm	Virginia	121
Duck River	Tennessee	86	Catoctin Creek		
George A. Dickel & Co.	Tennessee	87	Distilling Company	Virginia	122
H. Clark Distillery	Tennessee	88	Copper Fox Distillery	Virginia	123
Jack Daniel's Distillery	Tennessee	89	Davis Valley	Virginia	124
Knox	Tennessee	90	George Washington's		
Nashville Craft Distillery	Tennessee	91	Mount Vernon	Virginia	125
Nelson's Green Brier Distillery	Tennessee	92	Ironclad	Virginia	126
Old Dominick	Tennessee	93	MurLarkey	Virginia	127
Old Glory	Tennessee	94	Reservoir	Virginia	128
Ole Smoky Distillery	Tennessee	95	River Hill	Virginia	129
Popcorn Sutton Distilling	Tennessee	96	Silverback Distillery	Virginia	130
Prichard's Distillery at Fontanel	Tennessee	97	Virginia Distillery	Virginia	131
Prichard's Distillery at Kelso	Tennessee	98	Williamsburg Distillery	Virginia	132
Tenn South Distillery	Tennessee	99	Black Draft	West Virginia	133
Tennesseee Hills	Tennessee	100	Hatfield & McCoy Moonshine	West Virginia	134
Balcones Distilling	Texas	101	Heston Farm/ Pinchgut Hollow	West Virginia	135
Banner Distilling	Texas	102	HipsLipsFingerTips	West Virginia	136
Big Thicket Distilling	Texas	103	Isaiah Morgan	West Virginia	137
Bone Spirits	Texas	104	Mountain Moonshine /		
Dallas Distilleries	Texas	105	West Virginia Distilling	West Virginia	138
Firestone & Robertson Distilling	Texas	106	Rada Appalachian Spirits	West Virginia	139
Five Points	Texas	107	Smooth Ambler Spirits	West Virginia	140

NORTH WEST

US DISTILLERIES	STATE		US DISTILLERIES	STATE	
Alaska Distillery	Alaska	1	Mill Town	Idaho	8
Port Chilkoot	Alaska	2	Bozeman Spirits	Montana	9
8 Feathers	Idaho	3	Glacier Distilling	Montana	10
Bardenay	Idaho	4	Headframe Spirits	Montana	11
Grand Teton	Idaho	5	Montgomery	Montana	12
Idaho Bourbon	Idaho	6	Rattlesnake Creek	Montana	13
Koenig	Idaho	7	RoughStock	Montana	14

Steel Toe	Montana	15	Batch Distillery	Washington	50
Stonehouse	Montana	16	Black Heron Spirits	Washington	51
Trailhead Spirits	Montana	17	Blue Spirits	Washington	52
Whistling Andy	Montana	18	Carbon Glacier	Washington	53
Wildrye Distilling	Montana	19	Chambers Bay	Washington	54
Willie's	Montana	20	Chuckanut Bay Distillery	Washington	55
4 Spirits	Oregon	21	Copperworks Distilling	Washington	56
Big Bottom	Oregon	22	Deception Distilling	Washington	57
Bull Run	Oregon	23	Dominion	Washington	58
Camp 1805	Oregon	24	Double V Distillery	Washington	59
Cascade Peak Spirits	Oregon	25	Dry County Distillery	Washington	60
Clear Creek	Oregon	26	Dry Fly Distilling	Washington	61
Crater Lake Spirits / Bendistillery	Oregon	27	Ellensburg	Washington	62
Eastside	Oregon	28	Ezra Cox	Washington	63
Hard Times	Oregon	29	Fremont Mischief	Washington	64
House Spirits	Oregon	30	Golden	Washington	65
Immortal Spirits	Oregon	31	Heritage	Washington	66
Indio Spirits	Oregon	32	It's 5 Artisan Distillery	Washington	67
McMenamins Cornelius Pass Roadhouse	Oregon	33	J.P. Trodden	Washington	68
McMenamins Edgefield	Oregon	34	Mac Donald	Washington	69
New Deal	Oregon	35	Mount Baker Distillery	Washington	70
North Coast Distilling	Oregon	36	Old Soldier	Washington	71
Oregon Spirit	Oregon	37	OOLA Distillery	Washington	72
Ransom	Oregon	38	Sandstone	Washington	73
Rogue	Oregon	39	Seabeck Spirits	Washington	74
Rolling River Spirits	Oregon	40	Seattle Distilling	Washington	75
Stein	Oregon	41	Skunk Brothers Spirits	Washington	76
Stone Barn Brandyworks	Oregon	42	Tatoosh	Washington	77
Tualatin Valley	Oregon	43	Tinbender	Washington	78
Vinn	Oregon	44	Tucker Distillery	Washington	79
2 Loons Distillery	Washington	45	Walla Walla	Washington	80
2bar Spirits	Washington	46	Westland	Washington	81
3 Howls	Washington	47	Wishkah River	Washington	82
Bad Dog	Washington	48	Woodinville Whiskey	Washington	83
Bainbridge	Washington	49	Single Track Spirits	Wyoming	84
			Wyoming Whiskey	Wyoming	85

SOUTH WEST

US DISTILLERIES	STATE		US DISTILLERIES	STATE	
Arizona Distilling	Arizona	1	Anchor	California	8
Hamilton	Arizona	2	Ascendant Spirits	California	9
The Independent Distillery	Arizona	3	Ballast Point	California	10
Thumb Butte Distillery	Arizona	4	Bowen's	California	11
Tombstone	Arizona	5	Channel Islands	California	12
Alley 6	California	6	Charbay	California	13
Amador	California	7	Corbin	California	14

Craft Distillers	California	15
Do Good	California	16
Dry Diggings	California	17
Fog's End	California	18
Greenbar	California	19
Highspire	California	20
J. Riley	California	21
Krobār	California	22
Lost Spirits	California	23
Old World Spirits	California	24
Raff Distillerie	California	25
Saint James Spirits	California	26
Seven Stills	California	27
Sonoma Brothers	California	28
Sonoma County Distilling	California	29
Spirit Works Distillery	California	30
St. George Spirits	California	31
Stillwater Spirits	California	32
Sutherland Distilling	California	33
Tahoe Moonshine	California	34
Twisted Manzanita	California	35
Venus Spirits	California	36
10th Mountain	Colorado	37
Bear Creek	Colorado	38
Black Bear	Colorado	39
Black Canyon	Colorado	40
Blank and Booth Distilling	Colorado	41
Boathouse	Colorado	42
Breckenridge Distillery	Colorado	43
Colorado Gold	Colorado	44
CopperMuse	Colorado	45

Deerhammer Distilling	Colorado	46
Distillery 291 Colorado Whiskey	Colorado	47
Downslope Distilling	Colorado	48
Feisty Spirits	Colorado	49
Golden Moon	Colorado	50
JF Strothman Distillery	Colorado	51
KJ Wood Distillers	Colorado	52
Laws Whiskey House	Colorado	53
Leopold Bros.	Colorado	54
Mystic Mountain Distillery	Colorado	55
Old Town	Colorado	56
Peach Street Distillers	Colorado	57
Spirit Hound Distillers	Colorado	58
Stranahan's Colorado Whiskey	Colorado	59
Syntax Spirits	Colorado	60
Trail Town Still	Colorado	61
Wood's High Mountain Distillery	Colorado	62
Woodshed	Colorado	63
7 Troughs	Nevada	64
Frey Ranch	Nevada	65
Las Vegas Distillery	Nevada	66
The Depot Reno	Nevada	67
Don Quixote Distillery	New Mexico	68
Left Turn Distilling	New Mexico	69
Little Toad Creek Brewery & Distillery	New Mexico	70
Santa Fe Spirits	New Mexico	71
High West Distillery	Utah	72
Outlaw	Utah	73
Sugar House Distillery	Utah	74

Angel's Envy

**Founded in 2006 by Wes Henderson with the help of his father,
Lincoln Henderson, former master distiller at Brown Forman.
First bottling in 2010.
Bought by Bacardi in 2015.
A distillery is under construction at Louisville, KY.**

www.angelsenvy.com
Owner: Bacardi

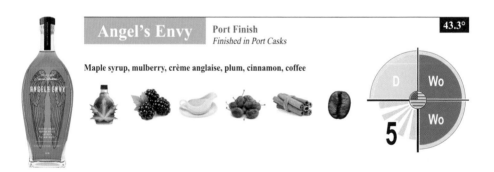

Angel's Envy — Port Finish — *Finished in Port Casks* — 43.3°

Maple syrup, mulberry, crème anglaise, plum, cinnamon, coffee

D | Wo
Wo
5

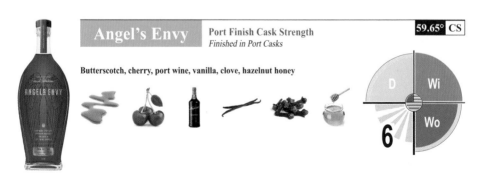

Angel's Envy — Port Finish Cask Strength — *Finished in Port Casks* — 59.65° CS

Butterscotch, cherry, port wine, vanilla, clove, hazelnut honey

D | Wi
Wo
6

Bulleit

**Brand created in 1987 by Thomas E. Bulleit Jr,
whose great-great-grandfather, Augustus Bulleit,
used to produce bourbon in the mid-19th century.**

Its recipe contains a high percentage of rye

Visitor centre at the former Stitzel-Weller Distillery, which was closed in 1991
3860 Fitzgerald Rd, Louisville, KY 40216
+1 502 810 3800
www.bulleit.com
Owner: Diageo

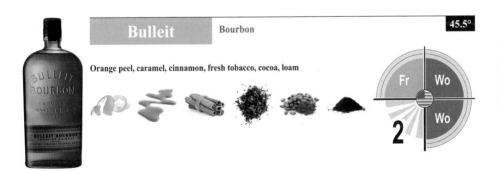

Bulleit — Bourbon — 45.5°
Orange peel, caramel, cinnamon, fresh tobacco, cocoa, loam

Bulleit — Rye — 45°
Cherry jam, nutmeg, gingerbread, rye, cocoa, allspice

Four Roses
Distillery

Brand registered in 1888 by Paul Jones Jr but in existence since the 1860s.
Distillery founded in 1910.
Top-selling bourbon brand after the end of Prohibition in the 1950s.
Acquired by the Japanese group Kirin in 2002.

1224 Bonds Mill Rd, Lawrenceburg, KY 40342
+1 502 839 3426
www.fourrosesbourbon.com
Owner: Kirin

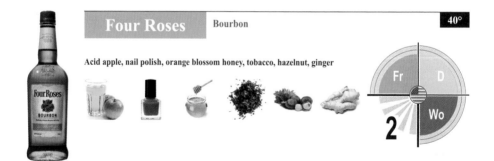

Four Roses Bourbon 40°

Acid apple, nail polish, orange blossom honey, tobacco, hazelnut, ginger

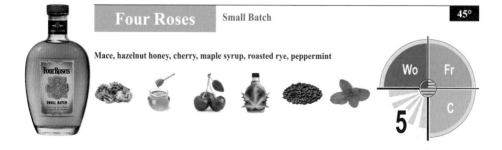

Four Roses Small Batch 45°

Mace, hazelnut honey, cherry, maple syrup, roasted rye, peppermint

George Dickel
Distillery

Founded in the 1870s by George Dickel.
Closed in 1910 after the introduction of Prohibition in Tennessee.
Rebuilt a mile away from the original site in 1958 by Ralph Dupps.

1950 Cascade Hollow Rd, Tullahoma, TN 37388
+1 931 857 4110
www.georgedickel.com
Owner: Diageo

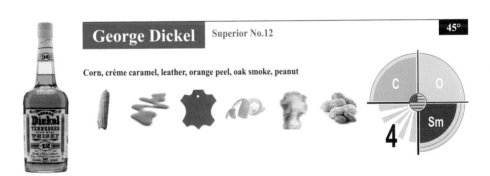

George Dickel Superior No.12 — 45°

Corn, crème caramel, leather, orange peel, oak smoke, peanut

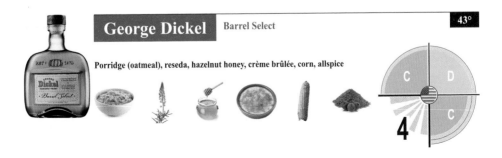

George Dickel Barrel Select — 43°

Porridge (oatmeal), reseda, hazelnut honey, crème brûlée, corn, allspice

Heaven Hill
Distillery

Founded in 1934 and now owned by the Shapira family.
All the master distillers are members of the Beam family.
Production has been provided by the Bernheim distillery since 1999.

Has more than a million casks and has filled more than
seven million since its creation

1311 Gilkey Run Rd, Bardstown, KY 40004
+1 502 337 1000
www.heavenhill.com
Owner: Heaven Hill

Evan Williams   Black Label 100 Proof   **50°**

Crème anglaise, cedar, beeswax, banana, hazelnut, peppermint

3

Evan Williams   Single Barrel Vintage 86 Proof   **43°**

Milk chocolate, ginger, orange blossom honey, charred oak, propolis, cinnamon

5

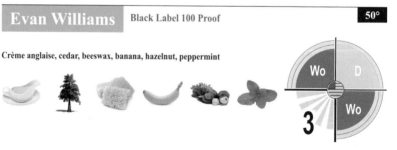

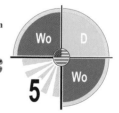

Evan Williams 1783 Small Batch

43°

Marzipan, corn, oak honey, orange peel, crème brûlée, apple

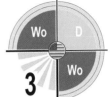

3

Henry McKenna 10 YO Single Barrel

50°

Peppermint, clove, butterscotch, orange peel, vanilla cream, malted barley

5

Rittenhouse 100 Proof

50°

Rye, plum, sesame oil, Seville orange, cinnamon, wintergreen

5

Bernheim Original 7 YO Small Batch

45°

Pine honey, reseda, white pepper, orange marmalade, ginger, Danish pastry

4

Elijah Craig   12 YO Small Batch   47°

Almond, encaustic, nutmeg, shoe polish, orange, cinnamon

5

Elijah Craig   Barrel Proof Small Batch   68.5° CS

Mulberry, coconut, honeysuckle, mango, eucalyptus oil, peach

9

Larceny   92 Proof   46°

Bread crust, butterscotch, kernel, molasses/treacle, allspice, vanilla

3

Old Fitzgerald   Prime   43°

Lemon blossom honey, almond, tobacco, green apple, incense, vanilla

2

Jack Daniel's
Distillery

Distillery founded in 1866 by Jasper Newton 'Jack' Daniel.
The oldest legally registered distillery in the US that is still operational.
The brand has used its famous square bottle since 1895.

The bestselling brand of North American whiskey,
with more than 100 million litres (26.4 million gallons) sold per year

182 Lynchburg Highway, Lynchburg, TN 37352
+1 931 759 6357
www.jackdaniels.com
Owner: Brown Forman Corp.

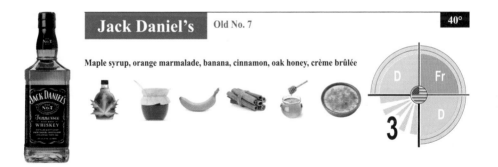

Jack Daniel's Old No. 7 — 40°

Maple syrup, orange marmalade, banana, cinnamon, oak honey, crème brûlée

Jack Daniel's Gentleman Jack — 40°

Butter, vanilla, apricot liqueur, liquorice, dark chocolate, lime tree honey

Jack Daniel's — Single Barrel Select — 45°

Cigar box, roasted corn, hazelnut honey, anise, clove, lemon peel

Wo · D · Wo · **5**

Jack Daniel's — White Rabbit Saloon — 43°

Mochaccino, banana, corn oil, ginger, black pepper, lemon peel

Wo · O · Wo · **4**

Jack Daniel's — Silver Select — 50°

Mandarine, muscovado, mace, pine resin, vanilla cream, cinnamon

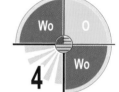

Fr · Wo · Wo · **6**

Jack Daniel's — Sinatra Select — 45°

Oak, crème brûlée, clove, banana, tarte tatin, vanilla

Wo · Wo · D · **4**

Jefferson's

Brand created in 1997 by Trey Zoeller and his father, Chet, a bourbon historian.
One of their ancestors was arrested in 1799 for 'the production and sale of spirit liquours'.
The name of the brand was chosen to pay tribute to the enquiring mind
of Thomas Jefferson, an immediately recognizable figure and name,
so budget marketing!

www.jeffersonsbourbon.com
Owner: Castle Brands

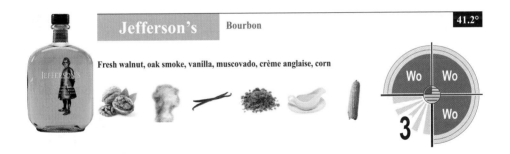

Jefferson's   Bourbon   41.2°

Fresh walnut, oak smoke, vanilla, muscovado, crème anglaise, corn

Jefferson's   Reserve   45.1°

Date, Sichuan pepper, salted butter caramel, leather, oak honey, ginger

Jim Beam
Distillery

**Brand created in 1935 by the successors of James Beauregard Beam.
The Beam family has owned its Kentucky distillery since 1795.**

The world's bestselling bourbon brand,
with more than 60 million litres (15.9 million gallons) sold per year

3350 Burks Spring Rd, Loretto, KY 40037
+1 502 543 9877
www.jimbeam.com
Owner: Beam Suntory Inc.

| Jim Beam | Original | 40° |

Reseda, caramel, corn, lemon peel, oak, resin

2

| Jim Beam | Devil's Cut | 45° |

Incense, roasted almond, manuka honey, pecan nut, vanilla, clove

3

Jim Beam — Black Extra Aged

43°

Caramel, vanilla, ginger, tobacco, roasted corn, black pepper

3

Jim Beam — Single Barrel

47.5°

Orange marmalade, reseda, white oak, corn oil, pecan nut, leather

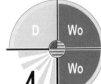

4

Jim Beam — Signature Craft 12 YO

43°

Benzoin, mango, crème anglaise, marzipan, orange blossom honey, hickory smoke

4

Knob Creek — Small Batch 9 YO 100 Proof

50°

White oak, maple syrup, hazelnut oil, liquorice cream, lingonberry, marzipan

4

Basil Hayden's

40°

Oolong tea, rye, orange blossom honey, nutmeg, leather, cinnamon

4

Baker's   7 YO 107 Proof

53.5°

Pine nut, Seville orange, toffee apple, oak smoke, coffee, leather

6

Booker's   6-8 YO 121-127 Proof

62°   **CS**

Banana, butterscotch, soursop, cedar, white pepper, liquorice

7

Old Grand-Dad   Traditional 86 Proof

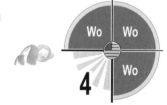

43°

White oak, rye, pecan nut, pepper, Cayenne pepper, orange peel

4

Maker's Mark
Distillery

The Burk distillery was founded in 1889.
Acquired by Bill Samuels Jr in 1953.
First marketed in 1958.

Rye is replaced by winter wheat in its recipe
One of the bestselling bourbon brands,
with more than 12 million litres (3.17 million gallons) sold per year

149 Happy Hollow Rd, Clermont, KY 40110
+1 220 865 2099
www.makersmark.com
Owner: Beam Suntory Inc.

Maker's Mark   Classic   `45°`

Wheat, fruit cake, shortbread, orange peel, walnut, butterscotch

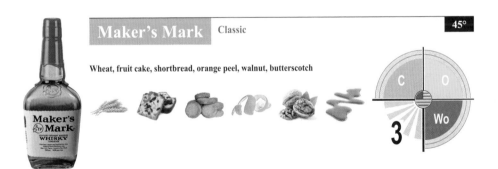

Maker's Mark   Cask Strength   `56.6°`

Coal, fruit cake, roasted almond, molasses/treacle, toffee, cinnamon

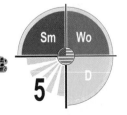

Michter's
Distillery

Founded in 1753 in Pennsylvania by John Schenk.
The brand was created in 1951 by Lou Forman.
The original distillery closed in 1989.
The brand was relaunched in the 1990s by Joseph J. Magliocco and
Richard Newman, around a unique expertise in ageing whiskey.
A new distillery has been in production since 2014 in Kentucky.

2351 New Millenium Drive, Shively, Louisville, KY 40216
+1 502 561 1001
www.michters.com
Owner: Michter's Distillery LLC

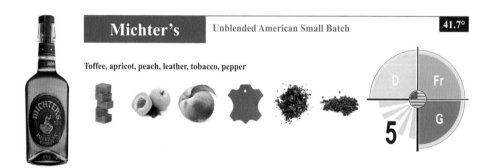

Michter's — Unblended American Small Batch — 41.7°

Toffee, apricot, peach, leather, tobacco, pepper

5

Michter's — Straight Rye Single Barrel — 42.4°

Black bread, wintergreen, black pepper, molasses/treacle, orange blossom honey, peony

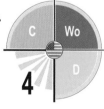

4

Michter's — Bourbon Small Batch

45.7°

Orange peel, crème brûlée, tarte tatin, fenugreek, white oak, muscovado

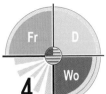

Fr | D
Wo
4

Michter's — Original Sour Mash

43°

Panetone, sandalwood, roasted almond, orange peel, allspice, cocoa

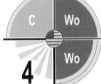

C | Wo
Wo
4

Michter's — 10 YO Bourbon

47.2°

Bitter chocolate, muscovado, mace, fenugreek, maple syrup, allspice

Wo | Wo
D
7

Michter's — 10 YO Rye

46.4°

Turmeric, roasted almond, spruce, leather, pine honey, black pepper

Wo | Wo
D
6

Old Forester

Founded in 1870 at Louisville by George Garvin Brown.
The first bourbon brand to be sold in bottles.
Production is currently carried out by the Brown Forman Distillery,
but a new distillery is due to open in the centre of Louisville in 2016
at 117 West Main St, in the building that the brand occupied from 1900 to 1919,
at the heart of Whiskey Row, the historical hub of the bourbon industry.

---

www.oldforester.com
Owner: Brown Forman

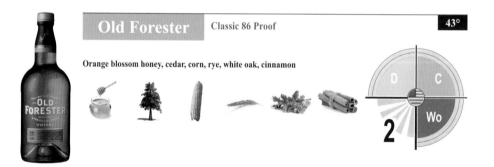

Old Forester — Classic 86 Proof — 43°

Orange blossom honey, cedar, corn, rye, white oak, cinnamon

2

Old Forester — Signature 100 Proof — 50°

Mochaccino, apple, toffee apple, roasted almond, vanilla cream, ginger

3

Old Potrero / Anchor
Distillery

Founded in 1993 in San Francisco by Fritz Maytag.
Anchor is also a brewery created in 1871 and acquired in 1965 by Maytag,
a true pioneer of American micro-breweries and micro-distilleries.
The distillery has two copper pot stills.

1705 Mariposa St, San Francisco CA 94107
+1 415 863 8350
www.anchordistilling.com
Owner: Anchor Distilling Co.

Old Potrero	Single Malt	45°

Black bread, ale, fenugreek, ginger, black pepper, buckwheat honey

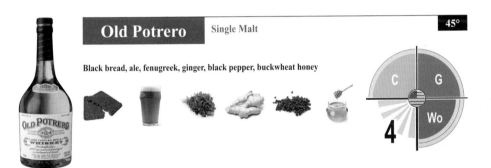

Old Potrero	18th Century Style	51.2°

Black bread, lemon meringue, cinnamon, peppermint, roasted rye, allspice

Sazerac
Distilleries

Founded in 1869 in New Orleans by Thomas H. Handy.
Sazerac was originally a cocktail based on Sazerac de Forges Cognac,
created around 1830, then a bar.
Today the group owns three distilleries:
Bartown in Bardstown, Kentucky;
Buffalo Trace in Frankfort, Kentucky;
A. Smith Bowman in Fredericksburg, Virginia.

www.sazerac.com
Owner: Sazerac Co.

Benchmark — Old No.8 — 40°

Orange blossom honey, vanilla, oak, plum, pepper, tobacco

2

Ancient Age — AAA 10 Star 90 Proof "Rye Recipe" — 45°

Cherry blossom honey, clove, rye, leather, toffee, oak smoke

3

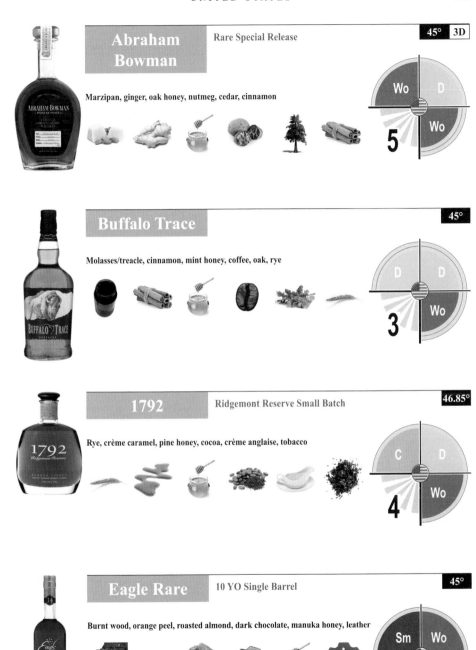

Abraham Bowman

Rare Special Release

45° 3D

Marzipan, ginger, oak honey, nutmeg, cedar, cinnamon

Wo | D
Wo

5

Buffalo Trace

45°

Molasses/treacle, cinnamon, mint honey, coffee, oak, rye

D | D
Wo

3

1792

Ridgemont Reserve Small Batch

46.85°

Rye, crème caramel, pine honey, cocoa, crème anglaise, tobacco

C | D
Wo

4

Eagle Rare

10 YO Single Barrel

45°

Burnt wood, orange peel, roasted almond, dark chocolate, manuka honey, leather

Sm | Wo
D

5

Eagle Rare — 17 YO — 45°

Cocoa, date, pine, roasted almond, vanilla, coconut

Wo | Wo
Wo

7

George T. Stagg — 15 YO — 68.5° CS

Thuja, fresh tobacco, mulberry, allspice, coffee ground, orange peel

Wo | Fr
Wo

8

Elmer T. Lee — Single Barrel — 45°

Apricot, leather, rye, caramel, vanilla cream, nutmeg

Fr | C
Wo

7

Blanton's — Original — 46.5°

Nail polish, orange blossom honey, muscovado, clove, ginger, banana

Fr | D
Wo

5

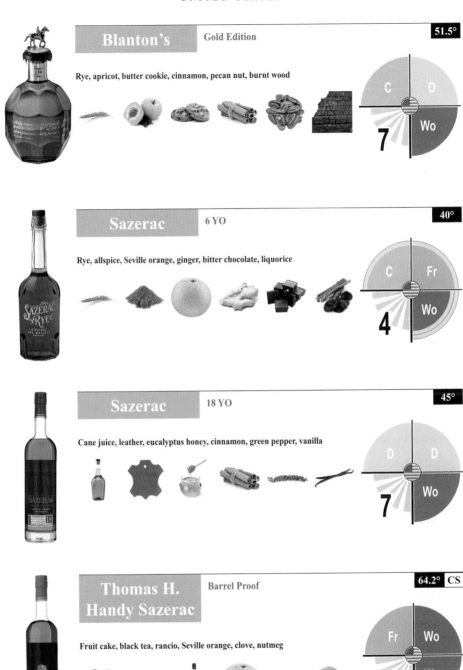

Blanton's Gold Edition   51.5°

Rye, apricot, butter cookie, cinnamon, pecan nut, burnt wood

C   O
Wo
7

Sazerac 6 YO   40°

Rye, allspice, Seville orange, ginger, bitter chocolate, liquorice

C   Fr
Wo
4

Sazerac 18 YO   45°

Cane juice, leather, eucalyptus honey, cinnamon, green pepper, vanilla

D   D
Wo
7

Thomas H. Handy Sazerac Barrel Proof   64.2° CS

Fruit cake, black tea, rancio, Seville orange, clove, nutmeg

Fr   Wo
Wo
8

William Larue Weller

Barrel Proof

Honeycomb, rancio, mochaccino, dried figs, orange blossom honey, white pepper

8

W. L. Weller

12 YO

45°

Sweet chestnut honey, reseda, praline, maple syrup, honeysuckle, cereal bar

6

Old Weller

Antique 107 Proof

53.5°

Butterscotch, reseda, cinnamon, almond honey, date, orange peel

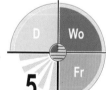

5

Hancock's Reserve

Single Barrel 88.9 Proof

44.45°

Clementine, vanilla, corn oil, mango, clove, cinnamon

4

Rock Hill Farms Single Barrel

50°

Cranberry, walnut, cocoa, butterscotch, anise honey, allspice

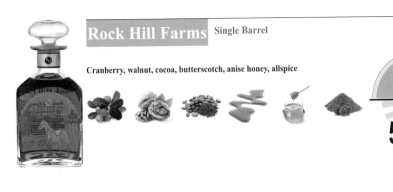

Fr | Wo

D

5

Old Charter 101 Proof

50.5°

Nail polish, raisin, corn, honeycomb, black pepper, almond

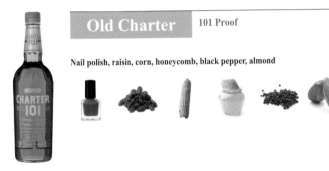

Fr | C

Wo

3

Stagg Jr.

67.2° CS

Chocolate, rye, oak honey, clove, cinnamon, burnt wood

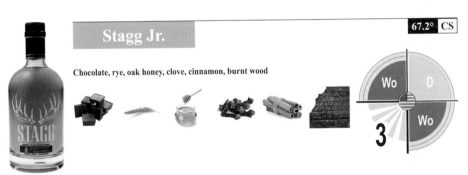

Wo | D

Wo

3

Colonel E.H. Taylor Small Batch Bourbon

50°

Cinnamon, corn, nutmeg, cereal bar, liquorice, tobacco

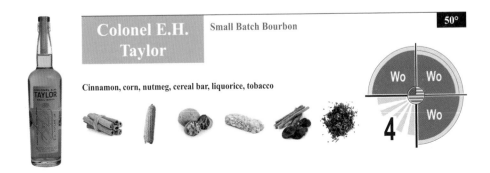

Wo | Wo

Wo

4

Pappy Van Winkle

15 YO Family Reserve

53.5°

Roasted almond, ground pepper, leather, dark chocolate, elderberry, caramel

Wo | O

Fr

5

Pappy Van Winkle

20 YO Family Reserve

45.2°

Pineapple, coconut, rancio, orange blossom honey, mace, fenugreek

Fr | Wo

Wo

8

Van Winkle

Rye 13 YO Family Reserve

47.8°

Nail polish, sweet chesnut, white pepper, prune, dark chocolate, mace

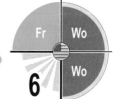

Fr | Wo

Wo

6

Wild Turkey
Distillery

Founded in 1855 by merchant Austin Nichols.
The original distillery was created in 1869 by the Ripy brothers
on the hill named Wild Turkey.
The brand name was chosen in 1940.

More than 12 million litres (3.17 million gallons) sold per year

1417 Versailles Rd, Lawrenceburg, KY 40342
+1 502 839 2182
www.wildturkeybourbon.com
Owner: Gruppo Campari

Wild Turkey   81 Proof 6-8 YO   **40.5°**

Coconut, almond, manuka honey, orange peel, mulberry, mocha

Wo   D   Fr   **3**

Wild Turkey   101 Proof 6-7-8 YO   **50.5°**

Plywood, hay, maple syrup, orange marmalade, caramel, vanilla

Wo   D   D   **3**

Wild Turkey   Rare Breed 6-8-12 YO   55°

Brioche, butterscotch, walnut, fresh tobacco, black pepper, orange blossom honey

6

Wild Turkey   Rye 4-5 YO   40.5°

Amber beer, nail polish, ground pepper, toffee, crème caramel, reseda

3

Russell's Reserve   10 YO Small Batch   45°

Cinnamon, fruit cake, molasses/treacle, bourbon vanilla, allspice, crème brûlée

6

Russell's Reserve   Single Barrel   55°

Sweet chestnut honey, soursop, milk chocolate, liquorice, peppermint, passion fruit/maracuja

7

Woodford Reserve
Distillery

**The distillery was created in 1838 and is the oldest still
operational distillery in Kentucky.**

Triple distillation in copper pot stills
Production on the site will soon be doubled with the addition of three new stills
Some batches are made from blends with whiskies from the column stills
of another distillery

7855 McCracken Pk, Versailles, KY 40383
+1 859 879 1812
www.woodfordreserve.com
Owner: Brown Forman Corp.

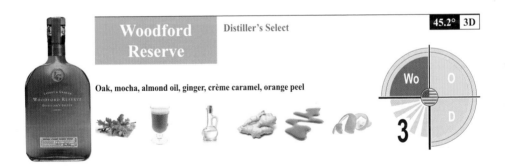

Woodford Reserve — Distiller's Select

45.2° 3D

Oak, mocha, almond oil, ginger, crème caramel, orange peel

Wo | O
3 | D

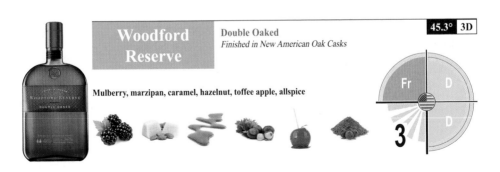

Woodford Reserve — Double Oaked
Finished in New American Oak Casks

45.3° 3D

Mulberry, marzipan, caramel, hazelnut, toffee apple, allspice

Fr | D
3 | D

Canadian distilleries

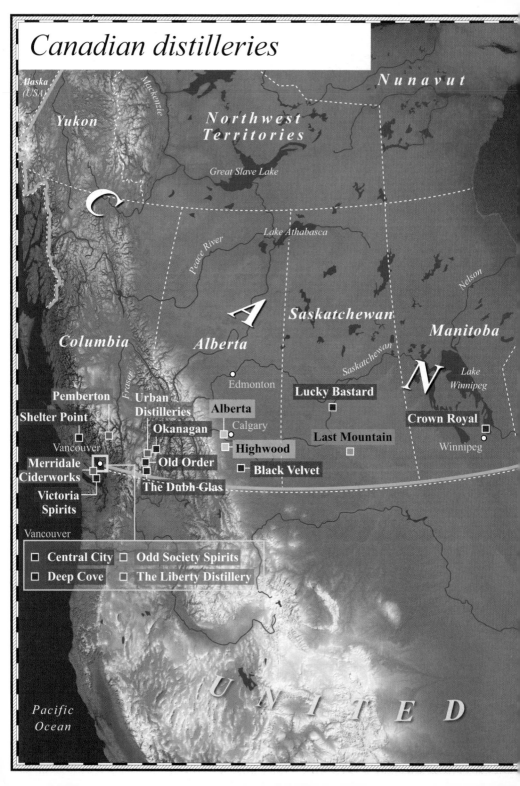

Alaska (USA)

Yukon

Northwest Territories

Nunavut

Mackenzie

Great Slave Lake

Peace River

Lake Athabasca

Saskatchewan

Nelson

Manitoba

Columbia

Alberta

Fraser

Edmonton

Lucky Bastard

Lake Winnipeg

Crown Royal

Pemberton

Urban Distilleries

Alberta

Calgary

Last Mountain

Winnipeg

Shelter Point

Okanagan

Highwood

Vancouver

Old Order

Black Velvet

Merridale Ciderworks

The Dubh-Glas

Victoria Spirits

Vancouver

☐ Central City	☐ Odd Society Spirits
☐ Deep Cove	☐ The Liberty Distillery

Pacific Ocean

UNITED

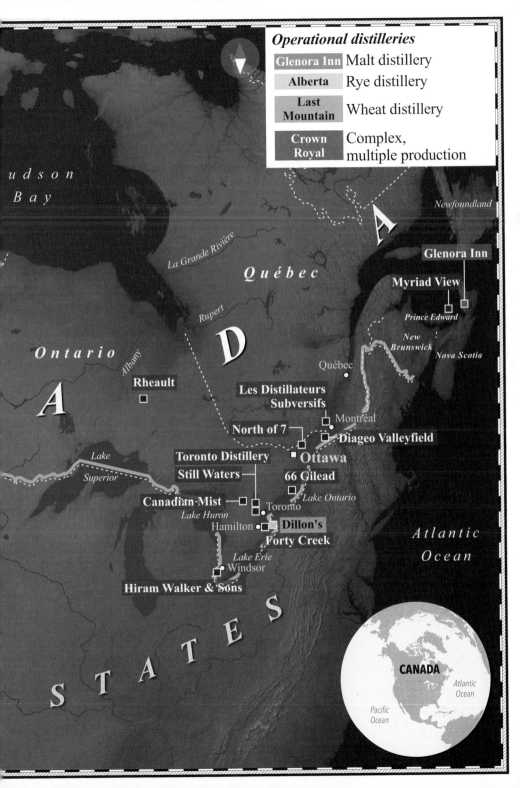

Operational distilleries

Glenora Inn	Malt distillery
Alberta	Rye distillery
Last Mountain	Wheat distillery
Crown Royal	Complex, multiple production

Hudson Bay

Newfoundland

A

La Grande Rivière

Québec

Glenora Inn

Myriad View

Prince Edward

Rupert

D

New Brunswick

Nova Scotia

Ontario

Albany

Rheault

A

Québec

Les Distillateurs Subversifs

Lake Superior

North of 7

Montréal

Diageo Valleyfield

Toronto Distillery

Still Waters

Ottawa

66 Gilead

Lake Ontario

Canadian Mist

Lake Huron

Toronto

Hamilton

Dillon's

Forty Creek

Atlantic Ocean

Lake Erie Windsor

Hiram Walker & Sons

S T A T E S

CANADA

Atlantic Ocean

Pacific Ocean

Alberta Springs 10 YO

40°

Rye, oak, lemon, vanilla, black pepper, galangal

2

Albert Premium Dark Horse

45°

Date, mocha, yellow grapefruit, crème caramel, dark chocolate, linseed oil

4

Black Velvet 8 YO
Reserve

40°

Rye, citron, caramel, white pepper, liquorice, prune

2

Canadian Club Chairman's Select 100% Rye

40°

Sweet chesnut, vanilla, rye, green curry, mace, metallic rail

3

Collingwood

.40°

Kaffir lime, grape, rye, marzipan, Sichuan pepper, rose

4

Collingwood   21 YO Rye

40°

Black bread, gorse bush, rose liqueur, coumarin, buckwheat honey, cardamom

6

Crown Royal   Hand Selected Barrel

51.5°

Brown sugar, ginseng, ganache, cigar box, brioche, liquorice cream

5

Forty Creek   Copper Pot Reserve

43°

Toffee, Seville orange, caramel, Mandarine Impériale, dark chocolate, galangal

2

Forty Creek   Barrel Select   40°

Macadamia nut, orange peel, walnut oil, green pepper, coriander, caramel

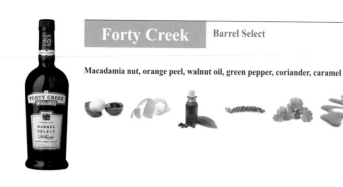

Wo | O
G
3

Forty Creek   Port Wood Reserve
Finished in Port Barrels   45°

Hazelnut, port wine, blackcurrant wine, kernel, wintergreen, raisin

Wo | Wi
Wo
4

Gibson's Finest   12 YO   40°

Rye, raspberry, lemon, butter, crème anglaise, pepper

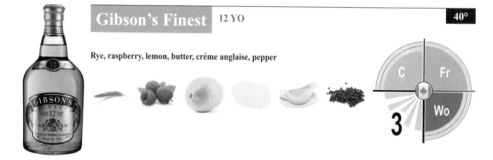

C | Fr
Wo
3

Gibson's Finest   Rare 18 YO   40°

Thuja, physalis, corn, brown sugar, vanilla, lemon

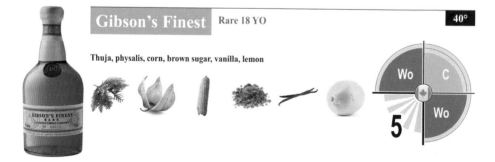

Wo | C
Wo
5

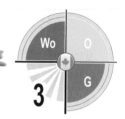

Canadian Rockies

21 YO for Taiwan

40°

Bran, kumquat, shea butter, vanilla, corn oil, lilac

5

Century Reserve

Lot 15-25

40°

Oak, bread crumb, gooseberry, marzipan, rooibos, pomelo

3

Highwood

25 YO Calgary Stampede

40°

Vanilla cream, cedar, lime, clove, caramel, ginger

3

Lot No.40

2012 Limited Edition

43°

Blackcurrant bud, crepe batter, beer, elderberry, cherry, cardamom

4

Masterson's 10 YO Straight Rye 45°

Cereal bar, leather, liquorice, linseed oil, fresh tobacco, grapefruit

C | Wo

G

4

Masterson's 10 YO Straight Rye French Oak 45°
Finished in a French Oak Cask

Damson, marzipan, French oak, orange blossom, cherry, green wood

Fr | Wo

Fr

5

Pendleton 1910 40°

Coumarin, mustard, green apple, muscovado, liquorice cream, pear

G | Fr

Wo

3

Pike Creek 10 YO Port Barrels Finish 40°
Finished in Port Barrels

Reseda, raspberry, strawberry liqueur, caramel, marshmallow, cinnamon

Wo | D

G

2

Snake River — Stamped 8 YO

40°

Lemon, sage, rye, orgeat syrup, vanilla, white pepper

3

Still Waters — 1+11

40°

Cereal bar, vanilla, black bread, caramel, green wood, lemon

2

Wiser's — 18 YO Limited Release

40°

Cereal bar, leather, pineapple, date, pastry cream, toffee apple

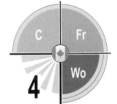

4

Wiser's — Small Batch

43.4°

Cinnamon, muesli, coconut, vanilla, chilli, lemon

3

CONTENTS

Rest of the world

Bakery Hill — Classic Malt

46° UN

Madarine, almond oil, pine honey, malted barley, nutmeg, vanilla

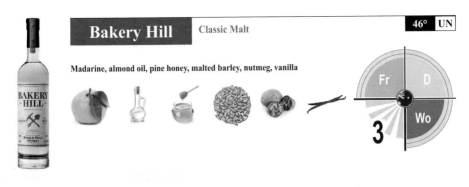

Fr | D
Wo

3

Bakery Hill — Double Wood
Finished in French Oak Casks

46° UN

Apricot, barley sugar, quince, shortbread, coumarin, milk chocolate

Fr | Fr
G

3

Bakery Hill — Peated Malt Cask Strength

61° UN CS

Burning pine needles, mandarine, pine honey, burnt wood, reseda, arnica

Sm | D
Wo

5

Sullivans Cove — Double Cask
Matured in French & American Oak Casks

40° UN

Fresh tobacco, cinnamon, lime tree honey, pear, pineapple, milk chocolate

G | D
Fr

2

Sullivans Cove — American Oak

47.5° UN

Nectarine, vanilla cream, apricot, barley sugar, orange blossom honey, white pepper

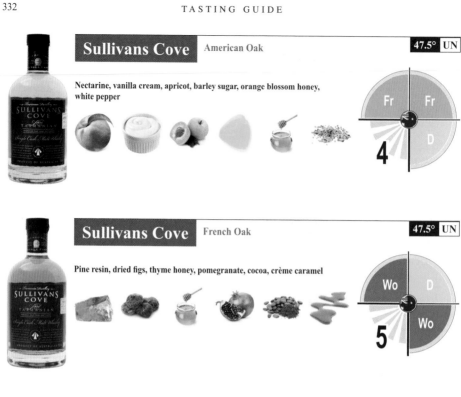

Fr / Fr / D

4

Sullivans Cove — French Oak

47.5° UN

Pine resin, dried figs, thyme honey, pomegranate, cocoa, crème caramel

Wo / D / Wo

5

Hellyer's Road — Original Roaring Forty

40°

Turpentine, papaya, cooked apple, sorrel, oak, juniper berry

Fr / Fr / Wo

2

Hellyer's Road — 10 YO

46.2° UN

Vanilla, grapefruit, papaya, malted barley, charcoal, crème anglaise

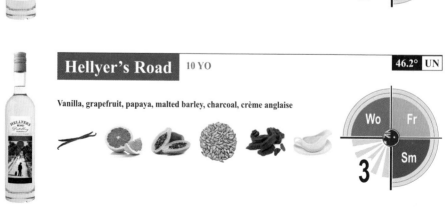

Wo / Fr / Sm

3

Hellyer's Road

Pinot Noir Finish
Finished in Pinot Noir Wine Cask

46.2° UN

Grapefruit peel, apricot, green malt, plywood, Pinot Noir, cocoa

3

Fr | C
Wi

Old Raven

Smoky Rabenbräu
Matured in Bourbon & PX Casks

55° UN

Pedro ximénez, peated malt, soot, raspberry, dark chocolate, barley malt syrup

      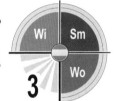

3

Wi | Sm
Wo

The Belgian Owl

Single Malt

46° UN

Pear, floral cream, vanilla cream, ginger, white oak, greengage

2

Fr | Wo
Wo

Lambertus

10 YO
Matured in French Limousin Oak cask

40°

Barley sugar, milk chocolate, crème brûlée, acacia honey, nutmeg, coffee

3

C | Wo
Wo

Goldlys — 12 YO Manzanilla Finish
Finished in Manzanilla Sherry Cask

43°

Almond honey, lemon peel, cereal bar, vanilla cream, liquorice, bread crumb

Hammer Head — 1989 23 YO

40.7°

Juniper berry, mace, plum, reseda, turmeric, acacia honey

Stauning — Traditional 3rd Edition
Matured in First Fill Ex-Bourbon Casks

49° **UN**

Linseed oil, malted barley, almond honey, muesli, barley, vanilla

Stauning — Peated 3rd Edition
Matured in First Fill Ex-Bourbon Casks

51° **UN**

Mown hay, peated malt, hickory smoke, leather, clove, pine

Stauning   Young Rye
Matured in New White Oak Barrels

53.3° UN CS

Sloe, rye, black bread, black pepper, cinnamon, Seville orange

English Whisky   Classic Single Malt

43°

Green malt, vanilla, mango, lilac, almond, malted barley

English Whisky   Peated Single Malt

43°

Oak smoke, star anise, creosote, mango, ginger, camphor

Teerenpeli   8 YO

43°

Bergamot, sweet almond, almond honey, vanilla cream, white oak, cinnamon

Glann ar Mor — Taol Esa
46° UN

Pineapple, sea spray, roasted barley, date, salt, lemon

Fr | C
Mi
5

Kornog — Peated Glann ar Mor
46° UN

Tar, grapefruit peel, Chablis, kiwi, peated malt, salt

Sm | Mi
Sm
5

Eddu — Silver
Matured in French Oak Casks
40°

Pear, orange marmalade, walnut, toffee apple, cinnamon, peppermint

Fr | Wo
Wo
3

Armorik — Classic Single Malt
Matured in Sherry & Bourbon Casks
46° UN

Crème anglaise, bread crust, panettone, leather, sea spray, galangal

Wo | C
Ma
3

P&M — Vintage
Matured in Corsican White Wine & Cap Corse Casks

42°

Strawberry tree honey, Seville orange peel, myrtle, eucalyptus honey, guarana, sweet chesnut

3

Brenne — Single Cask
Matured in French Oak & Cognac Casks

40°

Banana, toffee apple, soursop, vanilla cream, tarte tatin, leather

3

Domaine des Hautes Glaces — Les Moissons
Matured in Cognac, White Wine & New French Oak Casks

42° **UN**

Malted barley, peach, marzipan, lemongrass, truffle, almond

4

Blaue Maus — Fleischmann Single Cask Malt

40°

Hazelnut tree honey, banana, milk chocolate, pineapple, ground pepper, caramel

2

Slyrs — Single Malt
Matured in New American Oak Casks

43°

Apple compote, banana, almond honey, orange peel, malted barley, oak

Fr | D
C

2

Slyrs — PX Finish
Finished in PX Cask

46°

Pedro ximénez, malted barley, cocoa, molasses/treacle, toffee apple, white pepper

Wi | Wo
D

3

Amrut — Indian Single Malt

46° UN

Propolis, soursop, malted barley, cardamom, molasses/treacle, bergamot

Wo | C
D

2

Amrut — Peated

46° UN

Arnica, lemon, peat smoke, apple, star anise, mochaccino

Sm | Sm
G

3

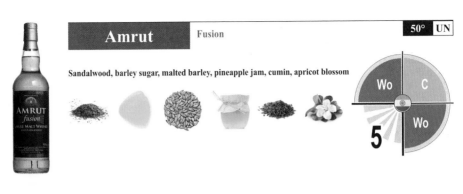

Amrut — Fusion

50° UN

Sandalwood, barley sugar, malted barley, pineapple jam, cumin, apricot blossom

Wo | C
Wo

5

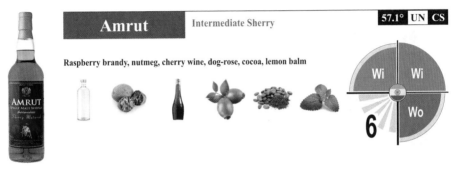

Amrut — Intermediate Sherry

57.1° UN CS

Raspberry brandy, nutmeg, cherry wine, dog-rose, cocoa, lemon balm

Wi | Wi
Wo

6

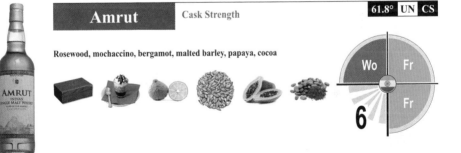

Amrut — Cask Strength

61.8° UN CS

Rosewood, mochaccino, bergamot, malted barley, papaya, cocoa

Wo | Fr
Fr

6

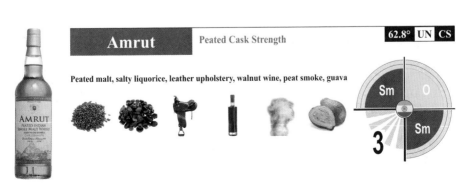

Amrut — Peated Cask Strength

62.8° UN CS

Peated malt, salty liquorice, leather upholstery, walnut wine, peat smoke, guava

Sm | O
Sm

3

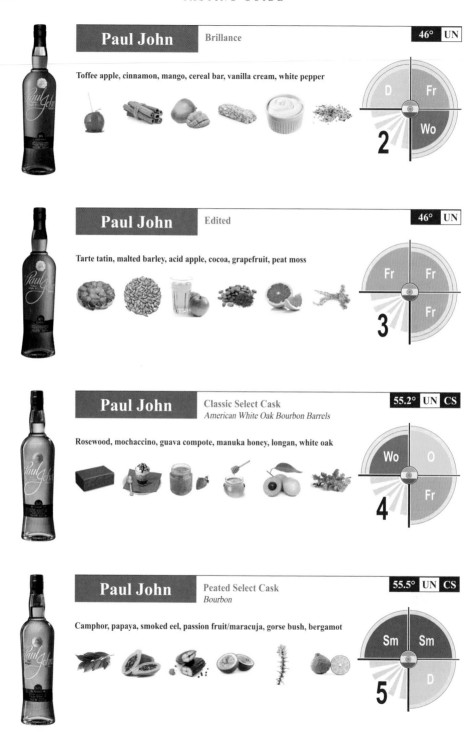

Paul John Brillance 46° UN

Toffee apple, cinnamon, mango, cereal bar, vanilla cream, white pepper

D | Fr
Wo
2

Paul John Edited 46° UN

Tarte tatin, malted barley, acid apple, cocoa, grapefruit, peat moss

Fr | Fr
Fr
3

Paul John Classic Select Cask
American White Oak Bourbon Barrels 55.2° UN CS

Rosewood, mochaccino, guava compote, manuka honey, longan, white oak

Wo | O
Fr
4

Paul John Peated Select Cask
Bourbon 55.5° UN CS

Camphor, papaya, smoked eel, passion fruit/maracuja, gorse bush, bergamot

Sm | Sm
D
5

Puni

Alba
Matured in Marsala Vergine & Pinot Noir Wine Casks

43°

Lemon blossom honey, vanilla, Pinot Noir, almond, salted butter caramel, pear

Millstone

Zuidam 12 YO
Matured in Sherry Cask

46° UN

Mulberry, chocolate malt, grapefruit peel, molasses/treacle, almond, mango

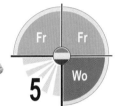

New Zealand Whisky

Double Wood
15 YO American Oak + NZ Red Wine French Oak

40°

Ganache, walnut, peony, tonka bean, peach wine, camphor

New Zealand Whisky

The Oamaruvian
16 YO Bourbon + NZ Red Wine Barrels

58.4° UN CS

Fudge, marron glacé, apricot brandy, walnut liqueur, praline, menthol

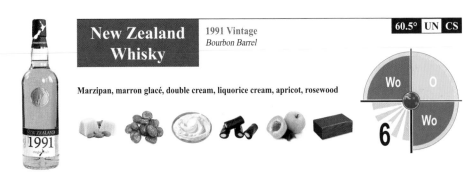

New Zealand Whisky

1991 Vintage
Bourbon Barrel

60.5° UN CS

Marzipan, marron glacé, double cream, liquorice cream, apricot, rosewood

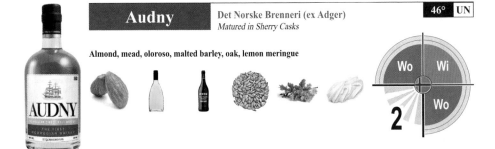

Audny

Det Norske Brenneri (ex Adger)
Matured in Sherry Casks

46° UN

Almond, mead, oloroso, malted barley, oak, lemon meringue

Three Ships

5 YO Premium Select

43°

Peated malt, reseda, pear compote, liquorice, peat oil, oak

Three Ships

Bourbon Cask Finish
Married in First Fill Bourbon Casks

43°

Manuka honey, white oak, ginger, pear, ground pepper, cinnamon

Three Ships

10 YO Single Malt
Matured in American Oak Casks

43°

Blood orange, peat smoke, myrtle, fresh tobacco, cumin, creosote

3

DYC

8 YO Special Blend

40°

Mown hay, heather honey, acid apple, vanilla, barley malt syrup, marzipan

      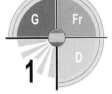

1

Mackmyra

Brukswhisky

41.4°

Oak moss, lemongrass, pear, juniper berry, liquorice, lemon

2

Mackmyra

Svensk Ek
Matured in American & Swedish Oak Casks

46.1° UN

Pear, lemon blossom honey, peach liqueur, green curry, almond, vanilla

3

Mackmyra — Svensk Rök — 46.1° UN

Tar rope, vetiver, smoked salmon, fresh tobacco, hickory smoke, turmeric

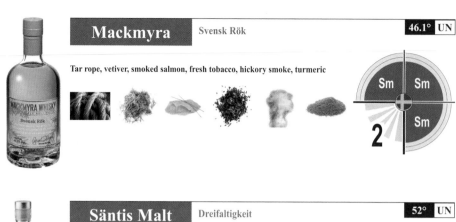

Sm | Sm
Sm
2

Säntis Malt — Dreifaltigkeit — 52° UN

Smoky mezcal, muscovado, eucalyptus honey, orange peel, soot, nutmeg

Sm | D
Sm
4

Langatun Rye — Old Eagle Pure Rye — 60.7° UN CS

Oak honey, raisin, Danish pastry, rye, acacia honey, crème brûlée

D | O
D
4

Kavalan — Single Malt — 40°

Wallflower, honey, mango, cinnamon, lemon essential oil, coconut

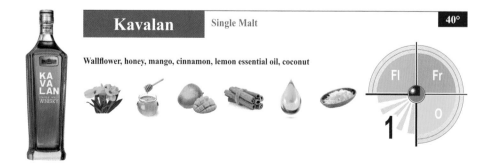

Fl | Fr
O
1

Kavalan

Concertmaster
Portuguese Ruby, Tawny + Vintage Port Wine Casks

40°

Mango, fig, strawberry tree honey, cinnamon, mulberry wine, rancio

2

Kavalan

King Car
Conductor

46° UN

Papaya, magnolia, banana, walnut, Angostura, cinnamon

3

Kavalan

ex-Bourbon Oak
Bourbon Barrels

46° UN

Pineapple, cinnamon, reseda, caramel, vanilla, rooibos

3

Kavalan

Sherry Oak
Small Oloroso Sherry Cask

46° UN

Raspberry wine, star anise, ganache, cardamom, oloroso, menthol

5

Kavalan
Solist ex-Bourbon Cask
2015 Bourbon Cask

59.4° UN CS

Vanilla, soursop, banana syrup, white pepper, coconut milk, green grapefruit

4

Kavalan
Solist Fino
2015 Fino Sherry Cask

57.8° UN CS

Walnut wine, gorse bush, Cynar®, fresh tobacco, cardamom, rooibos

5

Kavalan
Solist Sherry Cask
Sherry Cask

57.8° UN CS

Umeshu, turpentine, fig syrup, Angostura, blackcurrant wine, root chicory

6

Kavalan
Solist Vinho Barrique
2015 Vinho Barrique

58.6° UN CS

Cherry wine, peony, blackcurrant syrup, cardamom, walnut wine,
dark chocolate

4

Nantou
2010 Vintage
2010/2015 4 YO Bourbon Cask

57° | UN | CS

Vanilla cream, lemon meringue, coconut milk, ginger, papaya, guarana

Wo | O
Fr

3

Nantou
2009 Vintage
2009/2014 5 YO Sherry Cask

58° | UN | CS

Cherry wine, raisin, walnut wine, Iberico ham, star anise, cashew

Wi | Wi
Wo

3

Penderyn
Aur Cymru Madeira
Finished in Madeira Casks

46° | UN

Butterscotch, raisin, melon, cinnamon, mocha, vanilla

D | Fr
Wo

2

Penderyn
Peated

46° | UN

Peated malt, lime, kiwi, vanilla, hazelnut, peat smoke

Sm | Fr
Wo

2

PART III

EXPLORING
the different aspects of whisky

WHISKY TRAILS

Your whisky education will not be complete without first-hand experience of the people, the expertise and the *terroirs* that produce it. The journeys highlighted here offer just this: the chance to meet people with a common passion and explore extraordinary landscapes that combine shared experiences and individual discovery. There are many factors that contribute to the history and diversity of the individual whiskies and their makers. And, common to all distilleries, this is enshrined in the character of a region, the architectural arrangement of the site and the production method employed: from the most traditional to artisanal micro-distilleries, from malt to grain distilleries, from ancient underground sites to iconic distilleries lifting the veil on their rich past.

These trails are designed to help whisky-lovers make the most of their trip to the lands of malt according to how much time they have. They have been chosen because they are:

> *Practical:* recommending the key sites to visit as well as the most noteworthy view points;
>
> *Adaptable:* accounting for the duration of the trip: three days, one week, a fortnight;
>
> *Established:* following the most legendary whisky trails.

Scotland

– Campbeltown – Islay – Highlands (Islands and Western)
– Speyside and Highlands (Central, Eastern and Northern)
– Lowlands and Highlands

Japan

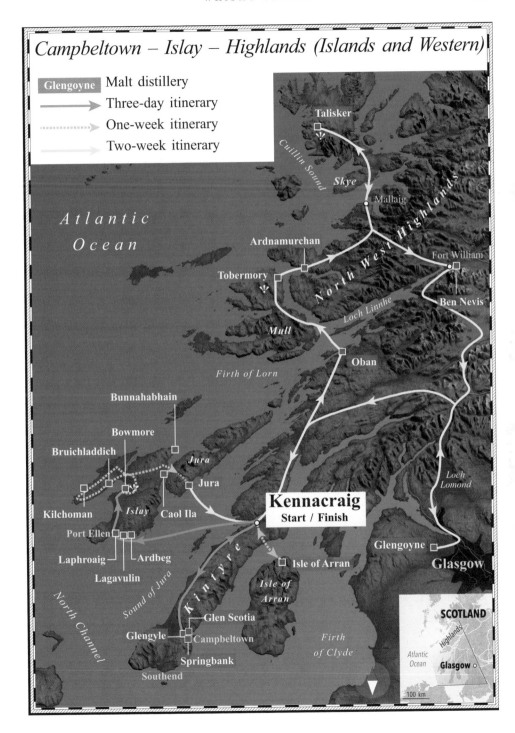

Campbeltown – Islay – Highlands (Islands and Western)

Glengoyne Malt distillery

→ Three-day itinerary

▸▸▸▸▸ One-week itinerary

→ Two-week itinerary

Atlantic Ocean

Talisker

Cuillin Sound

Skye

Mallaig

Ardnamurchan

North West Highlands

Fort William

Tobermory

Ben Nevis

Mull

Loch Linnhe

Firth of Lorn

Oban

Bunnahabhain

Bowmore

Bruichladdich

Jura

Loch Lomond

Jura

Kennacraig
Start / Finish

Kilchoman

Islay

Caol Ila

Port Ellen

Laphroaig   Ardbeg

Glengoyne

Glasgow

Lagavulin

Kintyre

Isle of Arran

Isle of Arran

Sound of Jura

North Channel

Glen Scotia

Glengyle   Campbeltown

Firth of Clyde

Springbank

Southend

SCOTLAND

Highlands

Atlantic Ocean

Glasgow ○

100 km

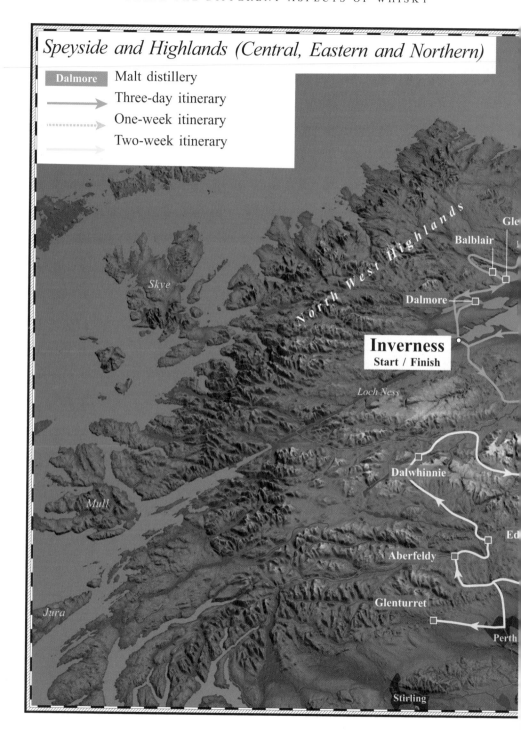

Speyside and Highlands (Central, Eastern and Northern)

Dalmore   Malt distillery
→   Three-day itinerary
┄┄►   One-week itinerary
→   Two-week itinerary

Skye

North West Highlands

Balblair

Gle

Dalmore

Inverness
Start / Finish

Loch Ness

Mull

Dalwhinnie

Ed

Aberfeldy

Jura

Glenturret

Perth

Stirling

Highland Park

St. Margaret's Hope

Orkney Islands

John O'Groats

Old Pulteney

Glenmorangie

Brora

North Sea

BenRiach

Benromach

Glenfiddich

Balvenie

Elgin

Spey

Glenglassaugh

S p e y s i d e

Strathisla

Macallan

Glendronach

Aberlour

Glenfarclas

Cragganmore

Royal Lochnagar

Glen Garioch

Aberdeen

Edradour

Fettercairn

Glencadam

Perth

Dundee

North Sea

Inverness

Elgin

Aberdeen

Highlands

SCOTLAND

Atlantic Ocean

100 km

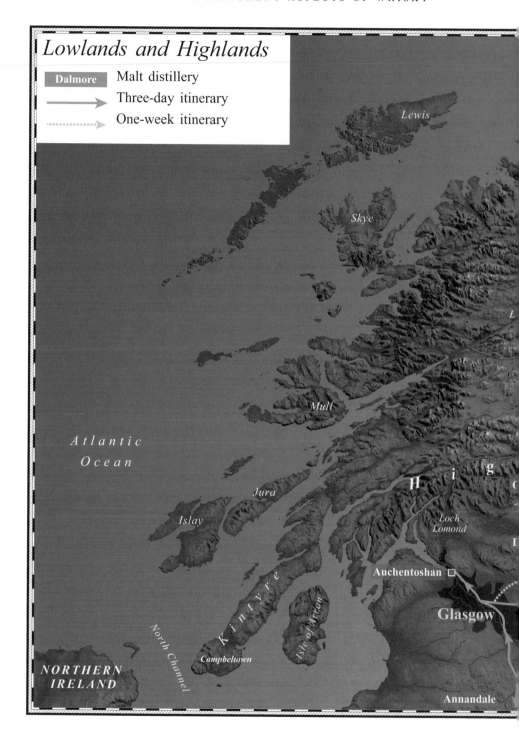

Lowlands and Highlands

Dalmore — Malt distillery
→ Three-day itinerary
▷ One-week itinerary

Lewis

Skye

Atlantic
Ocean

Mull

Jura

Islay

H i g

Loch
Lomond

Auchentoshan □

Kintyre

Isle of Arran

Glasgow

North Channel

Campbeltown

NORTHERN
IRELAND

Annandale

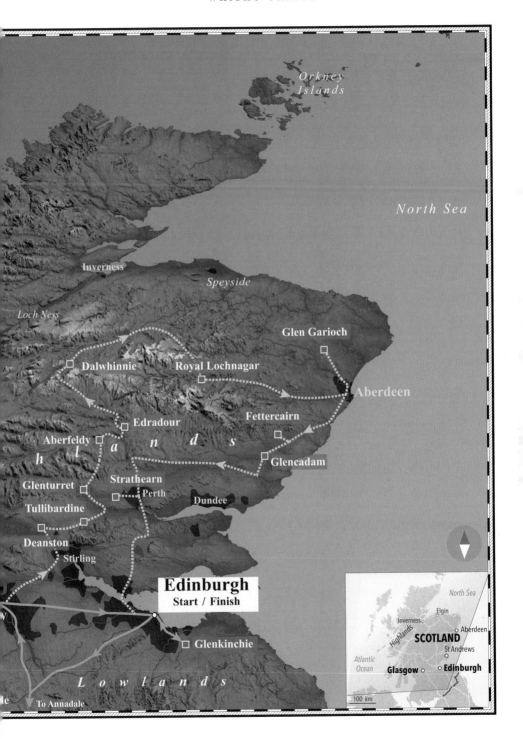

Orkney
Islands

North Sea

Inverness

Speyside

Loch Ness

Glen Garioch

Dalwhinnie   Royal Lochnagar

Aberdeen

Edradour   Fettercairn

Aberfeldy   *a*   *n*   *d*   *s*

h   *l*   Glencadam

Glenturret   Strathearn

Tullibardine   Perth   Dundee

Deanston

Stirling

Edinburgh
Start / Finish

Glenkinchie

L o w l a n d s

To Annadale

North Sea

Elgin

Inverness

Highlands   Aberdeen

SCOTLAND

St Andrews

Atlantic
Ocean   **Glasgow**   **Edinburgh**

100 km

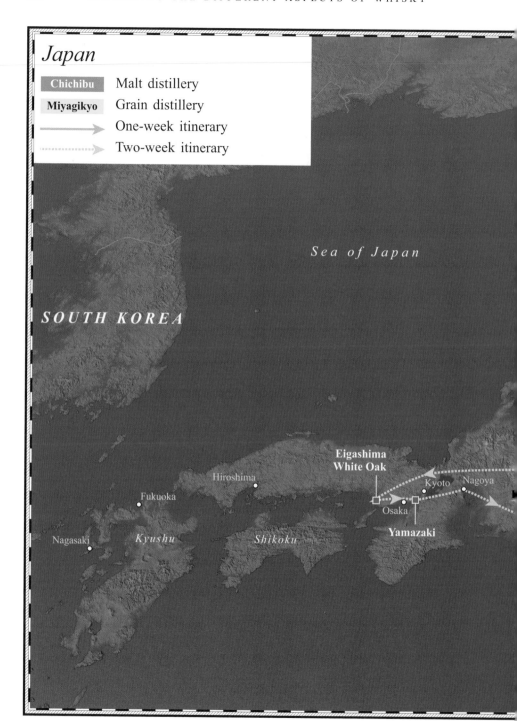

Japan

Chichibu	Malt distillery
Miyagikyo	Grain distillery
→	One-week itinerary
⇢	Two-week itinerary

Sea of Japan

SOUTH KOREA

Eigashima
White Oak

Hiroshima

Kyoto   Nagoya

Fukuoka

Osaka

Nagasaki   Kyushu   Shikoku   Yamazaki

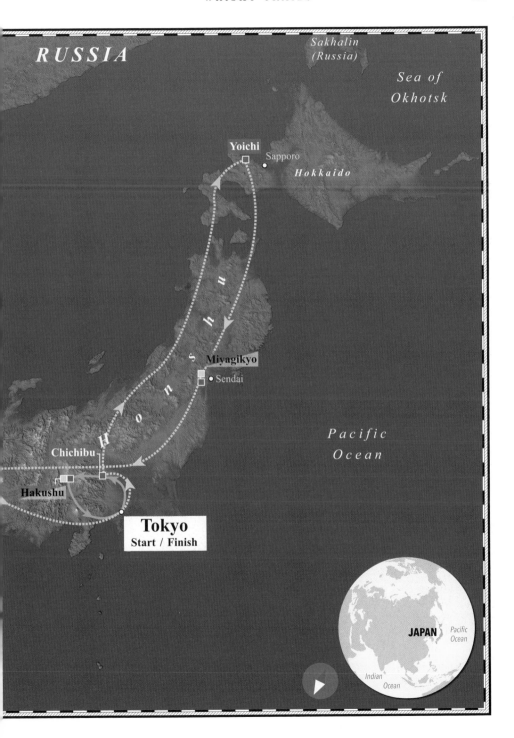

WHISKY AND FOOD PAIRING

A s when matching food with wine, the perfect pairing of a dish with a whisky is demonstrated by the fact that both are simply enhanced. The result of the pairing should be such that the sum of whisky plus dish is greater than the pleasure that would have been generated by one or other tasted on its own. In a sense, the perfect pairing should be a revelation: the truth of a harmony between the experience and things shared.

The whisky and food pairings listed here are grouped by the category of food to be served, then the whiskies are matched to particular dishes that best partner the whisky's individual aromas.

HORS D'OEUVRE

Whisky	Aromas	Food pairing
Balblair *Vint. 1983*	Lemon verbena, guava, honeysuckle, galangal	Fresh tomato tart
Caol Ila *18 YO*	Graphite, beach fire, lemon liqueur (liquor), black tea	Tapenade
Fettercairn *24 YO*	Walnut wine, slate, meat pie, mulberry wine	Bortsch
Glenglassaugh *39 YO Aleatico*	Meat pie, fig, green pepper, ginger	Samosa
Glen Scotia *18 YO*	Lemon honey, green pepper, green curry, peppermint	Coconut soup
Laphroaig *Triple Wood*	Liquorice cream, raisins, burnt grass, cream liqueur (liquor)	Eggs and bacon, herby chipolata, sweet-and-sour aubergine (eggplant)
Lochside *Blackadder 1981*	Buddha's hand, clementine honey, kaffir lime, agave, lemon essential oil	Grated carrot
North Port *28 YO*	Pebble, lemon verbena, citron, radicchio, sail locker, magnesium	Caesar salad

COLD MEATS

Whisky	Aromas	Food pairing
Aberfeldy *18 YO*	Heather honey, lilac, nutmeg, ginseng	Honey-roasted ham
Blair Athol *Manager's Dram*	Almond oil, libraries, sage, ginger	Rabbit terrine with tarragon, rabbit with thyme
Blanton's *Bourbon Gold Edition*	Rye, apricot, cinnamon, pecan	Pork loin sausage
Fettercairn *24 YO*	Walnut wine, slate, meat pie, mulberry wine	*Foie gras mi-cuit*
Glann ar Mor *Taol Esa*	Pineapple, roasted barley, date, salt, lemon	*Foie gras au torchon*
Millburn *25 YO*	Chestnut honey, Iberico ham, pineapple, lemon marmalade, nutmeg	*Bellota Iberico jambon*
Old Pulteney *21 YO*	Ginger, lemon essential oil, borage flower, white pepper, wet rock	Culatello ham
Woodford Reserve *Double Oaked*	Oak, caramel, walnut, maple syrup, spices	Parma ham (prosciutto)

VEGETABLES

Whisky	Aromas	Food pairing
Balblair *Vint. 1983*	Lemon verbena, guava, honeysuckle, galangal	Garden peas
Bunnahabhain *18 YO*	Dark malt, chestnut honey, leather upholstery, panelling, white pepper	Mushroom consommé, roasted chestnuts
Chivas Regal *18 YO*	Black olive, parsley, tomato, girolle mushroom	Roasted stuffed vegetables
Clynelish *BBR 1996*	Eucalpytus honey, earthy soils, lemon essential oil, angostura bark	Morel mushrooms, mushroom risotto
Fettercairn *24 YO*	Walnut wine, slate, meat pie, mulberry wine	Truffle

Glendronach *CS Batch 3*	Jujube honey, fresh tobacco, vine peach, beef broth, saffron, candied citrus	Paella
Glen Garioch *Vint. 1998 SC 670*	Elderflower, honeysuckle, clove, neroli	Asparagus
Glenglassaugh *39 YO Aleatico*	Meat pie, fig, green pepper, ginger	Artichoke *à la barigoule*
Lochside *DL 1989*	Chlorophyl, eucalyptus oil, lemongrass	Courgettes (zucchini) with mint
Sullivans Cove *French Oak*	Thyme honey, pine resin, dried fig, pomegranate, cocoa, caramel	Rack of lamb, courgette (zucchini) flower fritters, butternut ravioli
Van Winkle *Rye 13 YO Family Reserve*	Chestnut, prune, white pepper, dark chocolate, mace	Mushroom consommé

FISH AND SEAFOOD

Whisky	Aromas	Food pairing
Ardbeg *Ten*	Smoked herring, pineapple, molasses/treacle, salty liquorice	Pickled herring, anchovies
Arran *12 YO CS Batch 3*	Citrus peel, dark chocolate, ginger, elderberry	Blue lobster
Benromach *5 YO*	Parsley, chervil, mint	Razor shell (*navajas*), European bittersweet
Bladnoch *22 YO*	Mown lawn, citron, lemon verbena, longan	Steamed langoustines
Bowmore *100 Proof*	Sea spray, ginger, peat	Scallops, *botargo*
Bunnahabhain *Cruach-Mhòna*	Stalk, smoked oyster, maple smoke, lemon thyme, liquorice, white pepper	Smoked herring, smoked eel
Caol Ila *18 YO*	Graphite, beach fire, lemon liqueur (liquor), black tea	Smoked oyster
Caol Ila *WM 1982*	Abalone, lemon essential oil, green olive, charcoal, sea spray	Velvet crab soup

Clynelish 14 YO	Borage flower, sea spray, peated malt, sandy beach, malted barley, dill	Gravlax
Clynelish Manager's choice	Lemon essential oil, kumquat, pebble, pear	Spider crab
Craigellachie 17 YO	Jasmine, rose, lemon sorbet, lemongrass	Prawns (shrimp)
Glendronach CS Batch 3	Jujube honey, fresh tobacco, vine peach, beef broth, saffron, candied citrus	Octopus salad, bouillabaisse, pan-fried abalone, paella
Glen Garioch Vint. 1998 SC 670	Elderflower, honeysuckle, clove, neroli	Elver
Glengoyne 25 YO	Cranberry, leather upholstery, chocolate, Oloroso seco, bitter orange marmalade, liquorice	Lobster, spiny lobster
Glenlivet Archive 21 YO	Basil, mint, olive oil, sesame, ginger, honey	Tuna tartare, brown shrimp, clam
Glenmorangie Artein	Radicchio, limestone, peppermint, ganache	Roast langoustine
Glenmorangie Astar	Lemon, apricot, anise honey, almond	Monkfish, white fish with citrus
Glen Ord 23 YO	Kumquat, chicory, blue agave, havana, eucalyptus	Red mullet
Glenugie 1977 32 YO	Rosewood, encaustic, black sesame seed, ganache, mochaccino	Eel with tare sauce
Hibiki 17 YO	Peach, rose, lemon honey, cocoa, brioche, sandalwood	Gamberoni
Isle of Jura Samaroli 1997	Wet rock, pine resin, pebble, daikon	Salmon eggs, octopus in wine
Lagavulin 12 YO CS	Peat moss, grapefruit marmalade, wormwood, burnt grass	Teriyaki salmon, sautéed shellfish
Lochside MoS 1982	Passion fruit/maracuja, olive oil, hawthorn, angostura bark	Turbot, salt-crusted sea bass
Lochside Blackadder 1981	Buddha's hand, clementine honey, kaffir lime, agave, lemon essential oil	Marinated salmon, marinated mackerel
North Port 28 YO	Pebble, lemon verbena, citron, radicchio, sail locker, magnesium	Banka trout

Oban 21 YO	Strawberry tree honey, wet sand, mead, gingerbread, salt	Octopus curry
Old Pulteney 12 YO	Sea spray, malted barley, borage flower, Iberico ham	Marinated anchovies, burrata
Old Pulteney 21 YO	Ginger, lemon essential oil, borage flower, white pepper, wet rock	Crab, ceviche
Paul John Peated Select Cask	Camphor, bergamot, papaya, passion fruit	Braised black cod, sea bream carpaccio
Royal Lochnagar Triple Matured	Burning pine needle, barley sugar, ginger, oak, Espelette chilli pepper, malted milk	Grilled squid, mouclade (mussels with saffron)
Talisker Storm	Peat moss, sea spray, bandage, green pepper, oyster, white pepper	Oysters, smoked salmon, sashimi
Teaninich SV 1983	Wet sand, lime, clay, blue agave	Sea urchin
Van Winkle Rye 13YO Family Reserve	Chestnut, prune, white pepper, dark chocolate, mace	Cockles
Yamazaki Distiller's Reserve	Strawberry, cherry, yellow peach, persimmon	Sushi

MEAT

Whisky	Aromas	Food pairing
Aberfeldy 18 YO	Heather honey, lilac, nutmeg, ginseng	Moussaka
Aberlour a'Bunadh	Blackcurrant, chocolate, peony, black cherry, tamarind	Pigeon
Amrut Fusion	Pineapple, apricot, sandalwood, barley, voatsiperifery pepper	Lamb confit, chicken tajine, chicken tikka skewers
AnCnoc 22 YO	Berry honey, tarte tatin, barley malt syrup, roasted barley, green pepper	Chicken tandoori
Auchentoshan Three Wood	Blackcurrant, walnut honey, rosewood, lemongrass	Beef ribs, coq au vin

Aultmore *12 YO*	Herbal, hazelnut, girolle mushroom	Suckling lamb
Balblair *Vint. 1983*	Lemon verbena, guava, honeysuckle, galangal	Duckling
Balvenie *25 YO Triple Cask*	Rye, apricot, cinnamon, pecan	Beef *Pho Bo*, veal kidney, pork loin sausage
Blanton's *Bourbon Gold Edition*	Lemon, parsley, girolle mushroom, clove	Blanquette of veal
Bowmore *15 YO Laimrig*	Dark chocolate, cherry, maple smoke, almond, Oloroso	Reindeer with cranberries, braised game
Bowmore *17 YO*	Mochaccino, hazelnut, peated malt, nutmeg, petrichor, brown sugar	Barbary duck, mallard
Bruichladdich *Bere Barley*	Fern, barley malt syrup, lime tree honey, lemon, gorse bush, myrtle	Haggis
Clynelish *BBR 1996*	Eucalpytus honey, earthy soils, lemon essential oil, angostura bark	Chicken with *vin jaune* and morel mushrooms
Dalwhinnie *Distillers Edition*	Mown hay, roasted walnut, honey malt, tamarind, liquorice, radicchio	Spit-roasted grouse, quail eggs
Fettercairn *24 YO*	Walnut wine, slate, meat pie, mulberry wine	Confited beef shoulder, tournedos Rossini
Four Roses *Small Batch*	Sour cream, chilli, sea spray, mint	Chilli con carne
Glann ar Mor *Taol Esa*	Pineapple, roasted barley, date, salt, lemon	Quail tandoori
Glendronach *2002 Batch 8*	Fig liqueur (liquor), wet rock, caraway, Brown sherry	Pigeon pastilla
Glenfiddich *Vintage Cask*	Black olive, parsley, tomato, girolle mushroom	Daube Provençale, osso buco
Glenglassaugh *39 YO Aleatico*	Meat pie, fig, green pepper, ginger	Meat pie
Glengoyne *25 YO*	Cranberry, leather upholstery, chocolate, Oloroso seco, bitter orange marmalade, liquorice	Veal sweetbreads
Hibiki *17 YO*	Peach, rose, lemon honey, cocoa, brioche, sandalwood	Barbary duck
Highland Park *15 YO Loki*	Silica, lemon peel, sea spray, peat smoke	Pan-fried fois gras, pork *gyoza*

Kavalan *Solist Sherry Cask*	Plum, fig, blackcurrant, angostura, chicory (endive), hazelnut, hibiscus, pine nut	*Magret de canard*, duckling, lamb shanks
Lagavulin *12 YO CS*	Peat moss, grapefruit marmalade, wormwood, burnt grass	Tea smoked chicken
Lochside *DL 1989*	Chlorophyll, eucalyptus oil, lemongrass	Veal fillet (tenderloin)
Lochside *Blackadder 1981*	Buddha's hand, clementine honey, kaffir lime, agave, lemon essential oil	Pork chop, pork belly
Midleton *Power's 12 YO John Lane*	Cocoa, apricot, orange marmalade, honey, pepper	Duck, veal sweetbreads
Millburn *25 YO*	Chestnut honey, Iberico ham, pineapple, lemon marmalade, nutmeg	Veal *involtini*
Mortlach *Rare Old*	Chocolate, fruit cake, cherry honey	Deer steak
North Port *28 YO*	Pebble, lemon verbena, citron, radicchio, sail locker, magnesium	Veal strips
Sullivans Cove *French Oak*	Thyme honey, pine resin, dried fig, pomegranate, cocoa, caramel	Rack of lamb
Talisker *Storm*	Peat moss, sea spray, bandage, green pepper, oyster, white pepper	Kofta
Van Winkle *Rye 13YO Family Reserve*	Chestnut, prune, white pepper, dark chocolate, mace	*Gyoza satay*
Yamazaki *18 YO*	Ganache, fig, date, coffee, sandalwood	Braised veal sweetbreads

CHEESE

Whisky	Aromas	Food pairing
Aberlour *a'Bunadh*	Blackcurrant, chocolate, peony, black cherry, tamarind	Mimolette *vieille*
Aultmore *12 YO*	Herbal, hazelnut, girolle mushroom	Mature (sharp) Comté

Chichibu *On the way*	Honey malt, lily of the valley, malted barley, barley, persimmon, tarte tatin, rhubarb	Parmesan
Glen Moray *The Classic*	Malted barley, lemongrass, caramel, ginger	Brillat-Savarin
Highland Park *15 YO*	Heather honey, beach fire, ganache, candied citrus, orange, peated malt	Mature (sharp) Cheddar
Highland Park *SV CSC 22 YO*	Gorse bush, cherry, malted barley, heather honey	Saint-Nectaire
Midleton *Power's 12 YO John Lane*	Cocoa, apricot, orange marmalade, honey, pepper	Buffalo Mozzarella
Mortlach *18 YO*	Basil, mint, olive oil, sesame, ginger, honey	Goats' cheese
Talisker *Storm*	Peat moss, sea spray, bandage, green pepper, oyster, white pepper	Roquefort, Stilton
Yamazaki *18 YO*	Ganache, fig, date, coffee, sandalwood	Goats' cheese

DESSERTS AND PASTRIES

Whisky	Aromas	Food pairing
Amrut *Fusion*	Pineapple, apricot, sandalwood, barley, voatsiperifery pepper	Stem (preserved) ginger
Ardbeg *Ten*	Smoked herring, pineapple, molasses/treacle, salty liquorice	Citrus cream
Arran *12 YO CS Batch 3*	Citrus peel, dark chocolate, ginger, elderberry	Panna cotta
Chichibu *On the way*	Honey malt, lily of the valley, malted barley, persimmon, tarte tatin, rhubarb	Apple crumble
Craigellachie *18 YO*	Jasmine, rose, lemon sorbet, lemongrass	Dark fruit tart (blueberry, mulberry, fig, damson)
Dalmore *Cromatie*	Dates, Earl Grey tea, dark chocolate, pepper	Gingerbread
Glann ar Mor *Taol Esa*	Pineapple, roasted barley, date, salt, lemon	Ice cream, ginger, marshmallow

Glenmorangie *Artein*	Radicchio, limestone, peppermint, ganache	Watermelon
Glen Moray *The Classic*	Malted barley, lemongrass, caramel, ginger	Cheesecake
Hibiki *17 YO*	Peach, rose, lemon honey, cocoa, brioche, sandalwood	Blueberry tart
Highland Park *15 YO*	Heather honey, beach fire, ganache, candied citrus, orange, peated malt	Nougat glacé
Highland Park *25 YO*	Mown hay, Seville orange peel, grains of Selim, peat smoke, mulberry jam	Ginger sorbet
Kavalan *Solist Sherry Cask*	Plum, fig, blackcurrant, angostura, chicory (endive), hazelnut, hibiscus, pine nut	Fruit cake, fig tart
Littlemill *BBR 1992*	Wormwood, candied citrus, angelica	Summer fruits (peach, melon, cherry, plum, redcurrant)
Mortlach *Rare Old*	Chocolate, fruit cake, cherry honey	Cherries in syrup
Old Pulteney *12 YO*	Sea spray, malted barley, borage flower, Iberico ham	Melon
Yamazaki *Distiller's Reserve*	Strawberry, cherry, yellow peach, persimmon	Fruit charlotte

CHOCOLATE

Whisky	Aromas	Food pairing
Dalmore *Cromatie*	Dates, Earl Grey tea, dark chocolate, pepper	Chocolate with ginger
Glencadam *14 YO*	Orange peel, wild strawberry, chocolate malt, cranberry, ginger, hazelnut	Orangette, chocolate fondant
Glenmorangie *Companta*	Molasses/treacle, dark chocolate, liquorice cream, cranberry	Chocolate liquorice tart
Highland Park *SV CSC 22 YO*	Gorse bush, cherry, malted barley, heather honey	Dark chocolate mousse
Highland Park *25 YO*	Mown hay, Seville orange peel, grains of Selim, peat smoke, mulberry jam	Milk chocolate

WHISKY FLIGHTS

The following 'flights' allow you to taste and recognize different whiskies by style. In tasting the four whiskies grouped together for each 'flight' successively, you will equip yourself with the skill to be able to identify different regions, countries or particular types of whisky.

The colours of the circles follow those of the colour-coding commonly used by tasting clubs to identify whiskies.

REGIONAL FLIGHTS: THE FIVE WHISKY REGIONS OF SCOTLAND

Campbeltown

Kilkerran 6th Bourbon	Glen Scotia 15 YO	Springbank 10 YO	Longrow Peated

Highlands

Glengoyne 12 YO	Clynelish 14 YO	Glendronach 15 YO	Talisker Storm

Islay

Bruichladdich Islay Barley	Bunnahabhain 12 YO	Bowmore 12 YO	Laphroaig 10 YO

Lowlands

Auchentoshan Classic	Glenkinchie 12 YO	Bladnoch 15 YO	Auchentoshan Three Wood

Speyside

Glenlivet 12 YO	Balvenie Double Wood 12 YO	Cragganmore 12 YO	Glenfarclas 15 YO

DOMESTIC FLIGHTS: WHISKIES OF JAPAN, USA, CANADA, IRELAND

Japan

Suntory Hibiki 12 YO	Nikka from the Barrel	Yamazaki 12 YO	Yoichi 10 YO

USA

Jack Daniel's Glentleman Jack	Woodford Reserve Bourbon	Rittenhouse Rye 100 Proof	Wild Turkey Single Barrel

Canada

Crown Royal	Black Velvet 8 YO	Forty Creek Copper Pot	Whistle Pig Rye 10 YO

Ireland

The Irishman Founder's Reserve	Bushmills 10 YO	Power's 12 YO John Lane	Connemara Peated

INTERNATIONAL FLIGHTS: INTRODUCING THE WHISKIES OF THE WORLD

Kavalan
Single Malt

Mackmyra
First Edition

Sullivans
Cove Double
Cask

Amrut
Fusion

Three Ships
10 YO

English
Whisky Co.
Classic

Penderyn
Madeira
Finish

Glann Ar Mor
Kornog

PEAT FLIGHTS: EXTREME PEAT, WORLD PEAT, SOIL AND SEA

Extreme Peat

Port Charlotte
1slay Barley

Laphroaig
Triple Wood

Lagavulin
12 YO CS

Octomore
6.3

World Peat

Connemara
Peated

Amrut Peated

Glann ar Mor
Kornog

Bakery Hill
Peated Malt

Soil and Sea

Ardmore
Legacy

BenRiach
10 YO
Curiositas

Caol Ila
12 YO

Talisker
10 YO

WINE CASKS FLIGHT: VARIATIONS AROUND WINE CASKS

Glenmorangie
Nectar d'Or
(Sauternes)

Bunnahabhain
Eirigh Na
Greine

BenRiach
15 YO
(Madeira)

Balvenie
21 YO (Port)

SHERRY CASK FLIGHTS: VARIATIONS AROUND SHERRY CASKS

Glenkinchie
Distiller's Edition
(Amontillado)

Macallan
Sienna

Oban
Distiller's
Edition Fino

Benriach
15 YO PX

Oloroso

Glenmorangie
Lasanta

Dalmore
Vintage 2003

Macallan
Sienna

Bowmore
15 YO
Darkest

Pedro Ximénez

Auchentoshan
Solera

Benriach
15 YO PX

Laphroaig
PX Cask

Lagavulin
Distiller's Edition

NORTH AMERICAN WHISKEY FLIGHTS

Bourbon

Maker's
Mark

Four Roses
Small Batch

Elijah Craig
12 YO

Blanton's
Gold

Classic Whiskey Types

Mellow Corn

Wild Turkey
Rye

Jack Daniel's
Single barrel

Knob Creek

Rye

Jim Beam
Rye

Michter's
Straight Rye

Sazerac
Straight Rye

Old Potrero
Single Malt
Rye

THE MOST DISTINCTIVE WHISKIES

The following tables identify the most representative whiskies for each of the main aromatic families – those that have the most distinct aroma – the most floral, the most fruity, the most mineral, the most peaty, the most woody, and so forth.

Key to colour coding:

- Single Malt and other malt whisky
- Grain whisky
- Pot Still whisky
- Blend or blended whisky (grain and malt)
- Rye
- Bourbon
- Complex or American / Canadian Whisky
- Corn
- Tennessee Whiskey

CEREAL

Arran	*14 YO* **46° UN**
Bruichladdich	**The Laddie** *22 YO* **46° UN**
Bruichladdich	**Islay Barley 07-14** *2007/2014 Rockside Farm Bourbon Cask* **50° UN**
Chichibu	**The First** *2008/2011 3 YO Bourbon Barrel* **61.8° UN CS**
Dalmore	**Vintage 1990** *2012 Bourbon Matured* **51.8° UN CS SC 1**
Dalwhinnie	*15 YO* **43° UN**
George Dickel	*Barrel Select Tennessee 43°*
Glenmorangie	**Tùsail** *2015 Maris Otter Barley Private Edition 6th Release* **46° UN**
Glen Ord	**Singleton** *15 YO European & American Oak Casks* **40°**
Glen Scotia	*16 YO* **46° UN**
Glenrothes	*1995 Bourbon + Sherry Casks* **43°**
Highland Park	*Thor 16 YO Valhalla Coll.* **52.1° UN CS**
Highland Park	*Svein 2013 The Warrior Series* **40° TRE**
Nikka	*Coffey Malt 2013 45°*
Octomore	**06.1/167ppm** *2013 5 YO Scottish Barley Ochdamh-mòr* **57° UN CS**
Talisker	*1985/2013 27 YO Natural CS – Maritime Edition* **56.1° UN CS**

DULCET

Aberfeldy	*19 YO 1991/2010 Hogshead LMDW* **56.7° UN CS SC 2934**
AnCnoc	*22 YO Sherry + Bourbon Casks* **46° UN**
Angel's Envy	*Rum Finish Rye Finished in Rum Cask 50°*
Clynelish	*Berry Bros & Rudd 1996/2013 BBR Retro for LMDW* **57.1° UN CS SC 6421**
Langatun	*Old Eagle Pure Rye 60.7° UN CS*
Dalwhinnie	*25 YO 1987/2012 American Oak Special Release* **52.1° UN CS SC 431**
Glencadam	*15 YO* **40° UN**
Glendronach	Batch 8 *1993/2013 20 YO Oloroso Sherry Butt* **52.9° UN CS SC 3**
Glenmorangie	Astar *Missouri Ozarks Oak* **57.1° UN CS**
Highland Park	Ragnvald *2013 The Warrior Series* **44.6° UN TRE**
Littlemill	*The Whisky Agency 1989/2014 24 YO Refill Hogshead Liquid Library* **48.7° UN CS**
Jameson	*Signature Reserve Bourbon + Sherry Casks 40°*
Jameson	*Rarest Vintage Reserve Bourbon + Port Casks 46° UN*
Sazerac	*18 YO Straight Rye 45°*
Teaninich	*Signatory Vintage 1983/2013 29 YO Refill Sherry Butt* **57.5° UN CS SC 8071**
Yellow Spot	*12 YO Bourbon + Sherry + Malaga Casks 46° UN*

FLORAL

Glendronach	*1993/2013 20 YO Oloroso Sherry Butt LMDW* **59.7° UN CS SC 30**
Highland Park	**21 YO 47.5° UN CS TRE**
Lochside	*Malts of Scotland 1982/2014 32 YO Angel's Choice 55.2° UN CS SC 14019*

FRUITY

Amrut	**Cask Strength 61.8° UN CS**
Balblair	**Vintage 1983** *2013 Bourbon American Oak* **46° UN**
Bladnoch	*1990/2013 22 YO New Label* **51.7° UN CS SC 5070**
Ben Nevis	*1998/2013 15 YO 1st Fill Sherry Butt* **56.1° UN CS SC 586**
Booker's	*6-8 YO 121-127 Proof Straight Bourbon 62° CS*
Dalmore	*25 YO Tawny Port Finish Sherry Butt* **42°**
Famous Grouse	*40 YO* **47° UN**
Glencadam	*10 YO* **46° UN**
Glendronach	*1993/2013 20 YO Oloroso Sherry Butt LMDW* **59.7° UN CS SC 30**

Glen Garioch	**Vintage 1997/2012 14 YO 1st +2nd Fill Bourbon 56.7° UN CS SB 12 TRE**
Glengoyne	*12 YO* **43° UN**
Glen Grant	*1992 Cellar Reserve* **46° UN**
Glenmorangie	*Astar Missouri Ozarks Oak* **57.1° UN CS**
Glenmorangie	*Ealanta 1993/2012 19 YO Missouri White Oak Private Edition 1st Release* **46° UN**
Hibiki	*12 YO* 43°
Hibiki	*21 YO* 43°
Highland Park	**Loki 15 YO Valhalla Coll. 48.7° UN CS**
Highland Park	**Ragnvald 2013 The Warrior Series 44.6° UN TRE**
Highland Park	**Sigurd 2013 The Warrior Series 43° TRE**
Littlemill	*Archives 1988/2014 25 YO Bourbon Hogshead Holly Crab 51.9° UN CS SC 12*
Masterson's	*10 YO Straight Rye French Oak 47.8°*
Midleton	*Barry Crocket Legacy Bourbon + Virgin Oak Casks 46° UN*
Old Pulteney	**2014 35 YO Ex-Bourbon & Ex-Sherry Casks Limited Ed. 42.5° UN CS**
Redbreast	*12 YO CS Bourbon + Sherry Casks 59.9° UN CS*
Redbreast	*21 YO Bourbon + Sherry Casks 46° UN*
Rosebank	**1992/2014 21 YO Special Release Refill American Oak 55.3° UN CS**
Springbank	**2004/2013 9 YO Refill bourbon + Finished Fresh Gaja Barolo 54.7° UN CS**
Sullivans Cove	**American Oak 47.5° UN**
Teeling	**30 YO Single Malt Bourbon Barrel 46° UN**
Tomatin	**2014 14 YO Bourbon Barrel + Port Pipes 46° UN**
Zuidam	**Millstone 12 YO Sherry Cask 46° UN**

GRASSY

Aberfeldy	**19 YO** *1991/2010 Hogshead LMDW* **56.7° UN CS SC 2934**
Auchentoshan	**18 YO 43° 3D**
Balblair	**Vintage 1983/2013 Bourbon American Oak 46° UN**
Caol Ila	*Wilson & Morgan 2000/2012 12 YO Barrel Selection 20th Anry Ed. 48.5° UN SC*
Clynelish	*Berry Bros & Rudd 1996/2013 BBR Retro for LMDW 57.1° UN CS SC 6421*
Clynelish	*Signatory Vintage 1995/2012 16 YO Refill Sherry Butt CS Coll. 56.6° UN CS SC 12795*
Dalwhinnie	*1987/2012 25 YO American Oak Special Release 52.1° UN CS SC 431*

Glendronach	Batch 8 1996/2013 17 YO PX Sherry Puncheon 53.1° UN CS SC 1490
Lagavulin	2014 12 YO 14th Release Special Release 54.4° UN CS
Littlemill	Berry Bros & Rudd 1992/2013 20 YO 54.9° UN CS SC 10

MARINE

Ardbeg	Ten 2013 10 YO 46° UN
Bowmore	Maltmen's Selection 1995/2009 13 YO Sherry Butt Craftmen's Coll. 54.6° UN CS
Caol Ila	Wemyss Malts 1982/2014 Smoke on the Water Hogshead 46° UN
Clynelish	14 YO 46° UN
Glencadam	15 YO 40° UN
Glen Scotia	Signatory Vintage 1977/2012 35 YO Hogshead CS Coll. LMDW 52.5° UN CS SC 2750
Glen Scotia	SMWS 93.59 1999/2014 14 YO Refill Hogshead 60.6° UN CS
Highland Park	Loki 15 YO Valhalla Coll. 48.7° UN CS
Laphroaig	Highgrove 1999/2014 14 YO 46° UN SC 5163
Octomore	06.1/167ppm 2013 5 YO Scottish Barley Ochdamh-mòr 57° UN CS
Old Pulteney	2013 30 YO 40.1° UN
Port Askaig	Speciality Drinks Ltd 30 YO 51.1° UN CS
Talisker	Storm 2013 45.8° UN
Talisker	18 YO 45.8° UN

MINERAL

Bowmore	Berry Bros & Rudd 1994/2012 LMDW 53.6° UN CS SC 1705
Clynelish	Manager's Choice 1997/2009 11 YO 1st Fill Bourbon American Oak 58.5° UN CS SC 4341
Lagavulin	2012 12 YO 12th Release Refill American Oak 56.1° UN CS
Highland Park	Thor 16 YO Valhalla Coll. 52.1° UN CS
Longrow	18 YO 2013 46° UN
Longrow	CV 2010 46° UN
North Port	1977/2005 28 YO American Oak Rare Malts Selection 53.3° UN CS
Teaninich	Signatory Vintage 1983/2013 29 YO Refill Sherry Butt 57.5° UN CS SC 8071

OILY

Banff	*Cadenhead's 1976/2013 36 YO Bourbon Hogshead Small Batch* 49.8° UN CS SB
Blanton's	*Gold Edition YO Straight Bourbon* 51.5° CS
Caol Ila	*Wilson & Morgan 1995/2013 18 YO Barrel Selection Sherry Butt* 57.5° UN CS SC 10027
Clynelish	*Malts of Scotland 1989/2012 22 YO Bourbon Hogshead* 53.2 UN CS SC 12012
Clynelish	**Manager's Choice** *1997/2009 11 YO 1st Fill Bourbon American Oak* 58.5° **UN CS SC 4341**
Mortlach	*2014 25 YO Refill American Oak Casks* 43.4°
Old Pulteney	*2013 30 YO* 40.1°
Talisker	*2010 30 YO American & European Oak* 57.3° UN CS

SMOKY

Ardbeg	**Corryvreckan** *Ardbeg 2013* 57.1° **UN CS**
Ardbeg	**Uigeadail** *2013* 54.2° **UN CS**
Ardbeg	**Supernova SN2014** *Bourbon & Sherry Casks Ardbeg Committee Exclusive* 55° **UN CS**
BenRiach	*2005/2014 9 YO Peated / Virgin American Oak Hogshead Batch 11* 58.7° **UN CS**
Bowmore	**Maltmen's Selection** *1995/2009 13 YO Sherry Butt Craftmen's Coll.* 54.6° **UN CS**
Bowmore	*21 YO* 43°
Caol Ila	*12 YO* 43°
Chichibu	*Peated 2011/2015 3 YO Barrel + Hogshead* 62.5° **UN CS**
English Whisky Co.	*Peated Single Malt* 43°
Hakushu	*25 YO* 43°
Highland Park	*21 YO* 47.5° **UN CS TRE**
Highland Park	**Ragnvald** *2013 The Warrior Series* 44.6° **UN TRE**
Highland Park	**Dark Origins** *2014 1st Fill & Refill Sherry Casks* 46.8°
Kilchoman	**Loch Gorm** *2007/2013 Oloroso Sherry Casks* 46° **UN**
Kilkerran	*6th Release 2004/2014 10 YO Work in Progress - Bourbon Wood Pink Label* 46°
Kornog	*Sant Ivy 2015 1st Fill Bourbon Barrel* 59.6° **UN CS**

Lagavulin	*14ᵗʰ Release 2014 12 YO Special Release* **54.4°** UN CS
Lagavulin	*16 YO* **43°**
Laphroaig	*2014 10 YO* **58°** UN CS Batch 006
Laphroaig	**Highgrove** *1999/2014 14 YO* **46°** UN SC 5163
Longrow	*18 YO 2013* **46°** UN
Octomore	**06.3 Islay Barley/258ppm** *2009/2014 5 YO American Oak Cask* **64°** UN CS
Octomore	**06.2/167ppm** *2013 5 YO Ex Eau-de-Vie Limousin Oak Cask of Aquitaine* **58.2°** UN CS TRE
Port Charlotte	**Islay Barley** *2008/2014 6 YO* **50°** UN
Talisker	*2012 25 YO* **45.8°** UN
Talisker	*2010 30 YO American & European Oak* **57.3°** UN CS

SULPHURY

Fettercairn	*1984/2009 24 YO Rare Vintage* **44.4°**
Glen Ord	*SMWS 77.32 1987/2013 25 YO Refill Hogshead* **58.2°** UN CS SC
Glen Scotia	*Signatory Vintage 1977/2012 35 YO Hogshead CS Coll. LMDW* **52.5°** UN CS SC 2750

WINEY

Amrut	**Intermediate Sherry** *Bourbon / Sherry / Bourbon* **57.1°** UN CS
Bladnoch	*12 YO Black Face Sheep Label Sherry Matured* **55°** UN
Bruichladdich	**Sherry Classic** *2009 Fusion: Fernando de Castilla* **46°** UN
Chichibu	**Port Pipe** *2009/2013* **54.5°** UN CS
Clynelish	*Signatory Vintage 1995/2012 16 YO Refill Sherry Butt CS Coll.* **56.6°** UN CS SC 12795
Glencadam	*21 YO Sherry Cask The Exceptional* **46°** UN
Glendronach	**Batch 9** *1989/2013 22 YO PX Sherry Puncheon* **49.2°** UN CS SC 5470
Glendronach	**Batch 8** *1990/2013 22 YO PX Sherry Puncheon* **50.8°** UN CS SC 2971
Glendronach	**Batch 8** *1996/2013 17 YO PX Sherry Puncheon* **53.1°** UN CS SC 1490
Hakushu	*2014 Sherry Cask* **48°** UN CS
Karuizawa	*1981/2013 31 YO Sherry Butt Noh* **58.9°** UN CS SC 348
Kavalan	*Solist Sherry Cask* **57.8°** UN CS SC
Laphroaig	*2014 25 YO Bourbon & Oloroso Sherry Barrels* **45.1°** UN CS
Octomore	**02.2/140ppm** *2009 5 YO Orpheus Château Petrus* **61°** UN CS

Springbank	*2014 25 YO Bourbon & Sherry Cask* **46° UN**
Tobermory	*Adelphi 1994/2013 18 YO Sherry Butt* 58.8° UN CS SC 675031

WOODY

Aberfeldy	*16 YO Ramble* **56° UN CS**
AnCnoc	*18 YO Sherry + Bourbon Casks* **46° UN**
Angel's Envy	*CS Straight Bourbon Finished in Port Cask* 59.65° CS
Ballantine's	*Limited* 43°
Bernheim	*Original 7 YO Small Batch Straight Wheat* **45°**
Colonel E.H. Taylor	*Small Batch Straight Bourbon* 50°
Dalmore	*Cigar Malt Reserve Limited Edition* **44°**
Dewar's	*15 YO The Monarch* 40°
Eagle Rare	*17 YO Straight Bourbon* 45°
Elijah Craig	*12 YO Small Batch Straight Bourbon* 47°
Evan Williams	*1783 Small Batch Straight Bourbon* 43°
Forty Creek	*Port Wood Reserve* **45°**
Glen Garioch	*Vintage 1999/2013 Oloroso Sherry Cask Batch 30* **56.3° UN CS**
Glenmorangie	*Signet* **46° UN**
Grant's	*25 YO* 40°
Highland Park	*Cadenhead's 1985/2013 28 YO Bourbon Hogshead* **48.3° UN CS**
Highwood	*Century Reserve Lot 15-25 Rye* 45°
Jack Daniel's	*Silver Select Tennessee* **50°**
Jack Daniel's	*Sinatra Select Tennessee* **45°**
Michter's	*10 YO Straight Bourbon* 47.2° CS
Old Grand Dad	*Traditional 86 Proof Straight Bourbon* 43°
Russel's Reserve	*Single Barrel Straight Bourbon* 55° CS
NZ Whisky	*1991 Vintage Bourbon barrel* **60.5° UN CS**
Talisker	*1985/2013 27 YO Natural CS – Maritime Edition* **56.1° UN CS**
The Irishman	*Cask Strength Bourbon Barrels* 54° UN CS
Van Winkle	*13 YO Family Reserve Straight Rye* 47.8°
Wiser's	*Small Batch* **43.4°**

WHISKY HALL OF FAME

T he following directory lists, by vintage from 1928 to 1987, legendary whiskies from the 54 most prestigious distilleries and brands in the world. The years denote when the whiskies were put in barrel and when they were bottled.

■ : Single and other malt whiskies (distillery bottling)

▤ : Single and other malt whiskies (independent bottling)

1928
| | 1978 | Dalmore | *50 YO Crystal Decanter Dark Sherry* 52° UN CS SC |

1936
| | 1973 | Mortlach | *36 YO Sherry Wood Black Label G&M for Pinerolo* 43° |

1938
| | - - - | Macallan | *The Malt Handwritten Label* 43° |

1940
| | - - - | Macallan | *35 YO Gordon & MacPhail Sherry Wood Import Pinerolo* 43° |

1947
| | - - - | Macallan | *15 YO 80° Proof Rinaldi Import* 45.85° UN |

1951
| | 2001 | Macallan | *Matured in Sherry Wood Fine & Rare* 48.8° UN CS |

1952
| | - - - | Macallan | *15 YO 80° Proof Rinaldi Import* 45.85° UN |

1953
| | 2012 | Glenfarclas | *58 YO Spanish Sherry Cask* 47.2° UN CS SC 1674 |

	2003	Glenury Royal	*50 YO Special Release* **42.8° UN CS**

1954

	- - -	Macallan	*15 YO 80° Proof Sherry Cask Rinaldi Import* **45.85° UN**

1955

	1974	Bowmore	*Ceramic Decanter* **40°**
	- - -	Bowmore	*40 YO Bourbon Hogshead + Sherry Finish* **42° SC**
	1982	Glenlivet	*27 YO Hand Written Label Samaroli* **43°**
	1985	Highland Park	*30 YO Natural CS Oak Cask Intertrade* **53.2° UN CS**
	- - -	Macallan	*15 YO 80° Proof Sherry Wood Rinaldi Import* **45.85° UN**
	- - -	Strathisla	*48 YO Dark Sherry Cask G&M Private Coll.* **59.2° UN CS SC 407**

1956

	- - -	Bowmore	*Sherry Casks Islay Pure Malt* **43°**
	- - -	Glenfiddich	*29 YO Sherry Wood Intertrade* **50.6° UN CS**
	2005	Glen Grant	*49 YO 1ˢᵗ Fill Sherry Hogshead G&M LMDW* **46° UN**
	1986	Highland Park	*30 YO Gordon & MacPhail Intertrade* **55.6° UN CS**

1957

	- - -	Bowmore	*38 YO* **40.1° UN CS SC 216-220**
	1979	Glenrothes	*22 YO Cadenhead Dumpy Bottle* **45.7° UN**
	1978	Highland Park	*21 YO Sherry Wood Cadenhead Dumpy Bottle* **45.7° UN CS**

1982	Macallan	*25 YO The Anniversary Malt Import. Corade France* **43°**
- - -	Talisker	*100 Proof Gordon & MacPhail Black Label 57° UN CS*

1958

2007	Glen Grant	*48 YO G&M LMDW 50° UN*
1998	Highland Park	*40 YO* **44.2° CS**

1959

1984	Glen Moray	*Sherry Hogshead Cask Samaroli 46° UN*
1980	Highland Park	*21 YO James Grant Green Dumpy Italian Import* **43°**

1960

1999	Bunnahabhain	*39 YO Sherry Cask Douglas Laing OMC* **43.4° CS SC**
2007	Glenfarclas	*47 YO Sherry Hogshead The Family Casks* **52.4° CS SC 1767**
1977	Highland Park	*17 YO James Grant For Ferraretto Black Dumpy* **43°**
1978	Highland Park	*18 YO Dark Sherry James Grant Green Dumpy* **43°**
2013	Karuizawa	*52 YO Sherry Cask* **51.8° UN CS SC 5627**

1961

- - -	Bowmore	*50 YO Bourbon Hogsheads* **40.7° UN CS SC**
1997	Highland Park	*35 YO John Goodwin-CS 50° UN CS*
1987	Mortlach	*25 YO Samaroli 46° UN CS*

1963

1979	Glen Grant	*75 Proof 26 ²/³ Fl.oz. Berry Bros & Rudd Old Bond Street* **43°**
2014	Karuizawa	*50 YO Engraved Bottle* **59.4° UN CS SC 5132**

| 2003 | Strathisla | *40 YO Sherry Cask JWWW Old Train Line* 57.7° UN CS SC 2745 |

1964

1979	Bowmore	*Bicentenary* 43° UN CS
1993	Bowmore	*Black 1ˢᵗ Ed. 29 YO Sherry Cask* 50° UN CS
2000	Bowmore	*35 YO Oloroso Sherry Hogshead The Trilogy Series* 42.1° CS SC 3709
2002	Bowmore	*37 YO Fino Sherry Cask The Trilogy Series* 49.6° CS SC
2003	Bowmore	*38 YO Bourbon Cask The Trilogy Series* 43.2° CS SC
2008	Bowmore	*White 43 YO Bourbon Cask* 42.8° UN CS
2006	Glen Grant	*42 YO Sherry Butt Signatory Vintage* 52.8° UN CS SC 2632
2009	Highland Park	*Orcadian Vintage Series* 42.2° UN CS
2012	Karuizawa	*48 YO Sherry Cask* 57.7° UN CS SC 3603
2010	Longmorn	*46 YO 1ˢᵗ Fill Sherry Hogshead G&M* 51.3° UN CS SC 1033
1979	North Port	*15 YO Cadenhead Dumpy Bottle* 45.7° UN
1979	Saint Magdalene	*15 YO Cadenhead Black Label* 45.7° UN CS

1965

1988	Ardbeg	*23 YO Sherry Cask Cadenhead Mizuhashi TLS* 55° CS
- - -	Bowmore	*Typed Vintage Auxil* 43°
- - -	Bowmore	*22 YO Sherry Wood Prestonfield House* 43° SC 47
1985	Clynelish	*21 YO Duthie – Corti Brothers, Sacramento - Pelligrini* 43°
1989	Clynelish	*24 YO Cadenhead White Label - Sestante* 49.4° CS
2007	Glenfarclas	*41 YO Sherry Butt The Family Casks* 60° CS SC 417

- - -	**Glen Garioch**	*21 YO* **57° UN CS**
1994	Macallan	*29 YO Sherry Cask Signatory Vintage 49° UN SC 1058*
1993	Rosebank	*28 YO Sherry Cask Signatory Vintage Dumpy 53.4° UN CS*
1996	Springbank	*31 YO Sherry Wood Cadenhead Authentic Coll. 50.5° UN CS*

1966

1984	Bowmore	*Samaroli Bouquet 53° CS*
1988	**Bowmore**	*21 YO Sherry Wood Prestonfield House* **43°**
- - -	Bowmore	*35 YO Hogshead Kingsbury Celtic 43.7° CS SC 3300*
2001	Bowmore	*35 YO High Spirits' Coll. The Scottish Colourists 43.7° CS*
2002	**Bruichladdich**	*36 YO Legacy I American Oak Hogshead* **40.6° UN CS**
1985	Caol Ila	*19 YO Gordon & MacPhail - Intertrade 58.3° CS*
1998	Glenugie	*Samaroli Cream Label 55° UN CS*
1985	Laphroaig	*19 YO G&M for Intertrade 50.2° UN CS SC*
1996	Laphroaig	*30 YO Signatory Vintage - Dumpy 48.9° UN CS SC 561*
1986	Lochside	*32 YO Spanish Oak Butt 92.6 SMWS 62.3° UN CS*
2002	Lochside	*35 YO Premier Malts Malcolm Pride 51.3° UN CS SC 7541*
1990	**Springbank**	*24 YO Oak Sherry Cask Local Barley* **58.1° CS SC 1966 443**
1982	Tormore	*16 YO Sherry Wood Samaroli 57° CS*

1967

1995	Ardbeg	*28 YO Pale Oloroso Butt Signatory Vintage 53.7° CS SC 575*
- - -	Ardbeg	*28 YO Barrel Japan Scotch Malt Sales 53° CS*
1996	Ardbeg	*29 YO Sherry Cask Kingsbury 54.6° CS SC 922*
1999	**Balvenie**	*32 YO Vintage Cask* **49.7° UN CS SC 9908**

2008	Ben Nevis	*41 YO Very Dark Sherry Alambic Classique* **50.1° UN CS**
- - -	**Bowmore**	***Sherry Casks* 50°**
1983	Caol Ila	*16 YO R.W. Duthie - Narsai's USA 46°*
2010	**Glenglassaugh**	***The Manager's Legacy Refill Sherry Hogshead* 40.4° UN CS**
2006	Glen Keith	*38 YO Refill Sherry Butt G&M 53° UN CS SC 3876*
1989	Glenugie	*Sherry Wood Sestante Bird Label 59.5° UN CS*
2009	**Karuizawa**	***42 YO Sherry Cask* 58.4° UN CS SC 6426**
1982	Laphroaig	*15 YO Sherry Cask Samaroli – Duthie 57° CS SC*
1994	Laphroaig	*27 YO Oak Cask Signatory Vintage 50.1° CS SC 2957*
2008	Longmorn	*Sherry Hogshead G&M 50° UN CS SC 3348*
1988	**Springbank**	***20 YO Sherry Cask West Highland Malt* 46°**
1996	Strathisla	*Sherry Wood Samaroli. 57° UN CS*

1968

2000	**Balvenie**	***32 YO Vintage Cask* 51° UN CS SC 7297**
2006	**Bowmore**	***37 YO Bourbon* 43.4°**
2002	**Bunnahabhain**	***34 YO Sherry Casks Auld Acquaintance* 43.8° CS**
- - -	Caol Ila	*Gordon & MacPhail Cask Series Meregalli Import 58.5° CS*
1982	Caol Ila	*Samaroli Full Proof, Bulloch Lade & Co Ltd 57° CS SC*
2013	**Glendronach**	***44 YO Oloroso Sherry Butt Recherché* 48.6° UN CS SC 5**

- - -	Glen Garioch	*29 YO Individual Cask Bottling 57.7° UN CS SC 7*
- - -	Glen Garioch	*34 YO Individual Cask Bottling 55.4° UN CS SC 17*
2008	Glenlivet	*39 YO Reserve Vintage 50.9° UN CS SC 7629*
2010	Karuizawa	*42 YO Sherry Butt for LMDW 61° UN CS SC 6955*

1969

1984	Caol Ila	*15 YO Gordon & MacPhail Celtic Intertrade Import 58.5° CS*
1995	Glenlochy	*26 YO Rare Malts Selection 59° UN CS SC*
1969	Glenrothes	*Rare Vintage McNeill's Choice 53.4° UN CS SC 19217*
- - -	Longmorn	*19 YO Gordon & MacPhail 61.5° UN CS*
1985	Port Ellen	*15 YO Gordon & MacPhail Celtic Meregalli 64.7° CS*
2001	Port Ellen	*31 YO Douglas Laing OMC Alambic Classique 42.9° CS*
2009	Springbank	*40 YO Refill Sherry Butt SVCSC 54.4° UN CS SC 263*

1970

2005	Bowmore	*34 YO Sherry Signatory Vintage 56.6° UN CS SC 4689*
1984	Laphroaig	*Samaroli – Duthie 57.1° CS SC 4367*
1986	Laphroaig	*Samaroli – Duthie 54° UN CS*
2007	Springbank	*37 YO 1ˢᵗ Fill Oloroso Butt SVCSC 53.9° UN CS SC 1621*
1986	Talisker	*16 YO Gordon & MacPhail Intertrade Import 53.1° UN CS*

1971

2000	Brora	*29 YO Douglas Laing Old Malt Cask 50° UN*
2011	Glendronach	*40 YO Sherry Puncheon Taiwan 47.5° UN CS SC 1248*
- - -	Glen Garioch	*Sherry Wood Samaroli 59.6° UN CS*

2011	**Glen Garioch**	*40 YO North American Oak TWE* **43.9° UN CS SC 2038**
2004	Glen Keith	*32 YO SMWS 81.11* 56.4° UN CS SC
2005	Glen Keith	*33 YO Jack Wieber Old Train Line* 51.9° UN CS SC 473
2006	**Highland Park**	*34 YO 1ˢᵗ Fill Butt For Binny's Chicago* **53° UN CS SC 8363**
2007	Springbank	*35 YO Sherry Wood The Whisky Fair* 59° UN CS

1972		
2001	Ardbeg	*Ardbeggeddon 29 YO Sherry Cask USA DL OMC* 48.4° CS
2002	Ardbeg	*29 YO Douglas Laing Platinum Selection* 50.4° CS
2003	**Ardbeg**	*31 YO Bourbon Cask 2ⁿᵈ Release Velier* **49.9° CS SC 2782**
2004	**Ardbeg**	*31 YO Bourbon Hogshead France* **49.2° CS SC 2781**
1995	**Brora**	*22 YO Rare Malts Selection* **61.1° UN CS**
2003	Brora	*31 YO Douglas Laing Platinium Selection* 49.3° CS SC
2014	**Brora**	**13th Release** *40 YO Decanter World of Whiskies* **59.1° UN CS**
2000	Clynelish	*27 YO Hogshead 3Rivers Tokyo* 57.75° UN CS SC 14281
2012	**Glendronach**	*40 YO Oloroso Sherry Butt* **50.2° UN CS SC 713**
2010	**Glenglassaugh**	*38 YO Refill Hogshead Caminneci* **59.1° UN CS SC 2891**
2014	**Glenglassaugh**	*41 YO Refill Sherry Butt Rare Cask* **50.6° UN CS SC 2114**
- - -	Ledaig	*Isle of Mull Harold Currie Coll.* 51.9° UN CS SC
- - -	Ledaig	*18 YO James MacArthur Fine Malt Selection* 54.4° UN CS
2003	Longmorn	*30 YO SherryCask Kingsbury Japan* 50.2° UN CS SC 1100
2002	**Macallan**	*29 YO Hogshead Fine & Rare* **49.2° UN CS SC 4041**

1973

- - -	Ardbeg	*14 YO Sestante Green Label* **53.3° CS**
1988	Ardbeg	*20th Anniversary Samaroli* **57° CS SC**
2004	**Ardbeg**	***Manager's Choice Italy* 49.5° UN CS**
2004	**Balvenie**	***31 YO Vintage Cask* 49.7° UN CS SC 4266**
2006	Clynelish	*33 YO Signatory Vintage Prestonfield* **54.3° UN CS SC 8912**
2010	Glenury Royal	*37 YO Bourbon Hogshead The Whisky Agency* **42.1° UN CS**
2013	**Karuizawa**	***39 YO Sherry Butt* 67.7° UN CS SC 1607**
2003	Midleton	*30 YO Master Distiller's Private Coll.* **56° UN CS SC 41421**

1974

1993	Ardbeg	*19 YO Scotch Single Malt Circle* **55.1° UN CS SC4377**
1997	**Ardbeg**	***Provenance 23 YO Bourbon 1st Release* 55.6° UN CS SC**
2006	**Ardbeg**	***31 YO Bourbon Barrel LMDW* 52.5° UN CS SC 3309**
1987	Balvenie	*Duthie for Samaroli* **56° UN CS**
1986	Caol Ila	*12 YO Sherry Cask James MacArthur* **63° CS SC 74.23.1**
1991	Caol Ila	*17 YO Sherry Cask Signatory Vintage* **61.1° UN CS SC 5-9**
2003	**Glenfiddich**	***Private Vintage Queen Elizabeth II* 48.9° UN CS SC 2336**
2005	**Laphroaig**	***31 YO Sherry Cask LMDW* 49.7° UN CS**
- - -	**Longrow**	***16 YO Cork Cap Distillery label* 46° UN**
2005	Rosebank	*30 YO Sherry Butt Douglas Laing OMC* **55.6° UN CS SC 1595**

1975

1989	Ardbeg	*13 YO Gordon & MacPhail Intertrade* **54.8° UN CS**
2006	**Ardbeg**	***30 YO Fino Feis Ile 2006* 46.3° UN CS SC 4717**

| | 1998 | Port Ellen | *23 YO Oak Cask Signatory Vintage Coll.* **43° SC 155** |

1976

	1999	Ardbeg	*22 YO Sherry Butt Manager's Choice* **56° UN CS SC 2391**
	2001	Ardbeg	*25 YO Provenance* **57.5° UN CS**
	2002	Ardbeg	*25 YO Sherry Butt Feis Ile 2002* **53.1° UN CS SC 2390**
	2002	Ardbeg	*25 YO Sherry Butt Japan* **54.5° UN CS SC 2395**
	2008	Ardbeg	*31 YO Sherry Butt LMDW* **52.4° UN CS SC 2397**
	2008	BenRiach	*32 YO Hogshead Batch 5* **50.3° UN CS SC 2014**
	2009	Karuizawa	*32 YO Sherry Butt Noh* **63° UN CS SC 6719**
	2006	Lagavulin	*30 YO* **52.6° UN CS**
	- - -	Laphroaig	*Vintage* **43°**
	2006	Macallan	*29 YO Fine & Rare* **45.5° UN CS SC 11354**

1977

| | 2012 | Talisker | *35 YO Limited Ed.* **54.6° UN CS** |

1978

| | 2010 | Port Ellen | *31 YO Refill Sherry* **54.6° UN CS** |
| | 1998 | Saint Magdalene | *20 YO Refill European Oak* **62.7° UN CS** |

1979

	2005	Glenrothes	*25 YO Douglas Laing Platinium Selection* **51.9° UN CS**
	2008	Highland Park	*29 YO Return of the Vikings* **56.1° UN CS SC 413**
	2008	Yamazaki	*29 YO Japanese Mizunara Oak Cask* **55° UN CS SC RF1037**

1980

1992	Glenugie	*12 YO Oak Cask Cadenhead Authentic Coll. 59.8° UN CS*
2007	Laphroaig	*27 YO 5 Oloroso Sherry Casks 57.4° UN CS*
2002	Yamazaki	*22 YO White Oak Cask 50° UN SC 5J1367*

1981

2013	Karuizawa	*31 YO Sherry Butt Noh 58.9° UN CS SC 348*
2013	Karuizawa	*31 YO Sherry Butt Prendre le rythme 60.5° UN CS SC 78*
1991	Port Ellen	*Samaroli 57° CS SC*
2002	Talisker	*20 YO Sherry 62° UN CS*

1982

2004	Port Ellen	*21 YO Sherry Douglas Laing OMC 50° CS SC 414*

1984

2007	Yamazaki	*23 YO The Owner's Cask Sherry Butt 62° UN CS*
2009	Yamazaki	*25 YO American, Europ. & Japanese Mizunara Oak 48° UN*

1985

2007	Lagavulin	*21 YO Spanish Sherry European Oak Casks 56.5° UN CS*

1987

2004	Laphroaig	*17 YO Feis Ile 2004 55.2° UN CS SC 4299*
1999	Longrow	*Moon-Import Dreams-Mongiardino 45° UN SC 334*
2007	Yoichi	*20 YO 55° UN*

EVENTS AND FESTIVALS

The following calander is a list of the main whisky-related events and festivals that take place, month by month, around the world – so that you can be sure you don't miss anything!

B&SF	– Beer & Scotch Festival
SM&SW	– Single Malt & Scotch Whisky
W&BF	– Whisky & Beer Festival
WE	– Weekend
WF	– Whisky Festival
WL	– Whisky Live

EUROPE

January

Norway	Tromso WF
Netherlands	Special Whisky WE Amsterdam

February

Germany	Hanse Spirit Hamburg
	Finest Spirits
Belgium	WL Belgium Spa
Norway	Bergen International W&BF
Netherlands	Hielander WF Alkmaar
Sweden	WhiskyExpo Linköping

March

Germany	Whisky'n'more Bochum
	The Village Whisky-Messe Nürmberg
	Whisky Festival Radebeul
Austria	Wiener Whiskymesse
Belgium	WF Gent
Denmark	The Danish WF
Israel	WL Israel Tel Aviv
Norway	Trondheim WF
Netherlands	WF Noord
England	WL London
Switzerland	Whiskyschiff-Luzern

April

Germany	Whiskyfair Limburg
	Wustrow Spring WF
Scotland	Inverness WF
	Spirit of Speyside WF
England	The London Whisky Weekender

May

Germany	Wustrow Spring WF
	Kieler Whiskymesse
Scotland	Spirit of Speyside WF
	Perth Home of WF
	Spirit of Stirling WF
	Feis Ile, Islay Festival of Malt & Music
	The Edinburgh Whisky Stramash
Italy	Milano Whisky Day

June

Scotland	Whisky An'A'That X Festival
England	Bristol Whisky Festival

September

Germany	Cöperniker Whisky-Herbst Berlin
	Köpenicker Whiskyfest
	Whiskymesse Rüsselsheim

Scotland	Whisky Solstice Edinburgh
France	WL Paris
Netherlands	Maltstock
England	Liverpool WF
	Yorkshire WF
Sweden	Stockholm B&WF

October

Germany	Aquavitae die Messe
Irlande	WL Dublin
Netherlands	Pot Still Festival
England	The Whisky Exchange – Whisky Show
	Manchester WF
Poland	WL Varsovie
Sweden	Stockholm B&WF

November

Germany	Whisk(e)y Pur Festival
	Rostocker Whiskymesse
Scotland	Drambusters Whisky Festival
Italy	Milano Whisky Festival
Norway	Oslo WF
Netherlands	International Whisky Festival Holland
	WL La Haye
England	Whisky Sessions Manchester
Switzerland	Whiskyship Zürich

December

| Serbia | WL Belgrade |

AMERICA

January

| Canada | Victoria WF |

February

| Canada | The Spirits of Kingston |
| USA | WL New York |

March

USA	WL Washington DC
	Whiskies of the World Expo
	The Nth Ultimate Whisky Experience Las Vegas

April

Canada	Cowichan Valley Whiskey Festival
USA	Hop Scotch Spring B&SF
	WhiskyFest Chicago
	SM&SW Extravaganza Houston

May

Canada	Spirit of Toronto
USA	SM&SW Extravaganza Dallas
	SM&SW Extravaganza Denver

September

Canada	Durham Festival Spirits
	Hopscotch Festival Kelowna
USA	Kentucky Bourbon Festival Bardstown
	WhiskyFest New York
	WL San Francisco

October

USA	SM&SW Extravaganza Chicago
	SM&SW Extravaganza Washington
	WhiskyFest San Francisco

November

Canada	Hopscotch Festival Vancouver
USA	SM&SW Extravaganza Boston
	SM&SW Extravaganza Seattle
	WL Los Angeles
	SM&SW Extravaganza Los Angeles

December

| USA | SM&SW Extravaganza Fort Lauderdale |

ASIA, AUSTRALASIA AND AFRICA

January

Indonesia	WL Jakarta

February

Japan	Saitama Whisky Session – Chichibu WF
	WF Kyoto

April

Australia	WL Perth

May

South Africa	WL Pretoria
Australia	The Whisky Show Sydney
	WL Adelaide
	WL Canberra
Japan	Bar Show Whisky Expo Tokyo

June

South Africa	WL Cape Town
Australia	The Whisky Show Melbourne
	WL Sydney
Japan	WF Osaka

July

Australia	WL Melbourne

August

South Africa	WL Soweto
Australia	WL Brisbane
Taiwan	WL Taipei

September

China	WL Shanghai
Japan	WL Tokyo

October

Canada	WL Toronto
Singapore	WL Singapore

November

South Africa	WL Sandton City
Japan	WF Tokyo

December

Taiwan	Whisky Luxe Taipei

THE SCOTCH MALT WHISKY SOCIETY CODES

T he following tables list the distillery codes used by The Scotch Malt Whisky Society in numerical and alphabetical order.

CODES IN NUMERICAL ORDER

Single Malts		38	Caperdonich	76	Mortlach	114	Longrow
1	Glenfarclas	39	Linkwood	77	Glen Ord	115	AnCnoc
2	Glenlivet	40	Balvenie	78	Ben Nevis	116	Yoichi
3	Bowmore	41	Dailuaine	79	Deanston	117	Cooley *Unpeated*
4	Highland Park	42	Ledaig	80	Glen Spey	118	Cooley *Peated*
5	Auchentoshan	43	Port Ellen	81	Glen Keith	119	Yamazaki
6	Glen Deveron	44	Craigellachie	82	Glencadam	120	Hakushu
7	Longmorn	45	Dallas Dhu	83	Convalmore	121	Arran
8	Tamdhu	46	Glenlossie	84	Glendullan	122	Croftengea
9	Glen Grant	47	Benromach	85	Glen Elgin	123	Glengoyne
10	Bunnahabhain	48	Balmenach	86	Glenesk	124	Miyagikyo
11	Tomatin	49	St. Magdalene	87	Millburn	125	Glenmorangie
12	BenRiach	50	Bladnoch	88	Speyburn	126	Hazelburn
13	Dalmore	51	Bushmills	89	Tomintoul	127	Port Charlotte
14	Talisker	52	Old Pulteney	90	Pittyvaich	128	Penderyn
15	Glenfiddich	53	Caol Ila	91	Dufftown	129	Kilchoman
16	Glenturret	54	Aberlour	92	Lochside	130	Chichibu
17	Scapa	55	Royal Brackla	93	Glen Scotia	131	Hanyu
18	Inchgower	56	Coleburn	94	Old Fettercairn	132	Karuizawa
19	Glen Garioch	57	Glen Mhor	95	Auchroisk	**Grain Whisky**	
20	Inverleven	58	Strathisla	96	Glendronach	G1	North British
21	Glenglassaugh	59	Teaninich	97	Littlemill	G2	Carsebridge
22	Glenkinchie	60	Aberfeldy	98	Lomond *Inverleven*	G3	Caledonian
23	Bruichladdich	61	Brora	99	Glenugie	G4	Cameronbridge
24	Macallan	62	Glenlochy	100	Strathmill	G5	Invergordon
25	Rosebank	63	Glentauchers	101	Knockando	G6	Port Dundas
26	Clynelish	64	Mannochmore	102	Dalwhinnie	G7	Girvan
27	Springbank	65	Imperial	103	Royal Lochnagar	G8	Cambus
28	Tullibardine	66	Ardmore	104	Glencraig	G9	Loch Lomond
29	Laphroaig	67	Banff	105	Tormore	G10	Strathclyde
30	Glenrothes	68	Blair Athol	106	Cardhu	G11	Nikka *Coffey Grain*
31	Isle of Jura	69	Glen Albyn	107	Glenallachie	G12	Nikka *Coffey Malt*
32	Edradour	70	Balblair	108	Allt-a-Bhainne	G13	Chita
33	Ardbeg	71	Glenburgie	109	Mosstowie	G14	Dumbarton
34	Tamnavulin	72	Miltonduff	110	Oban	**Bourbon Whiskey**	
35	Glen Moray	73	Aultmore	111	Lagavulin	B1	Heaven Hill
36	Benrinnes	74	North Port	112	Inchmurrin	B2	Bernheim
37	Cragganmore	75	Glenury Royal	113	Braes of Glenlivet	B3	Rock Town

CODES IN ALPHABETICAL ORDER

Aberfeldy	60	Convalmore	83	Glen Moray	35	Mortlach	76
Aberlour	54	Cooley *Peated*	118	Glen Ord	77	Mosstowie	109
Allt-a-Bhainne	108	Cooley *Unpeated*	117	Glenrothes	30	Nikka *Coffey Grain*	G11
AnCnoc	115	Cragganmore	37	Glen Scotia	93	Nikka *Coffey Malt*	G12
Ardbeg	33	Craigellachie	44	Glen Spey	80	North British	G1
Ardmore	66	Croftengea	122	Glentauchers	63	North Port	74
Arran	121	Dailuaine	41	Glenturret	16	Oban	110
Auchentoshan	5	Dallas Dhu	45	Glenugie	99	Old Fettercairn	94
Auchroisk	95	Dalmore	13	Glenury Royal	75	Old Pulteney	52
Aultmore	73	Dalwhinnie	102	Hakushu	120	Penderyn	128
Balblair	70	Deanston	79	Hanyu	131	Pittyvaich	90
Balmenach	48	Dufftown	91	Hazelburn	126	Port Charlotte	127
Balvenie	40	Dumbarton	G14	Heaven Hill	B1	Port Dundas	G6
Banff	67	Edradour	32	Highland Park	4	Port Ellen	43
Ben Nevis	78	Girvan	G7	Imperial	65	Rock Town	B3
BenRiach	12	Glen Albyn	69	Inchgower	18	Rosebank	25
Benrinnes	36	Glenallachie	107	Inchmurrin	112	Royal Brackla	55
Benromach	47	Glenburgie	71	Invergordon	G5	Royal Lochnagar	103
Bernheim	B2	Glencadam	82	Inverleven	20	Scapa	17
Bladnoch	50	Glencraig	104	Isle of Jura	31	Speyburn	88
Blair Athol	68	Glen Deveron	6	Karuizawa	132	Springbank	27
Bowmore	3	Glendronach	96	Kilchoman	129	St. Magdalene	49
Braes of Glenlivet	113	Glendullan	84	Knockando	101	Strathclyde	G10
Brora	61	Glen Elgin	85	Lagavulin	111	Strathisla	58
Bruichladdich	23	Glenesk	86	Laphroaig	29	Strathmill	100
Bunnahabhain	10	Glenfarclas	1	Ledaig	42	Talisker	14
Bushmills	51	Glenfiddich	15	Linkwood	39	Tamdhu	8
Caledonian	G3	Glen Garioch	19	Littlemill	97	Tamnavulin	34
Cambus	G8	Glenglassaugh	21	Loch Lomond	G9	Teaninich	59
Cameronbridge	G4	Glengoyne	123	Lochside	92	Tomatin	11
Caol Ila	53	Glen Grant	9	Lomond *Inverleven*	98	Tomintoul	89
Caperdonich	38	Glen Keith	81	Longmorn	7	Tormore	105
Cardhu	106	Glenkinchie	22	Longrow	114	Tullibardine	28
Carsebridge	G2	Glenlivet	2	Macallan	24	Yamazaki	119
Chichibu	130	Glenlochy	62	Mannochmore	64	Yoichi	116
Chita	G13	Glenlossie	46	Millburn	87		
Clynelish	26	Glen Mhor	57	Miltonduff	72		
Coleburn	56	Glenmorangie	125	Miyagikyo	124		

CONVERSION TABLES

The conversion tables below show the equivalent units of measurement for both alcohol content and volume. This is essential for understanding the differences between traditional measurements, as used in the UK, and the metric system now used exclusively in the United States and other parts of the world.

% ABV / UK proof / US proof									
% ABV Alcohol by volume	40	43	45.7	46	50	51.4	57	60	100
UK proof	70	75.25	80	80.5	87.5	90	100	105	175
US proof	80	86	91.4	92	100	102.8	114	120	200

Litre / US gallon / Imperial UK gallon								
				Bourbon Barrel	*B/S Hogshead*	*Puncheon Sherry Butt*	*Port Cask*	*Gorda*
Litre (L)	1	3.78541	4.54609	190	245	500	550	600
US gallon – *US gal*	0.264172	1	1.20	50	65	132	145	159
Imperial UK gallon – *Imp. gal.*	0.219969	0.83	1	42	54	110	121	132

Centilitre, Imperial fluid ounce, US fluid ounce									
							Litre	*US gal.*	*Imp.gal.*
Centilitre (cl)	1	2.84	2.96	4	70	75	100	378.54	454.61
Imperial fluid ounce – *UK fl.oz.*	0.352	1	1.04	1.41	24.64	26.4	35.2	132.49	160
US fluid ounce – *US fl.oz.*	0.338	0.96	1	1.35	23.67	25.36	33.81	128	153.72

INDEX

INDEX BY BRAND

INDEX BY COUNTRY

Scotland – Islay

Ardbeg

Scotland – Lowlands

Scotland – Speyside

Wales

Abbreviations:

CS: Cask Strength
Coll.: Collection
†: Closed Distillery
Ed.: Edition
HP: Heavily Peated
IB: Independent Bottler
LPA: Litres of Pure Alcohol
NAS: No Age Statement
OB: Official Bottling
ppm: parts per million
PX: Pedro Ximénez
SC: Single Cask
TRE: Travel Retail Exclusive
UN: Unchill-filtered
Vint.: Vintage
YO: Year Old
3D: Triple Distilled
4D: Quadruple Distilled

Key to colour coding:

Single Malt and other malt whisky
Grain whisky
Pot Still whisky
Blend or blended whisky (grain and malt)
Rye
Bourbon
Complex or American/Canadian whisky
Corn
Tennessee whiskey

Tasting notes: